To James,

May God continue
bless you alw...

Kind regards,

Divine Will, Restless Heart

Mary E. C. Drew
,12/25/2010

D1062009

Divine Will, Restless Heart

The Life and Works
of
Dr. John Jefferson
Smallwood

1863–1912

Mary E. C. Drew

Copyright © 2010 by Mary E. C. Drew.

Library of Congress Control Number: 2010907791
ISBN: Hardcover   978-1-4535-1197-8
                Softcover   978-1-4535-1196-1
                Ebook   978-1-4535-1198-5

All rights reserved. No part of this book may be reproduced or transmitted in any form or by any means, electronic or mechanical, including photocopying, recording, or by any information storage and retrieval system, without permission in writing from the copyright owner.

This book was printed in the United States of America.

To order additional copies of this book, contact:
Xlibris Corporation
1-888-795-4274
www.Xlibris.com
Orders@Xlibris.com
79952

CONTENTS

ACKNOWLEDGMENTS..11

INTRODUCTION 13

Chapter 1:   Origin..17

Chapter 2:   Thousand Deaths 25

Chapter 3:   Spring 1865..32

Chapter 4:   The Butler School:
              The Early Days of Hampton 37

Chapter 5:   Shaw Days 47

Chapter 6:   Unquenchable Thirst:
              Wesleyan Academy at Wilbraham 56

Chapter 7:   Finding His Mother.......................................59

Chapter 8:   Visionary..62

Chapter 9:   Temperance, Industrial
              and Collegiate Institute...................................72

Chapter 10:   Years of Growth 83

Chapter 11:   Course of Study 102

Chapter 12:   Mary, Don't You Weep 111

Chapter 13:   The Race Problem...116

Chapter 14:   Remaining on Southern Soil........................122

Chapter 15:   Prayed Just as Hard as He Worked 125

Chapter 16:   Lincoln Memorial Hall In Honor
              of the Great Emancipator...............................130

Chapter 17:   Dedication of Lincoln Memorial Hall 138

Chapter 18:   "My Work Is Finished"..................................144

Chapter 19:   Smallwood Memorial Institute 149

Chapter 20:   Lawsuit 152

Chapter 21:   Smallwood-Corey Memorial Industrial
and Collegiate Institute...183

Chapter 22:   Marcus Garvey /
Universal Liberty University 189

EPILOGUE   Moonlight on the James..199

Smallwood's Speech 201

SELECTED BIBLIOGRAPHY...207

PHOTOGRAPHY CREDITS 223

NOTES..229

INDEX...283

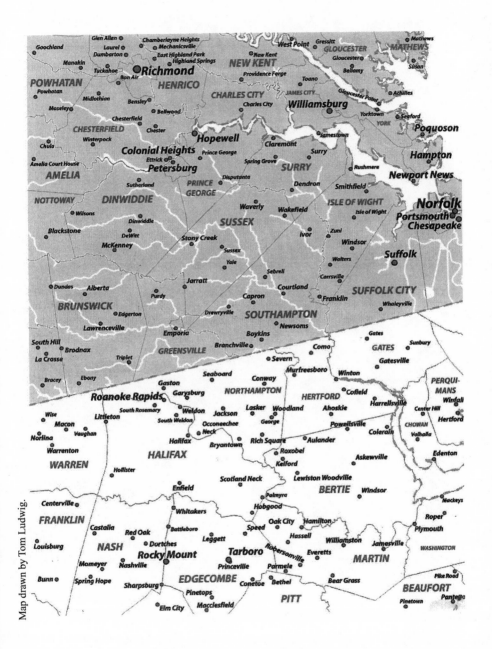

Map drawn by Tom Ludwig.

In memory of Eddie Chambers Jr. and Flora Tann-Chambliss

To my great-aunt,
Mrs. Willie L. Lassiter,
whose abiding love, memories,
and keen sense of the unrevealed
history of Dr. John J. Smallwood
were the basis for the creation
of this book.

ACKNOWLEDGMENTS

Writing this book has been exhilarating, fulfilling, and adventurous. It has been a labor of love that is very endearing to me. The finished work would not exist were it not for the help of many people whose commitment and enthusiasm were instrumental. I would like to acknowledge as many of them as possible, with my sincere thanks.

A special thanks to Eve Gregory at the Surry County Historical Society in Surry County, Virginia, who laid the foundation on which this project was developed, in addition to the following individuals who unselfishly shared documents, photos, and oral history collections, as well as the generous giving of their time in researching for this book: Rev. James Harrison, Barbara Hopper, James Atkins, Clarence Fields, Natarsha Berkley, Gail P. Clayton, Jeanne Holmes, Claude Keeson, Donzella Maupin, Andreese Scott, Sonya Basnight, Carolyn Baker, Sarah Barnes-Vallandingham, Lucious Edwards, Selicia Gregory-Allen, Carolyn Goudie, Lucinda Glover, Jonathan "Troy" Wiley, Barbara Davis, Janice Babb, Dennis Babb, Angela Thorpe, Tisha Young, John Jackson, Dr. Neir Mark, Judy Miller, Dr. Freddie Parker, Dr. Nathaniel Fullwood, Amanda Mathis, Octavious Spruill, Joyce V. Davis, Leslie Mehta, Lakai Terrell, Rick Francis, Bruce Turner, Dr. Scot French, Mrs. Parker, Luther and Annie Jones, Pamela Wood, Mary Miner, Rev. Jeremiah Wright, Helen Lucas, Charlotte Baskerville-Brown, James Brown, Ralph Price, Jean Moore, Marvin T. Jones, Genora Tann-Bishop, Jacqueline Bishop-Boone, Flora Tann-Chambliss, Wilhelmina Bishop-Carver, Joann Carver-Hardie, Joyce Lawrence, Eva Josey-Mangum, Jean Josey-Bowers, Rev. Dorothy Ruffin, Rev. Charles Eason, Billie Josey-Dunham, Shirley Townes, Al Lassiter, Mildred Debreaux, Virginia Poaches, Dr. Gloria Williams,

Clarence Lassiter, and to my family, for their unwavering enthusiasm and support for this project.

Finally, a special thanks to my great-aunt, Mrs. Willie L. Lassiter, whose desire it was to share her uncle's life work with others. Her superb memory at 110 years of age undergirds every page of this book.

INTRODUCTION

Today, the Temperance, Industrial and Collegiate Institute is little more than a highway marker[1] on the side of Route 10 in Surry County, Virginia, but it was once a thriving 65¾-acre campus bustling with students, teachers, administrators, workers, and even tourists. One of the nation's first schools dedicated to the education of emancipated slaves after the Civil War, the institute was the life's work of its founder, Dr. John Jefferson Smallwood, who dreamed of a world in which blacks could become productive citizens and proud Americans through education—by becoming "intelligent men and women," he declared. His vision of "one common country, for one common people"[2] underlay the foundation of the institute, which was designed to instill "Temperance and Morality, Industry and Economy, Intelligence and Race Pride" in American blacks.[3]

Dr. Smallwood, who preached a message of temperance and nonviolence, was the grandson of Nat Turner, the leader of the slave revolt in Southampton County, Virginia, in 1831.[4] The calling of one man laid upon the soil of America the foundation for the calling of the other, both under the authority of an omnipotent and omnipresent God. It was Nat Turner's divine calling to free black Americans from the ravages of slavery in the antebellum South through the use of armed struggle. And so he answered the call and forfeited his life so that others of his kind might live free. Dr. Smallwood, on the other hand, urged emancipated blacks toward a kind of quiet revolution, one achieved not through bloodshed but through a collective uplifting of the people of his race through a message of race and self-pride.

During his lifetime, Dr. Smallwood delivered lectures on race relations throughout the United States and abroad and corresponded with such iconic American figures as Frederick Douglass, Booker T. Washington, and Elizabeth Cady Stanton. His story is part of the rich fabric of experiences that helped shape the nation's perceptions of race and race relations, but his life and works have, until now, remained largely unknown.

I first knew Dr. Smallwood only as Uncle John, a mysterious figure whose presence haunted the stories of bygone days that my grandfather told me when I was a little girl. Granddaddy knew no more about Uncle John than that he had built a school for "colored people" somewhere near Richmond, Virginia; in fact, it was not until September 2007 that I learned, for the first time, Uncle John's full name. The occasion of the discovery was a conversation with my then-107-year-old great-aunt, Dr. Smallwood's niece. She was able to share several photos of her uncle and a few stories about him that had been passed down through the family's rich tradition of oral history. Almost immediately, I began to search for more information about Uncle John, now known to me as Dr. John Jefferson Smallwood.

My journey to bring Dr. Smallwood's life and works to light has led me across state lines, through the dusty archives of many a county library. The greatest aid in my search has undoubtedly been the collection of Dr. Smallwood's papers that is now housed in the archives of Hampton University Library, where countless hours spent sifting through innumerable boxes of papers revealed practically everything I needed—newspaper clippings, journal articles, photographs, letters, and a myriad of other historical documents. Particularly useful among these papers was a four-page letter from December 1903, handwritten by Dr. Smallwood himself and addressed to a Dr. Hollis Frissell, principal of the Hampton Normal and Agricultural Institute, known today as Hampton University. In the letter, Dr. Smallwood methodically wrote a miniature autobiographical sketch of his life, beginning with personal recollections from his early childhood and continuing on to the establishment of his Temperance, Industrial and Collegiate Institute. Relying heavily on this document, as well as a wealth of other archival records and oral family history, the present volume follows Dr. Smallwood from his birth into slavery, through his childhood and emancipation in rural North Carolina, and his education at Hampton, Shaw, Wesleyan Academy and Trinity College, to the establishment of the Temperance, Industrial and

Collegiate Institute, which Dr. Smallwood envisioned as a catalyst for the social, moral, and spiritual elevation of American blacks. Although Dr. Smallwood's dream to build a school for his people was fulfilled, its existence was limited to only four decades, from 1892 to 1928. Death claimed Dr. Smallwood at an early age before he could ensure that the school would continue to function in perpetuity. The official court records of several lawsuits over the Smallwood estate attest to the years of financial woes and general mismanagement that plagued the once-thriving institute after his death.

In what follows, I have made every effort to tell the story of John Jefferson Smallwood in a factual and straightforward manner. In setting forth the details of his life and works, I must give credit to the many researchers who preceded me and laid the foundation for my research. I must also say many thanks to Uncle John for making what could have been a difficult and arduous process an enjoyable journey. His cache of collected papers at Hampton University not only provided much of the information contained in this volume but also enabled me to uncover a deep and enduring connection to the very real, rich history of my family.

CHAPTER ONE

ORIGIN

In 1607, the first English immigrants made a permanent settlement in America at Jamestown in the colony of Virginia. Only thirteen years later, the first cargo of human slaves arrived. It was another forty-three years before the English king Charles II issued the charter that created the Carolina colony and settlers began leaving Virginia, with their slaves, for the fertile soil, economic opportunities, and religious freedom of the new territory. The new settlement was named Carolina in honor of King Charles I, the father of the present king. Land grants were offered by the crown to encourage migration to the region around the Albemarle Sound and the rivers that emptied into it. This territory, between the Cape Fear and Roanoke rivers, was the site of the first permanent settlement by the English in what is now North Carolina.[1]

By 1670, this region was populous enough to warrant subdivision into smaller territories, called precincts. First, the original Albemarle Precinct was divided to create the Chowan Precinct, and this territory, in turn, was divided to form the Bertie Precinct in 1722.[2] When the term "precinct" was changed to "county" in 1738, these territories became known as Chowan County and Bertie County, respectively.[3] The division of Bertie County in 1741 created Northampton County, which took its name from George, Earl of Northampton.[4] The population of Chowan, Bertie, and Northampton counties continued to grow as settlers, many of them Quakers, moved from Virginia and other eastern Carolina counties. Some settlers came to these lands from as far away as Pennsylvania to establish farms and cultivate the lucrative crops of corn, tobacco, and peanuts.[5]

Toward the end of the eighteenth century, in 1797, 177 years after the first shipment of African slaves arrived in Virginia, a girl in her early teens was taken off a cargo ship at Jamestown, Virginia. Legend had it that she was abducted by slave traders along the Nile River region of North Africa,[6] and that she was an Afro-Israelite and a direct descendant of royalty.[7] Nothing is known about her first two years in the New World, but records show that in 1799, she was put on an auction block in Suffolk, Virginia, and sold to a man named Benjamin Turner in Southampton County, a Virginia territory that shared a border with Northampton County, North Carolina.[8]

Turner named this olive-complexioned young slave Nancy, and she came to be called Nancy of the Nile because of her alleged origin. Nancy had tremendous difficulty adjusting to slave life, and her often-rebellious behavior frequently resulted in severe beatings. On October 2, 1800, she gave birth to a son who was given the name of Nathaniel, or Nat, Turner, in keeping with the tradition of identifying slaves by their master's last name.[9]

That same year, just over the Carolina border in Beaufort County, North Carolina, Marcus W. Smallwood, the third child of Charles and Sally Smaw Smallwood, was born. His parents, distant descendants of the Smallwoods who left England for America in the 1600s, had presumably migrated to the area in search of prosperity, like other settlers.[10] By the 1830s, the family was quite well-to-do, and Marcus W. Smallwood himself was the owner of a considerable amount of property in Northampton County on the plantation known as Rich Square.[11]

Originally a fertile tract of land 640 acres square, Rich Square had developed into a town over the course of the eighteenth century;[12] by 1815, however, it had been sold several times, resulting in a reduction of the original territory by just over 100 acres. In 1838, the last surviving son of the last owner of Rich Square divided the remaining 539 acres and began to sell off individual pieces of the Rich Square land.[13] Most of these pieces were purchased and reconsolidated by Marcus W. Smallwood; in fact, between 1830 and 1870, he would become one of the most active buyers and sellers of real estate that the area of Rich Square had ever known.[14] He even earned the nickname "Rich Squire" because his property formed the bulk of the Rich Square land.[15]

By January 26, 1831, Marcus W. Smallwood had taken up residence at the Rich Square plantation and was living in a house on the northwest portion of the land known as Bryantown Road.[16] The name probably derived from a resident with the surname of Bryan or Bryant from the earliest days of Northampton County, possibly as far back as the mid-1700s.[17] In 1831, Marcus also assumed the position of postmaster at the second post office to be established in the county.[18] Later, he would become a farmer, a county magistrate, and owner of a general store and the first steam-powered sawmill in the vicinity; from 1856 to 1859, he would serve as a state representative.[19] But Marcus never married.[20] Instead, he devoted himself to tending his considerable property, managing his various enterprises, and attending to public service activities.

Charles and Sally Smallwood's other children also did well for themselves. They owned considerable property, in addition to being active in political affairs. The second Smallwood son, John Smaw Smallwood, represented Beaufort County in the general assembly of North Carolina in 1818.[21] The fourth son, Samuel Smaw Smallwood, represented Beaufort County in the general assembly from 1829 to 1836.[22] The fifth son, Thomas Smallwood, who also remained in Beaufort County, owned real estate and three slaves by 1850.[23] In 1851, he was the deputy sheriff of Beaufort County, and in 1870, he and his family moved onto Marcus's land in Rich Square to operate the steam mill.[24] The Smallwoods' sixth and youngest son, T. T. Piladese, worked as a physician in Beaufort County in 1850.[25] By 1860, he had moved to Bertie County, North Carolina, where he owned eighty-seven slaves and properties with a real estate value of $22,000. Overall, his personal assets were valued at $73,120.[26]

As Marcus W. Smallwood was settling in as postmaster in the town of Rich Square, his neighbors in Southampton County, Virginia, were about to experience a catastrophe so shocking that it would change the course of the nation's history. It would all begin with the son of Nancy of the Nile, Nat Turner, who was preparing to focus the attention of a horrified nation upon "one of the cruelest systems of slavery ever established by mankind."[27] No one, not even Nat's fellow residents in the obscure backwater of Southampton County, Virginia, suspected the events that would soon unfold along the Carolina border. Neither did Marcus W. Smallwood know that he would eventually become indirectly linked to

Nat Turner, a man who despised the slave system that he was himself so much a part of.

Nat Turner was a literate, pious man of high intelligence who had a reputation for honesty and hard work.[28] He claimed to have received frequent visions that he interpreted as divinely inspired. He took these visions so seriously, in fact, that he was convinced by one to return to his owner after a successful escape in 1821.[29] Although his lot as a slave was to labor in the fields, Nat was permitted to preach to both whites and blacks and to conduct Baptist services as far north as Richmond, Virginia, and southward into North Carolina as well. His influence in these areas is attested to by the fact that his fellow slaves gave him the nickname of "the Prophet."[30] Known for his charismatic leadership abilities, Nat was, by early manhood, able to persuade others to do his will.[31]

By early 1828, Nat was convinced that he "was ordained for some great purpose in the hands of the Almighty."[32] On May 12 of that year, while working in the fields, he claimed to have been interrupted by a loud noise above him, "and the Spirit instantly appeared to me and said the Serpent was loosened, and Christ had laid down the yoke he had borne for the sins of men, and that I should take it on and fight against the Serpent, for the time was fast approaching when the first should be last and the last should be first."[33] This vision and his own revulsion for slavery and the human misery it imposed convinced Nat that he had been called upon by God to carry forth a mission to "arise and prepare myself, and slay my enemies with their own weapons."[34] He believed that blacks could not be delivered from bondage until they were confident in the knowledge that slavery was not divinely ordained, as whites had led them to believe.[35] Therefore, confiding in his four most trusted friends, Henry, Hank, Nelson, and Sam, he began to watch for divine signals that would tell him when and how to begin his mission.[36] In the meantime, he continued to labor in the fields, preach, pray, plan, and wait for a sign.[37]

As Nat waited, he acquired a new slave owner. In 1828, he became the inherited property of Putnam Moore, the nine-year-old son of Thomas Moore, his previous owner, who had died earlier that year.[38] Thomas Moore had purchased Nat for the sum of four hundred dollars after the death of Samuel Turner, the son of Nat's original owner, Benjamin Turner, in 1822. At the same time, Nat's wife, Cherry, and their children were sold to a different plantation in Southampton County, allowing Nat only limited contact with his family.[39] Thomas Moore's widow, Sally Francis Moore, married Joseph Travis in 1829, a year after her husband's death, and Travis took over supervision of young Putnam's slaves, Nat included.[40]

On February 12, 1831, the signs that Nat had been waiting for began to appear. He interpreted the occurrence of an annular solar eclipse as a vision of a black man's hand covering the sun, and he and his followers began planning in earnest. Later that year, on August 13, another solar eclipse occurred. This time the sun appeared to be surrounded by a blue green haze. Nat was convinced that this was the final signal, and he and a band of armed slave insurgents decided to strike a "blow at slavery" within the week.[41] This "blow" ultimately rocked the foundation of the slaveholding South and shattered its complacency forever.[42]

On the afternoon of Sunday, August 21, 1831, around three o'clock, Turner met at Cabin Pond with his four chosen followers and two new recruits named Will and Jack to plan the rebellion. He had originally planned to strike on July 4—Independence Day—but had been forced to postpone the insurrection because of illness and a lack of adequate planning.[43] On August 21, while Nat's followers feasted on a roasted pig and drank apple brandy, Nat delivered a speech informing his men about their plan, their mission, and their purpose.[44] He reminded them that their actions would start a war against slavery—a war for freedom—and directed them to make their way into Jerusalem, the seat of Southampton County, where he predicted they would reign in victory.[45] In order for the revolt to be successful, he said, they must "spare neither age nor sex."[46]

At 2:00 a.m. on August 22, 1831, Nat and his fellow revolutionaries, armed with rackets and knives,[47] burst out of the dense forest of southeastern Virginia and embarked on a quest that many before them had only attempted—a successful slave revolt. In their commitment to gain not only their own freedom but also the freedom of all people victimized by the vicious and evil system of slavery, they dispelled the myth of the docile Negro who accepted his lot and "carved a trail of death"[48] that would remain etched in the minds of Southerners, both black and white, for generations to come.[49]

Nat and his men traveled from farm to farm, killing entire families, sparing only a few residences, such as the one where Nat's wife and children lived.[50] And as the army of slaves cut its way through the countryside, it gained more and more recruits and confiscated weapons and ammunition.[51] By noon on Monday, August 22, 1831, Turner's army, now sixty strong, had left a trail of dead men, women, and children, and chaos had spilled over the borders of Southampton County.

News of the revolt spread like wildfire across surrounding counties, neighboring states, and eventually the entire country. Everywhere, fear hung in the air because Nat Turner had not yet been captured, and his whereabouts and whether he was still recruiting slaves for his army of insurgents were unknown.[52] It was not long before white volunteers and farmers united and a militia was assembled.[53] Gripped with fear, local townspeople near Southampton County prepared for the onslaught of the revolutionaries and hoped that the massacre might soon be stopped. The town of Murfreesboro, North Carolina, located about sixteen miles from Rich Square and approximately fourteen miles from the starting point of the revolt, was the largest town near Southampton County and the first town to hear of the revolt.[54] The rumor that Nat Turner and his men were approaching had already spread through Murfreesboro when a runner from Northampton County came to warn residents that the revolutionaries were only eight miles away and were headed their way.[55] Although this rumor proved untrue, others arose and became the cause of much fear and panic. The white residents of Murfreesboro believed that the rebels were advancing toward their town and that Turner and his men were only a mile and a half away. Again, it was a false alarm. Nonetheless, panic and fear spread throughout "Southampton, Hertford, Gates, Northampton, Halifax, and adjoining counties," and many of those who lived in Southampton County sought refuge in adjacent counties.[56] The intensity of the moment and the "demoralizing news" of the revolt were described by residents as having the same effect that might "in after years, have been caused by a nuclear blast not far distant."[57] One Murfreesboro resident, upon hearing that Turner and his men were approaching, fell dead on the spot.[58] A growing sense of paranoia among the white population of Murfreesboro triggered suspicions that many of the town's black residents were in cahoots with Nat Turner, and as a result, many blacks, both slave and free, were put under restrictions or house arrest. An uprising or outright warfare initiated by blacks had been, for a number of years, the great fear of many whites and had been deemed the "most dreaded nightmare of Armageddon."[59]

Only twenty-four hours after the revolt had broken out, however, the band of revolutionaries began to fall apart. After encountering resistance from local white residents, much of Turner's army ended its rebellion on the morning of Tuesday, August 22, leaving about sixty white victims.[60] Turner himself, identified as the leader of the revolt by whites who had survived the attacks, retreated to a point near Cabin Pond with two of his surviving men. Still determined to win the war against slavery, he instructed them to go out and find other insurgents. They never returned.[61]

For the next six weeks, Nat Turner lived in a field in a hole he had dug with his sword, using fence rails to conceal himself.[62] On October 30, 1831, he was captured and brought to Jerusalem in chains to stand trial. There a vicious and angry crowd awaited him, but his commitment to what he believed was his mission—emancipation—never wavered.[63] When reminded of the failure of his revolt, he replied that "the saviour of man had been executed, but that his cause had not failed."[64]

In the weeks before Turner's capture, panic and fear among Southern whites translated into retaliation against the black race. Some Negroes were "taken in different directions, and executed every day,"[65] while others were shot or beheaded, their heads stuck on poles to rot. Many other acts of violence were committed against blacks as a result of the uprising. In the aftermath of the revolt, it is estimated that as many as two hundred or more innocent Negroes were killed in retaliation, compared to the approximately sixty whites who fell victim to Nat Turner's rebellion.[66]

Even long after its conclusion, Nat Turner's revolt was a source of fear for Southern whites and Negroes alike. One resident of Northampton County described Turner as a man who was "to be more feared than soul-burning Satan,"[67] and for many years after Turner's death, his name was invoked as a scare tactic to get good behavior from children. In Rich Square, for example, children were told that "Nat Turner would go to people's house, get the baby out of the cradle, catch it by the heels, and then run away and hide."[68]

On November 11, 1831, Nat Turner and his fellow insurgents were hanged.[69] Turner himself went to the gallows without showing the slightest hint of emotion. In fact, one account, published in Richmond's *Times*, stated that he not only seemed "reckless of his fate, but actually hurried the executioner to the performance of his duty."[70]

Turner's execution marked the end of the last major slave rebellion in Virginia and the last time that slavery was seriously challenged in the South. One historian noted that Nat Turner's insurrection "was a landmark in the history of slavery . . . It was the forerunner of the great slavery debates, which resulted in the abolition of slavery in the United States and was, indirectly, most instrumental in bringing about this result." [71]

After Turner's death, two of his sons reportedly remained in the county of Southampton, with one eventually making his way to Ohio, while Nat's wife and daughter were sold south to slave traders.[72] Just over two decades later, this daughter would become the property of Marcus W. Smallwood.

After the Insurrection, Giles Reese [Cherry's master]
hid Cherry and the children . . . No records exist of
one daughter. She could have lived and had children.
There is the probability she was the property of
another master in her adult years. Any children born
to her would have been known by the name of that
master . . . instead of the last name of Turner.¹

—*Bruce Lawrence Turner*
Great-great-great-grandson of Nat Turner

CHAPTER TWO

THOUSAND DEATHS

In 1850, approximately nineteen years after Nat Turner's revolt, Marcus W. Smallwood was still living on Bryantown Road in Rich Square, Northampton County, North Carolina. He continued to own most of the land in the area, was working as a farmer, and had three slaves.² Now around fifty years old, he was living at the home of Mrs. Martha Josey, the fifty-year-old widow of Stephen Josey. The Joseys' son, William, also lived in the house and acted as overseer of the Josey property.³

Martha Josey also owned a considerable amount of land in the town of Rich Square. Her husband had purchased 100 of the 640 acres of the original Rich Square tract in 1753,⁴ and she herself owned twenty-five slaves by the mid-1800s.⁵ One of these slaves, Oscar Josey, had been fathered by her late husband. Oscar and his brother George lived nearby in the home of a local white family, Mr. and Mrs. William Norwood.⁶ Mr. Norwood was a man of considerable wealth. He owned a horse-drawn wagon gin⁷ and a general store that housed a post office⁸ and served as postmaster in Rich Square in 1877.⁹ He was also the first mayor of Rich Square after the town was incorporated in 1883.¹⁰

By 1860, one year before the Civil War, Marcus W. Smallwood owned an enormous amount of real estate and personal property. His real estate alone was valued at $17,000, and his personal property amounted to an additional $36,000, a sum that included thirty-two slaves—fourteen males and eighteen females.[11] Smallwood had owned only three slaves in 1850, but in the decade before the war, he either inherited or purchased an additional twenty-nine. The exact year, Marcus W. Smallwood acquired ownership of these slaves is unknown, as it was common practice, in property valuations, to categorize slaves as general "property" rather than catalogue them as human beings or list them individually by name. The Smallwood slaves themselves, like most Negroes at that time, were prohibited by law from learning to read or write; as a consequence, most of their written history was never documented but was transmitted solely through oral recollections. For the most part, these oral histories have proven accurate and can be verified, except in the case of details that family tradition failed to record. Because of the nature of the source materials, however, there are still many unknown facts about the Smallwood family.

What is known is that sometime between 1855 and 1858 or 1859, Nat Turner's daughter, now in her mid-to late thirties, was sold out of the state of Virginia into North Carolina, along with her slave husband, called David, [12] and three of her eleven children.[13] It is not clear how many times she had been sold before she was brought to North Carolina because the slave trade in Virginia was substantial and records of sale were often poorly kept. According to a statement made in the mid-1800s by fugitive slave William W. Brown, "[T]he precise number of slaves carried from the slave-raising to the slave-consuming states we have no means of knowing. But it must have been very great, as forty thousand were sold and carried out of the state of Virginia in one single year!"[14] Thus there is little chance that accurate records of her sale or trade were kept before her export from Virginia.

There is even some uncertainty about her name. After her arrival in North Carolina, she was known as "Mary Eliza,"[15] but this may not have been the name given her at birth as it was not unusual for slaves' names to be changed when they were sold or traded and became the property of a different owner. It was also common for a slave's name to be changed if there was a slave with the same name already living on a plantation. If this was the case with Mary Eliza, her name could possibly have been changed several times, depending on the number of times she had been sold.

In any case, the enumerator of the 1900 U.S. Federal Census recorded that Mary Eliza was born in June 1820 in Virginia, the same state where she reported that both of her parents were born.[16] The three children who were sold with Mary Eliza and David into North Carolina were also born in Virginia—Tobias (born ca. 1850), Thomas (born ca. 1852), and Emma (born ca. 1854). Mary Eliza's other eight children had either been sold from her, or she had been sold from them, at the time she was exported from Virginia.[17] What happened to them is unknown. As soon as Mary Eliza arrived in North Carolina, she gave birth to another daughter, whom she named Elizabeth, or Betty, in 1858.[18]

That Mary Eliza, only in her mid-thirties, had given birth to eleven children prior to being sold into North Carolina was not unusual.[19] As was the case with many female slaves, birthing could begin as early as thirteen years of age, and possibly younger, depending on a girl's age at menarche. By twenty years of age, most slave females were expected to have had at least four or five children.[20] Mary Eliza herself was around thirty years old when she gave birth to Tobias, her ninth child, who was sold with her into North Carolina. Given that she had already borne eight other children before Tobias's birth, she was undoubtedly a very young teenager—possibly twelve or thirteen—at the time she began bearing children.

In Virginia, Mary Eliza apparently belonged to a slaveholder named Bryant, as she was given the surname "Bryant" when she was sold into North Carolina.[21] At the time, there were several slave-owning Bryant families who lived in the area of Rich Square.[22] In fact, it is possible that the name of Bryantown Road, where Marcus W. Smallwood lived, was derived from the large number of Bryants who settled in the northwest section of Rich Square after the formation of Northampton County in 1741.[23] It is unclear how long Mary Eliza belonged to the Bryant slaveholder, but she became the property of Marcus W. Smallwood within a short time of her arrival in Northampton County. Whether her husband, David,[24] and her two sons, Tobias and Thomas, were ever the property of Marcus W. Smallwood is unknown, but they were put up for sale soon after their arrival in North Carolina, and Mary Eliza had to witness yet again the debasement of her loved ones as they were sold like mere chattel.

A typical scene from a mid-1800s slave auction in Northampton County is preserved in the account of Andrew Boone, an ex-slave who lived in a town less than six miles from the town of Rich Square. Boone drove a two-horse wagon when slaves were carried to market and had occasion to observe a number of auctions during the period in which Mary Eliza and her family resided in Northampton County. In an interview conducted many years after the abolition of slavery, Boone described how "dey sold slaves jes' like people sell hosses now. I saw a lot of slaves sold on de auction block. Dey would strip 'em stark naked. A nigger scarred up or whaled an' welted up wus considered a bad nigger an' did not bring much. If his body wus not scarred, he brought a good price."[25] Similarly, William Wells Brown described a slave auction as the "most cruel, revolting and atrocious scene" he had ever witnessed and stated that only God could know the "human agony and suffering" of the horrors of the slave trade:

> There was on the boat [i.e., slave ship] a large room on the lower deck, in which all slaves were kept, men and women, all chained together. The slaves were then carried to the slave-pen [for auction]. Here the slaves were placed in a negro-pen, where those who wished to purchase could call and examine them. The negro-pen is a small yard, surrounded by buildings, from fifteen to twenty feet wide, with the exception of a large gate with iron bars. The slaves are kept in the building during the night and turned out into the yard during the day. After the best of the stock was sold at private sale at the pen, the balance was sold at public auction. Such are but uncommon occurrences in the slave states. At these auction-stands . . . human beings are sold with as much indifference as a farmer in the north sells a horse or sheep.[26]

This type of scene was one that Mary Eliza, unfortunately, witnessed many times. Not only was she bought and sold a number of times herself and made to endure the sale of her husband and two eldest sons once they arrived in North Carolina, but she was soon forcibly separated from yet another of her children. On September 19, 1863, not long after she became the property of Marcus W. Smallwood, Mary Eliza gave birth to another son—John Jefferson Smallwood. Within six months of his birth, John Jefferson was separated from his mother.[27]

The experiences of Mary Eliza were typical of most slaves in the mid-1800s. Separation of a slave mother from her children, even in their infancy, was commonplace, and it is impossible to comprehend the agony that Mary Eliza and other slave women must have felt when they saw their children, as well as other family members, sold away, many of them never to be seen again. William and Ellen Craft, who chronicled their own successful escape from slavery in *Running a Thousand Miles for Freedom*, tried to capture the feelings of a mother robbed of her children on the auction block when they wrote, in 1860, "O, deep was the anguish of the slave mother's heart, / When called from her darlings forever to part; / ... That poor mourning mother, of reason bereft, / Soon ended her sorrows and sank cold in death."[28] Similarly, in 1861, the abolitionist reformer Harriet Jacobs, herself a former slave, depicted the horror and anguish of a slave mother on the eve of an auction:

> She sits on her cold cabin floor, watching the children who may all be torn from her the next morning; and often does she wish that she and they might die before the day dawns. She may be an ignorant creature, degraded by the system that has brutalized her from childhood; but she has a mother's instinct, and is capable of feeling a mother's agonies. On one of these sale days, I saw a mother lead seven children to the auction-block. She knew that *some* of them would be taken from her, but they took *all*. The children were sold to a slave-trader, and their mother begged the trader to tell her where he intended to take them; this he refused to do. How *could* he, when he knew he would sell them, one by one, wherever he could command the highest price? I met that mother in the street, and her wild, haggard face lives to-day in my mind. She wrung her hands in anguish, and exclaimed, "Gone! All gone! Why *don't* God kill me?" I had no words wherewith to comfort her. Instances of this kind are daily, yea, of hourly occurrence.[29]

Women like Mary Eliza must indeed have broken the "night-silence with the shrieks of [their] breaking heart"[30] countless times as they witnessed, over and over again, the sale of their family members. The slave system crippled them, crushing their spirits under day-to-day drudgeries and the constant threat of "slave-prisons, slave-auctions, handcuffs, whips, chains, bloodhounds and other instruments of cruelty,"[31] and left them without any means of preventing the auctions or of getting their loved ones back. For Mary Eliza, the daughter of Nat Turner, the man who had fought so violently against the abhorrent treatment of his people, the anguish of the auctions must have been only too pointed.

When the infant John Jefferson was taken from Mary Eliza, it is unclear whether she herself was sold outside of Rich Square or whether she was simply moved to a different plantation within the same town. Whatever Mary Eliza's exact location, it is clear that she remained somewhere in the vicinity of Rich Square, because records indicate that, in August 1865, only two years after John Jefferson's birth, she bore Marcus W. Smallwood a daughter, whom she named Mary Eliza, after herself, in keeping with the Smallwood family custom.[32] John Jefferson's accounts state that he himself remained at Rich Square on the plantation of his birth,[33] with or near Marcus W. Smallwood,[34] who would later in his life serve as somewhat of a father figure to him in the absence of his real father, whom he often referred to as David Lawrence (Smallwood), who had been sold away from the family.[35]

Taken from his mother at an early age, young John Jefferson had an experience similar to that of Frederick Douglass, who wrote of his own separation from his mother in his autobiography:

> My mother and I were separated when I was but an infant—before I knew her as my mother. It is a common custom, in the part of Maryland from which I ran away, to part children from their mothers at a very early age. Frequently, before the child has reached its twelfth month, its mother is taken from it, and hired out on some farm a considerable distance off, and the child is placed under the care of an old woman, too old for field labor. For what this separation is done, I do not know, unless it be to hinder the development of the child's affection toward its mother, and to blunt and destroy the natural affection of the mother for the child. This is the inevitable result.[36]

In John Jefferson's case, however, enforced separation did not hinder or destroy the natural affection he felt for his mother. Throughout most of his life, he never stopped longing, searching, and praying for her and for the day when he would see her again. He was determined to find her and never gave up hope or stopped looking for her. Most importantly, he never stopped loving her.[37]

It's all hard, slavery and freedom, both bad when
you can't eat.[1]

—*Andrew Boone, ex-slave*
Northampton County, North Carolina.

CHAPTER THREE

SPRING 1865

At the time of John Jefferson's birth, on September 19, 1863, America was in the grips of a Civil War. Although the war would forever change John Jefferson's life and the lives of many other Americans, he himself was completely oblivious to it, and quite understandably so. He was only an infant—an infant without a mother.

Only a year and three days before John Jefferson's birth, on September 22, 1862, President Lincoln issued a proclamation warning rebellious slaveholding states that if they did not return to the Union by January 1, 1863, all slaves in them would be "forever free."[2] Despite this proclamation, the war, and the secession of Southern states continued.[3] North Carolina—with a total population of 999,622 and a slave population of 331,059—was one of several states that had already seceded from the Union by 1861.[4] At the time of his birth, John Jefferson Smallwood was one of 6,804 slaves who resided in Northampton County, a county with more slaves than whites.[5] The main reason that Northampton contained such a large slave population was its role in producing four staple crops that required an enormous amount of manual labor—corn, cotton, peanuts, and tobacco.[6] Agriculture in Northampton County, and in North Carolina as a whole, was the primary source of income for many white Southerners, because it presented them with opportunities to amass a good deal of wealth.[7]

Many of the slaves in Northampton County, John Jefferson included, lived on the plantations of their owners, usually in primitive slave cabins.[8] These cabins were generally built of logs and covered with slabs, and their chimneys were built of sticks and mud, with a coating of clay mud daubed over them. Mud also covered any cracks in slave houses.[9] Slaves themselves toiled relentlessly on the plantations of their owners, usually from "sun to sun" without any monetary compensation, their hard work benefiting only their masters.[10] John Jefferson, like most slave children, worked in whatever way his small body could. More than likely, he was made to accompany older slaves to the fields so that he could become accustomed to the arduous tasks of fieldwork.

And, like most other slave children, young John Jefferson was not taught to read. Any attempts by slaves to become literate were typically forbidden and often resulted in punishment that ranged from minor, such as whipping, to severe, such as hanging. Andrew Boone, a slave in Northampton County during the time of the Civil War, acknowledged being forbidden to read or write, although he was taught to count: "Dey learned us to count dis way. Ought is an' ought, an' a figger is a figger, all for de white man an' nothin' for de nigger."[11] Boone further described one of the types of punishment that he and others, like John Jefferson, might have received if they attempted to learn how to read and write:

I saw a lot of slaves whupped an' I wus whupped myself. Dey whupped me wid de cat o' nine tails. It had nine lashes on it. Some of de slaves wus whupped wid a cobbin paddle. Dey had forty holes in 'em an' when you wus buckled to a barrel dey hit your naked flesh wid de paddle an' everywhur dere wus a hole in de paddle it drawed a blister. When de whuppin' wid de paddle wus over, dey took de cat o' nine tails an' busted de blisters. By dis time de blood sometimes would be runnin' down dere heels. Den de next thing wus a wash in salt water strong enough to hold up an egg.[12]

On the warfront, many Northamptonians heeded the call to serve the Confederacy, with an estimated one thousand troops serving from the county, a site for several Confederate training camps. Despite the strong Confederate presence, Union activity in the area of Northampton had begun even before Lincoln's warning to the rebellious South. In fact, on February 20, 1862, between the hours of 11:00 a.m. and 2:00 p.m., while many of the local farmers were busy planting their crops, the village of Winton, North Carolina, located on the Chowan River in Northampton's neighboring county of Hertford, was burned by Union troops en route to destroy the bridges of the Seaboard and Roanoke Railroad across the Nottaway and Blackwater rivers. Winton, approximately twenty-four miles from Rich Square, was reportedly the first town in North Carolina burned by Union troops during the Civil War.[13]

Two months before John Jefferson's birth, in July 1863, Union Troops invaded Northampton County's soil again. An estimated five thousand Union soldiers, commanded by Colonel S. P. Spear, marched through Northampton County over the Roanoke River toward the bridge of the Wilmington and Weldon Railroad. This railway was essential for the Confederacy; it allowed military supplies to be sent from Wilmington, North Carolina, to General Lee in Virginia. Fearing an attempt to disrupt supply lines, Confederate intelligence watched the Union soldiers closely as they tramped onto Northampton County soil and headed for the railway bridge. General Matt Ransom, a Northampton County native who had served as a commissioner to the Confederate government in Montgomery, Alabama prior to the war, was sent to stop the movement of the five thousand Union soldiers with a mere two hundred troops.[14]

On the morning of July 28, 1863, as the Confederates stopped to bathe and eat at the millpond known as Boone's Mill, Colonel Spear's Union troops, en route to destroy the railroad bridge, caught them off guard.[15] But Ransom's troops rallied and, for nearly three hours, exchanged intense fire with Spear and his men. When Spear's troops began a flanking movement around them, Ransom's men pulled a bluff and forced Spear and the Union forces to retreat to Winton, North Carolina. In the end, the railroad bridge was not destroyed, and the crops of 1863 and 1864 were spared.[16]

From the spring of 1864 until the summer of 1865, perhaps unbeknown to John Jefferson, several events were unfolding that would shape his life forever. Early in 1864, President Lincoln placed General Ulysses S. Grant in charge of the Union armies.[17] Grant, with support from General William Tecumseh Sherman, took the war directly into the heartland of the Confederacy, after much intense and coordinated planning on how to cripple the Southern army on all fronts.[18] In the fall of 1864, the city of Atlanta surrendered to Sherman after persistent attacks by his Union forces. Union solders had been instructed to demolish fields, livestock, railroads, bridges, and whatever else they felt compelled to destroy.[19] Meanwhile, Grant carried an attack against Richmond.[20]

In November 1864, President Lincoln was reelected to a second term of office, and the continued victories of Generals Grant and Sherman gave all indications that the war would soon end. Accordingly, the new year and the passing of the Thirteenth Amendment, which forever abolished slavery in America, brought joy and jubilation to millions of slaves.[21] Three months after abolition was put into effect, on April 9, 1865, the war officially ended, after four long and bloody years.[22]

During the closing weeks of the Civil War, in the spring of 1865, Union soldiers again trampled the familiar soil of Northampton County. As farmers in Northampton were preparing their crops for harvest, word came that an estimated eight thousand mounted Union troops and artillery had moved across the county into the Seaboard area of North Carolina, approximately nineteen miles from Rich Square. The mission of the Union army was to destroy livestock, ruin fields, smash bridges, and tear up rail lines.[23] Union soldiers placed their artillery alongside the railroad and dug up embankments, with the intention of destroying the train from Norfolk, Virginia, en route to Weldon, North Carolina, or possibly Richmond, Virginia. On this train were approximately two thousand Confederate troops.[24] Disaster was averted when the Confederates got wind of the danger lurking ahead of them. As the train approached, they backed down. The battle that could have been never happened.[25]

Meanwhile, as Union soldiers continued to move across Northampton County, according to oral family history, little John Jefferson had gone with Marcus W. Smallwood to his general store in the town of Rich Square, not too far from Union-occupied Seaboard.[26] Apparently, he had heard Marcus W. Smallwood and others talking about the "Yankee," and as was the case with many other Negroes in the South, it had been instilled in him that the Yankees were bad people who would either harm or kill him. Andrew Boone, another Northampton County slave, described the fear that much of the local slave population felt for the Yankees: "Dey tole us dat de Yankees would bore holes in our shoulders an' work us to carts. Dey tole us we would be treated a lot worser den dey wus treating us."[27] Like Boone and most of his fellow slaves, little John Jefferson, too, was perhaps afraid of the Yankees.

Known by local residents to be an extremely bright child who possessed an intelligence superior to that of most children his age, as

Union soldiers and their horses came closer to the place where John Jefferson was sitting, he knew he had to do something, and fast. As the horses' hooves tramped closer, John Jefferson ran to the steps of the store and tried to warn Marcus Smallwood of the impending danger.[28]

As the mounted Union soldiers drew ever nearer, he became more and more persistent in trying to get Marcus W. Smallwood's attention. Because he was causing such a ruckus outside of the store, Marcus W. Smallwood walked to the door and stepped outside.[29]

But it was already too late. The Union soldiers were upon him. One of them grabbed Smallwood, by now a man of considerable age, and struck him repeatedly. John Jefferson later described that day as one of utter chaos.[30]

Little John Jefferson could do nothing but cry. He knew, even at his very young age, that Marcus W. Smallwood was all the family he had. To see him, the only person who had played anything of a paternal role in his life, beaten almost to death, was beyond belief. John Jefferson repeatedly wailed as he witnessed the bloody beating. Feeling sorry for this pitiful young boy, the soldiers stopped the beating. As they were departing, one of them told Smallwood that the only reason they had not killed him was because of "that Negro boy." In gratitude, Marcus W. Smallwood, one of the wealthiest men and largest landowners in the town of Rich Square, promised John Jefferson that he would send him to school.[31] And that is exactly what he did.

In Oct 1870 to June 1871 I was a poor pupil at Hampton. I was sent home in June 1871 and told by the late Gen. Armstrong not to return <u>not because I was a "bad student"</u> or had violated any of the laws of that Institution, not because I had disrespected any of the officials or teachers, but because <u>I had no money</u> and <u>no parents to vouch for me.</u>

—John J. Smallwood
Letter to Dr. H. B. Frissell, Principal,
Hampton Normal and Agricultural Institute
Hampton, Virginia
December 26, 1903

CHAPTER FOUR

THE BUTLER SCHOOL: THE EARLY DAYS OF HAMPTON

When John Jefferson arrived at the Butler School on the campus of Hampton Normal and Agricultural Institute in October 1870, it must have seemed liked a dream come true.[1] Like Booker T. Washington,[2] who would attend Hampton two years later, in 1872, he too must have thought that Hampton was "the greatest place on earth, and not even Heaven presented more attractions."[3] For John Jefferson, having the opportunity to go to school must have felt like heaven right here on earth.

The Butler School was the first school in the United States to be opened for freedmen. Established at Fort Monroe (also known as Fortress Monroe) in Virginia in 1861, during the early years of the Civil War and two years before John Jefferson's birth, the school was named for General Benjamin Franklin Butler, a Massachusetts politician and Union officer who served as commander of the Union forces at Fort Monroe, the most powerful fort in the United States during the Civil War.[4] General Butler, who in civilian life was a prominent lawyer, was a forerunner for the liberation of Negro slaves and had already liberated thousands by the time of Lincoln's Emancipation Proclamation.[5]

Shortly after Butler was assigned command of Fort Monroe in Hampton, Virginia, and of the Department of Virginia, in 1861, on May 23, three Negro slaves who had escaped from their masters in Hampton were brought before him.[6] According to the Fugitive Slave Act, a federal law passed by Congress on September 18, 1850, a runaway slave had to be returned to his rightful owner.[7] But Butler was not like other generals, who typically complied with the act and promptly returned runaways to their masters. Butler defied the law and refused to send the fugitive field hands back to their owners when he learned that they were about to be sent farther south to work on coastal fortifications for the Confederacy. The slaves' masters demanded that their "property" be returned to them, based on the provisions of the act,[8] but General Butler confiscated the slaves, dubbing them "contraband of war," as with any property in use by the enemy during a time of war.[9] The War Department supported Butler's interpretation of the laws of war and refused to enforce the Fugitive Slave Act against the runaways.[10]

Before long, Fort Monroe became inundated by hordes of fugitive slaves as General Butler found himself with at least $60,000 worth of property on his hands, as more and more slaves sought refuge fleeing to Union lines around Fort Monroe, which later earned the nickname "Freedom's Fortress." He wrote to his superiors in Washington, seeking advice and guidance on the disposition of this confiscated human property. Backed by the War Department who sided with General Butler's unique interpretation of the laws of the war, he was instructed to feed, shelter, and employ the slaves in suitable and appropriate jobs.[11] Congress itself took matters a step further, by emancipating slaves in the District of Columbia and prohibiting Union officers from sending fugitives back to their owners.[12] The term "contraband" soon caught on as common vernacular, and throughout the Union army, it became standard policy in the confiscation of fugitive slaves.[13] Congress also extended to President Lincoln the discretionary power to use Negro troops in the war against the Confederacy,[14] and General Butler, in turn, was able to make extensive use of Negro troops within his own department during the war.[15]

That same year, in 1861, General Butler made a request to the American Missionary Association (AMA) to establish a school for freedmen.[16] In response to his request, Rev. Lewis C. Lockwood, a missionary with the AMA, was sent to Fort Monroe on September 3, 1861. There, he established the first day school for freedmen and employed Mrs. Mary Peake as the first teacher.[17] Mrs. Peake, a free Negro woman in Hampton, taught the first class of twenty contraband children under the shade tree of the great live oak—now known as the Emancipation oak—at the head of the Hampton Hospital.[18] Mrs. Peake died in 1862, and the Butler School, named in honor of General Butler, was established as a school for freedmen the next year.[19]

Again assigned as commander of the greatly expanded Department of Virginia and North Carolina, when General Butler returned to Fort Monroe in November 1863, after having been defeated at Big Bethel on June 10, 1861, and having commanded an expeditionary force on August 10, 1861, that, in conjunction with the United States Navy, took Forts Hatteras and Clark in North Carolina,[20] in addition to having commanded the troops that accompanied Admiral Farragut in taking New Orleans in May 1862 in which he was made military governor of the city,[21] he found that the school's contraband children were in great need of supplies and provisions, despite the dedicated efforts of many Northern missionaries who had devoted themselves to educating the refugees. Feeling that the situation warranted immediate attention, Butler was instrumental in securing government funding for the school's buildings. Thanks to his efforts, the Butler School building was erected in 1863 near the Emancipation oak, where Mrs. Peake had taught the first students only two years before.[22] When the school opened its doors, six hundred students ranging from ages five to twenty-four attended.[23] These students were the offspring of freedmen.[24] Initially, many of the teachers who had come from New England states[25] and who had served as missionaries in the Hampton area after the Civil War[26] criticized the students because of their lack of appropriate attire and manners. The missionaries failed to understand the harsh conditions and extreme deprivation under which these children had lived as ex-slaves and descendants of slaves. Most of these children, if not all of them, had come directly from plantations and from situations in which they had to contend with disease, ragged clothing, hunger, lack of medical care, and other bleak conditions.[27] In addition, some of the students had been without parents—with no one to care for them or teach them how to care for themselves.

After having some degree of contact with the Butler School children, however, it was not long before many of the teachers realized that even though most of their pupils had come from extremely dehumanizing situations, their thirst for knowledge was so intense that it overshadowed their dehumanization. Many of the students were bright and possessed an enthusiasm and an eagerness for learning,[28] and their determination kept the morale of the staff high, despite the fact that there were many reasons for discontent, including overcrowding, lack of supplies and instructional materials,[29] ostracism, threats, and community attempts to prevent teachers from providing educational opportunities to freedmen.[30] Even in the face of these difficulties, many teachers remained optimistic about the Butler School children and believed that they deserved the same type of education that they had received themselves.[31]

In the spring of 1864, several months later, after General Butler's return, as the Butler School continued to operate and educate many students, which was the desire of General Butler, the war continued. General U. S. Grant, general in chief of all the Union armies, conferred with Butler at Fort Monroe in early April regarding his plan to attack the Confederates. The plan was for Butler to go up the James River, seize City Point on the south bank of the river, and then make an advance on Richmond while Grant would be simultaneously attacking General Lee's army in Northern Virginia, forcing it back toward Richmond. Grant's object was not solely to capture Richmond, but to destroy Lee's army. In his operations against Richmond, Butler's forces, under his command, were driven back to Bermuda Hundred, a peninsula between the James and Appomattox rivers. Butler's army was completely shut off from further operations directly against Richmond. The Confederates immediately sealed the neck of the peninsula as Butler's army was contained on Bermuda Hundred, thus resulting in an enormous number of wounded men and causalities. However, Grant's military skills allowed him to slip across the James River to Butler, and with their combined efforts, they attacked Petersburg, forcing Lee to come to the aid of city. [32] This incident, coupled with the fiasco of Fort Fisher that occurred later that year in

December 1864, where Butler was in charge of the expedition that failed, contributed mightily to the ending of his military career. [33] Meanwhile, as the war and General Butler's military career were both coming to an end, the Butler School was thriving and beginning to embark upon a new phase of education for the newly freed slaves.

After the Civil War ended, in 1866, General Oliver Otis Howard, commissioner general of the Freedmen's Bureau in Washington DC,[34] appointed General Samuel Chapman Armstrong as superintendent of the Ninth District of Virginia,[35] a position that put General Armstrong in charge of ten counties in Tidewater, Virginia, with headquarters at Hampton.[36] General Howard himself, as soon as the Civil War began with the surrender of Fort Sumter, had been appointed Colonel of the Third Maine Volunteer Infantry Regiment[37] and had temporarily commanded a brigade at the First Battle of Bull Run. He was later promoted to brigadier general and was given command of his brigade effective September 3, 1861.[38]

On March 3, 1865, Congress had established the Bureau of Refugees, Freedmen and Abandoned Lands, or the Freedmen Bureau, which had been signed into legislation by President Lincoln.[39] The Freedmen's Bureau Bill, initiated by President Lincoln, created the Freedman's Bureau, which assigned agents throughout the South to help the newly freed slave transition from slavery to freedom.[40] The bureau's main focus was to provide the following: food, clothing, medical care, and jobs, as well as, establish homes, ensure justice for the freedmen, manage abandoned or confiscated property, regulate labor, establish schools, and make provisions for the orphans.[41] The bureau's objective was to also minimize violence against freedmen. In 1865, 1866, and 1867, mobs throughout the South, in opposition to freedmen obtaining an education, burned school buildings and churches used as schools; teachers were flogged or driven away and, in some instances, murdered. [42] Some of the opposition from Southerners regarding the freedmen obtaining an education grew out of the notion that an educated Negro was a dangerous Negro[43] and the fear that an education would spoil them as field hands. In addition to opposing the cost of educating the freedman, others argued that racial equality was being advocated by Northern teachers. However, the opponents failed to realize that ex-slaves were not the only individuals who benefited from the services offered through the Freedmen's Bureau. In many cases, the bureau also provided aid for poor whites.[44]

General Howard, while serving as commissioner of the Freedman's Bureau, which he held the position from May 1865 to July 1874, was known for promoting the welfare and education of former slaves, freedmen, and refugees.[45] On November 20, 1866, General Howard and nearly a dozen or more men of various professional backgrounds met in Washington DC to discuss plans for a theological seminary to train colored ministers. Additionally, some of the men in attendance desired to include some industrial features other than ministry for the institute. General Howard, as he had previously done with other educational associations, offered to erect, by the bureau, a suitable building, if they would provide a proper lot. A motion was made, and the new institution was named the Howard Theological Seminary. Several days later, on December 4, 1866, Normal and Theological Institute for the Education of Preachers and Teachers was the new title adopted. On January 8, 1867, the idea of a university that would have many separate departments acting together under one board of trustees was discussed. As a result, the board of trustees voted to change the name of the institution to Howard University, which was approved by the president of the United States on March 2, 1867. General Howard, known for playing a role in the founding of Howard University, served as president from 1869 to 1874.[46]

Armstrong, like Howard, too, had served in the Civil War. Armstrong had served at Fort Monroe as superintendent of black affairs during the Civil War,[47] in the capacity of leader of the Eighth and Ninth regiments of the United States Colored Troops. His experiences with the Negro troops and close association with them sparked an interest in their needs. General Armstrong was optimistic about the potential progress of Negroes and believed that, if given an opportunity, they would become self-reliant and responsible citizens.[48]

Upon accepting the appointment to the Ninth District, General Armstrong directed his energies toward assisting newly freed slaves. The son of a missionary to the Sandwich Islands (which later became the U.S. state of Hawaii), Armstrong's father, having overseen the teaching of writing, arithmetic and reading to the dark-skinned Polynesians in Hawaii, Armstrong himself envisioned a school similar to the one he had witnessed used by his father to educate the Polynesians whose situations in many respects were very similar to the ex-slaves.[49] He viewed his new post as an opportunity to help the ex-slaves he found in the Hampton area who were homeless, jobless, unskilled, and without the means to become self-sufficient.[50] His immediate task was to provide education, training, and jobs for the many Negroes who were living in squatter camps in the Hampton area,[51] and he found that, despite their destitute conditions, many ex-slaves were hungry for education. And it was education, he believed, that was not only the best vehicle for but also the only permanent solution to the advancement of thousands of former slaves.[52] His overall mission was to implement a plan that would allow the Negro to become self-reliant. [53]

In the spring of 1867, General Armstrong received $19,000 in donations from private donors, as well as the Freedmen's Bureau and the American Missionary Society, to purchase land and buildings for the establishment of educational facilities for Negroes. One such building was the Butler School.[54] The following year, in April 1868, Hampton Normal and Agricultural Institute opened its doors, with General Armstrong as its founder and principal.[55] Two years later, in June 1870, the institute received its charter from the state. Soon afterward, the AMA turned over full ownership of the Butler School to General Armstrong and the board of trustees.[56]

Word of the opening of a school in Hampton, Virginia, must have come to the small town of Rich Square fairly quickly. Like Booker T. Washington when he learned of a school for freedmen in Virginia,[57] John Jefferson might too have overheard talk about the Butler School from local residents of Rich Square or one of the surrounding towns, or perhaps Marcus W. Smallwood, seeking to make good on his promise, had searched for such a school to send John Jefferson to. Either way, Marcus W. Smallwood kept his promise, and when the fall term commenced on Monday, October 3, 1870, Marcus W. Smallwood made sure John Jefferson would be one of several students in attendance at the Butler School, now the property of Hampton Normal and Agricultural Institute.[58]

At the time of John Jefferson's enrollment that first Monday morning in October, he was a very young seven-year-old, having just turned seven a mere fourteen days earlier. Not only was Hampton, Virginia, quite different in terms of size and population from his small hometown of Rich Square, North Carolina, but it was also (perhaps unbeknown to young John

Jefferson) of great historical significance. Not only did Hampton contain the United States' first established school for freedmen, but it was also not far from the site where the first slaves had landed when they were brought to America. And in full view of the Hampton Institute was the cemetery containing the bodies of nearly six thousand U.S. soldiers and the granite monument to the martyrs who had first fought for the freedom of Negro slaves like John Jefferson. Not far away from the institute, the flag of Fort Monroe could be seen. It was erected near the site where General Butler had refused to send back the three fugitive slaves who had come seeking refuge from their masters. It was here too that the Jefferson Barracks had provided medical treatment to fifteen thousand ill and wounded soldiers from the armies of Generals McClellan and Grant during the Civil War.[59] The school itself was located near the site where President Lincoln's Emancipation Proclamation was read, the same site where Mrs. Peake taught the first class of contraband students in 1861.[60]

When John Jefferson arrived on the campus at Hampton Normal and Agricultural Institute, there stood before his eyes a one-room school building, the Butler School, built in the shape of a Greek cross.[61] It was 30 feet wide and 180 feet from end to end, with many tall windows and latticed porches. Inside was one great room without partitions. Benches could be arranged to form classes with long rows of desks. One can only imagine that for a child you processed an intellect that far surpassed his peers and who yearned for such as opportunity to acquire knowledge, surely, for John Jefferson, this was beyond belief.

Older students from the institute served as instructors for John Jefferson and his classmates at the Butler School. Suitable buildings for residence were available at the institute to accommodate John Jefferson and other students.[62] The cost for room and board was $7.50 per month. Tuition was $1.00 per month and cost of fuel was $0.75. Students who had difficulty paying could offset some of these expenses through practical labor.[63] In an effort to reduce school expenses, students were expected to spend their vacations at home, from the middle of June to October.[64]

John Jefferson, now a student at Hampton, was learning grammar, geography, arithmetic, reading, and writing. He would be the first in his family and one of the first in the long legacy of his race to learn to read, spell, add, subtract, write, and study geographical features of the earth, without fear of retribution.[65] John Jefferson by no means took this privilege for granted. Being a child who possessed an innate propensity to learn, he was intelligent enough to know that, not too long before, not much longer than five years, in fact, he would have been forbidden to take advantage of this opportunity to get an education—an opportunity that his forbears had been denied and one that had often resulted in danger, and sometimes even death, for themselves or their families.

Things were going just fine for John Jefferson at school, but things back at home, in Rich Square, were not going as well for Marcus W. Smallwood. By 1866, Marcus W. Smallwood had sold most of his land. Things had changed drastically since the war. Because the South had lost, Confederate money was of no value, and Marcus W. Smallwood, like many other white Southerners, knew that the end of prosperity was at hand.[66] Only two years after the sale of most of his land, the remaining tracts were sold at public auction on July 14, 1868.[67]

Marcus W. Smallwood, in the twilight years of his life and no longer occupied with the business of buying and selling land, now began to spend time with his daughter, John Jefferson's younger sister, Mary Eliza, who was five years of age. Mary Eliza, named after her mother, later told her children about an incident with her father. One day, as Marcus W. Smallwood was preparing to leave for town, she ran out of the house toward his horse-driven wagon and asked if she could go with him. Marcus W. Smallwood was initially at a loss for words. It was 1870. How could he explain to his five-year-old daughter that she could not accompany him? She vividly recalled him telling her that he could not take her with him, but he did not give her a reason why she could not go. As tears streamed down her face and she began to cry uncontrollably, Marcus W. Smallwood picked her up and sat her on the back of the wagon and told her that he could not take her with him but that he could send her to school and give her a plantation. Still crying, she told him that she did not want either of those things—she just wanted to go with her daddy. Years later she would come to understand the reason why she was not allowed to accompany her father or even acknowledge him as her father, or be acknowledged by him, in public: she was half-white, and if she were seen with this white man by the local white residents, she could easily have been identified as his daughter, which could have gotten Marcus Smallwood into a lot of trouble.[68]

Unfortunately, by the time Mary Eliza had grown older and had developed a better understanding of the world in which she lived, she was unable to take her father up on his offer of an education and land. Even if she had desired to do so, once she came to realize the value of his offer, it was too late. Soon after he made his promise, Marcus W. Smallwood died.[69]

John Jefferson had only been at Hampton a couple of months when Marcus W. Smallwood's death occurred. More than likely the event must have been very traumatic for him. In a sense, Marcus W. Smallwood was the only parental figure he had ever known. And yet on top of Smallwood's death, John Jefferson received some more heartrending news. Without any money or anyone to vouch for him, John Jefferson was told by General Armstrong himself, president of Hampton, not to return after the 1870–1871 school year had ended.[70]

Though in 1871, nearing the end of John Jefferson's first year at the Butler School, the trustees gave the use of the building (Butler School) to Elizabeth City County for a colored free school, which aligned it with the new public school system of Virginia. While the cost of attending the Butler School during his second year would have been free, John Jefferson still would not have been able to take advantage of this opportunity due to the fact that he had no parent or parental figure to vouch for him. [71]

When summer vacation came at the end of the school year at Hampton Normal and Agricultural Institute, John Jefferson, despondent and brokenhearted over the death of the man who had been his only semblance of a parental figure and having lost all hope of ever receiving an education, sadly said good-bye to his friends and teachers, never to see them again. He packed his belongings and cried all the way back home.

In the fall of 1876 I went to Shaw University under Rev. Dr. H. M. Tupper. I had studied the "Old Webster Spelling Book"—one hundred times—I had read every public speech and newspaper I could get at that time. I remained at Shaw University 1875-'76-'77, teaching upon the plantations of my birthplace during the summer months.[1]

—John J. Smallwood
Letter to Dr. H. B. Frissell, Principal
Hampton Normal and Agricultural
Institute, Hampton, Virginia
December 26, 1903

CHAPTER FIVE

SHAW DAYS

When John Jefferson returned to Rich Square that June, he had an extremely heavy heart. Disappointed at being ordered not to return to Hampton and saddened by the thought that he would never again have a chance at an education, John Jefferson was filled with great despair. He was indeed brokenhearted, but more so than that, he had lost his closest friend and confidant. When Marcus W. Smallwood died, John Jefferson was robbed of the only semblance of a parental figure he had ever known. He was alone—again. And sadly, he had not gotten the chance to say good-bye. From this point forward, Marcus W. Smallwood's physical presence would no longer play a part in John Jefferson's life—only his essence. This part of Marcus W. Smallwood would remain with John Jefferson for the rest of his life and would ultimately serve as a solid foundation upon which he would make his mark in life.

When he arrived in Rich Square that summer, John Jefferson began working on one of the largest cotton farms in the Roanoke Valley.[2] The cotton had been planted in May, a month before his arrival, and he was immediately given the arduous task of plowing and chopping the grass from the cotton plants. John Jefferson chopped until the middle of June, and once the bolls opened up around September, he began picking the cotton.[3]

For the next five years, John Jefferson worked on the farm, plowing, planting, chopping cotton and peanuts, baling vines and hay, and mauling rails—grueling work for a grown man, much less for a child of young John Jefferson's age. But John Jefferson still possessed an insatiable thirst for knowledge and continued to learn as much as he could on his own, building on the instruction he had acquired while studying at Hampton. Even while toiling all day, he could often be found at the end of a field row perusing the *Old Webster Spelling Book*, which he studied "one hundred times." He had such a voracious appetite for reading that he read every speech and newspaper he could get his hands on[4] and spent most of his time in the evenings studying after he had completed the multitude of chores assigned to him. Although he was poor, he showed a propensity to seek and acquire knowledge by whatever means he could; he possessed an intrinsic desire to learn and was extremely bright.[5] He yearned for the opportunity to learn in a classroom environment as he had when he was a student at Hampton, but he had no money and no parents, and at the time, learning as he worked was the best he could do.

Tired of the day-to-day drudgery of fieldwork and still yearning to be reunited with his mother, John Jefferson ran away from Rich Square a couple of months before he reached his twelfth birthday, during the summer of 1875. With no paper sack in his hands but a clear understanding of where he was going and what and whom he was searching for, John Jefferson walked sixty miles to the town of Franklin, Virginia, searching for his parents. Apparently he had heard whispers of his parents' being from Southampton County; perhaps even Marcus W. Smallwood had once told him. In any case, John Jefferson went to Southampton County in search of his mother.[6] It is doubtful that, at the time he ran away, he was aware that his grandfather, Nat Turner, had lived in Southampton County some forty-four years before.[7]

While in Southampton County, John Jefferson wandered around the area of Franklin, Virginia, and its surrounding towns, perhaps going from person to person asking if anyone had seen his mother. In his search, he realized that he was at a disadvantage: when he was asked for his mother's description, he could give no answer, because he had no memory of his mother and would not have recognized her even if she were standing before him. Neither could he remember the sound of her voice. This was a double tragedy for John Jefferson—one that caused him much emotional and mental pain.

As he continued his search from cabin to cabin, asking former slaves if anyone had seen his mother, John Jefferson soon realized that he was not alone. Many of the ex-slaves whom he met were perhaps victims of this same predicament. It is quite possible that they all felt his pain, as they, too, searched for and inquired about their own lost loved ones. They, too, like John Jefferson, had been displaced from family members by the barbarous system of slavery. Many children who had been slaves and who were now free had no way of finding their parents, their siblings, or even extended family members, as was the case with John Jefferson, who, technically, was considered an orphan. With Rich Square being a small closely-knit community, it is quite possible that John Jefferson, like so many other children who had been orphaned, was cared for by local colored residents in the town. With orphanage at its height after the Civil War, the caring of these children by other colored people in the community saved the government much expense.[8]

After searching for many days and nights, hungry, brokenhearted, and disappointed again, with no luck finding his parents, John Jefferson began the tedious sixty-mile walk back to Rich Square. When he arrived in Rich Square, a couple of weeks before his twelfth birthday, John Jefferson received the best news he had heard since Marcus W. Smallwood told him to pack his bags and prepare for the trip to Hampton. He had been accepted to study at Shaw University in Raleigh, North Carolina, for the fall term, which began in October.

Ten years before John Jefferson's enrollment in Shaw University, a thirty-four-year-old white man,[9] Dr. Henry Martin Tupper, left Monson, Massachusetts, with his wife and arrived in Raleigh, North Carolina, on October 10, 1865, to serve as a missionary to freedmen in the South.[10] Dr. Tupper's request to serve as a missionary had been granted by the American Baptist Mission Society in New York, and he was assigned to train Negroes to become leaders and ministers in the Baptist Church.[11] Immediately upon Dr. Tupper's arrival in Raleigh, he saw the need to provide biblical instruction to freedmen, owing to the fact that Negroes and whites were no longer allowed to worship together after the Civil War. Additionally, he desired to train leaders and to establish churches and other associations for freedmen.[12]

Five months after Dr. Tupper arrived in Raleigh, a series of events occurred that drastically enhanced his school. In February 1866, Tupper realized he needed to purchase a site for a building to provide the full range of services that he had envisioned for the freedmen who attended the school. He then wrote to the Home Mission Board, requesting a monetary advance.[13] His desire was to purchase land to build a two-story building for religious and educational purposes—one story to be used for general education and the other for religious instruction.[14]

Within a couple of months, the board granted Tupper's request, providing him with the funds to move forward on the plan for his school. With the monetary advance from the board and the five hundred dollars he had saved as a Union soldier, Tupper purchased the land needed for the site of his school on February 23, 1866. In the spring of that year, construction of the building that would serve as both school and church began at the corner of Blount and Cabarrus streets in Raleigh.[15] By the summer of 1866, the first floor of Tupper's building was completed, and the second story was added in the spring of 1867.[16] By the fall of 1868, several rooms on the second story were furnished to provide boarding and dormitory space.[17] By February 1870, the school had grown enough to warrant the purchase of additional property to accommodate the students.[18] Tupper himself remained committed to the idea of building an institution to provide an education for freedmen and continued to solicit funds to expand his school.[19]

The first building erected on the newly expanded site was Shaw Hall, named in honor of Elijah Shaw, who donated a large amount of money to the school.[20] By the summer of 1872, Shaw Hall was fully completed. At the time of John Jefferson's enrollment in Shaw University, it was one of two major structures on campus, the other being Estey Seminary.[21] Shaw Hall was four stories high and served as a dormitory, a library, and an instructional facility. Estey Seminary was an all-female facility that provided training for women in music, sewing, cooking, and other related areas. The seminary was renowned for housing some of the finest women from the best families in the state.[22]

In October 1875, having traveled over one hundred miles, John Jefferson arrived on the campus of Shaw University under the instruction of the Rev. Dr. Henry M. Tupper.[23] Filled with anxiety and excitement, John Jefferson had left the comforts of a small rural town for the city of Raleigh, which boasted a population of over seven thousand people. Much like his hometown of Rich Square, Raleigh had more Negroes than whites: Negroes comprised 53 percent of the population.[24]

What John Jefferson witnessed upon his arrival in Raleigh was quite different from what he was accustomed to seeing in his hometown. In Raleigh, there were approximately seven hundred Negroes employed in steady jobs, many of them unskilled occupations, such as servants, laundresses, laborers, and waiters. There were also thirteen colored professionals (including eight preachers, four teachers, and one physician) and thirty-one Negro businesses owners (including restaurateurs, blacksmiths, undertakers, cabinetmakers, boardinghouse managers, shoemakers, city market dealers, harness makers, grocers, and barbers).[25] This environment was very different from anything John Jefferson had experienced in his hometown of Rich Square, where most Negroes were employed as field hands, farm laborers, laundresses, and domestic workers. Seeing Negroes employed in these various positions, John Jefferson was optimistic about his future, as well as the future of other Negroes.

Compared to small-town Rich Square, the city of Raleigh must have been breathtaking to twelve-year-old John Jefferson, who must have imagined a world of possibilities when he arrived, full of excitement, on the campus of Shaw University. There before his eyes were the magnificent newly constructed Estey and Shaw Hall facilities, the latter of which would be his place of residence for the next four years. His precise mode of travel is not known, but chances are that he was transported either by a horse-drawn wagon or by rail. Walking was, of course, another option and was, in 1875, a common means of transportation, even over long distances. To John Jefferson's advantage, many classmates from his hometown of Rich Square and its surrounding towns had already taken this momentous journey in pursuit of an education, and it is quite possible that he may have traveled to Raleigh in company with other students.

One of his classmates who had arrived a year or two prior to his enrollment was Nicholas Franklin Roberts, who hailed from the town of Seaboard, North Carolina, near John Jefferson's hometown of Rich Square. Dr. Roberts was one of the first graduates of the college department at Shaw University, and upon graduation he was made professor of mathematics in the university. He was also vice president of the university and was later named acting president (effective November 12, 1893, to March 14, 1894) after Tupper's death.[26] Along with N. F. Roberts, another of John Jefferson's classmates was Manassa T. Pope, who traveled from John Jefferson's hometown of Rich Square to attend Shaw University in 1874. Upon graduation from Shaw, Pope studied at Shaw's Leonard School of Medicine and was a graduate of its first medical class in 1886. He was also one of the first Negro physicians licensed by the board.[27] Dr. Pope later ran unsuccessfully for mayor of Raleigh in 1919. Born to free parents, Dr. Pope was one of only seven Negroes eligible to vote in Wake County, Raleigh, North Carolina, in the early twentieth century. [28]

When John Jefferson arrived on Shaw's campus in October 1875, he had turned twelve—the minimum age for admission—only a little over a week before.[29] To attend the university, all males had to present testimonials or a record of unblemished character, and all students were required to perform satisfactorily, compared to their peers, on examinations.[30] John Jefferson was eager for the challenge. He had undoubtedly waited a long time for this opportunity, which, like his admission to Hampton, was a privilege that, unfortunately, only very few Negroes were afforded. It was certainly an opportunity that would not have been available to him, or to any other Negro, at the time of his birth, only twelve years earlier.

John Jefferson's intrinsic desire for and love of learning served him well at Shaw. Long before his admittance, the countless times he had studied the *Old Webster Spelling Book* and read every speech and newspaper in his possession helped him to develop his own pattern of studying and learning that, when combined with the tools and applications he had acquired at Hampton, made matriculation from Shaw somewhat effortless. Unlike the many days after he had left Hampton, he would now be able to receive instruction within the confines of a newly built classroom, with a faculty of five-well trained instructors, rather than reading alone at the end of a row of peanuts or cotton or under a shade tree.[31]

On his first day of class, John Jefferson was one of ninety-four students enrolled in the preparatory department.[32] And although his program of study was rigorous—including classes in arithmetic, penmanship, spelling, grammar, physical geography, history, map drawing, etymology, and English analysis—he remained optimistic about the challenges he faced. He was no stranger to hard work, and it was not long before he was accepted into the normal department, which required mastery of all courses in the preparatory department, in addition to passing a critical and rigid examination. Within a short time, John Jefferson had completed all course work and passed the exam.[33] He was elated, not so much because he had progressed so quickly, but because he was absorbing all the knowledge he could, in terms of both academics and the business aspect of operating a school. His knowledge of his surroundings was keen, and he studied not only his school work but also Dr. Tupper and how he operated his school.

The normal department course of study consisted of more advanced courses than the preparatory department and afforded John Jefferson as well as his classmates the opportunity to prepare themselves to become teachers.[34] When John Jefferson returned for his second year at Shaw, he was one of two hundred students enrolled in the classical (college) department. The classical (college) curriculum was even more rigorous than the program of the normal department and required John Jefferson to take Latin three of the four years of the program during each of its three terms—October to December, January to March, and March to May.[35] John Jefferson was also introduced to Greek, trigonometry, geometry, ancient history, geology, logic, Butler's analogy, zoology, chemistry, moral and natural philosophy, botany, rhetoric, and English literature.[36] A degree of AB was conferred on students who completed the classical (college) department curriculum, whereas diplomas were given to students who completed the normal or scientific courses of study.[37]

In addition to his academics, John Jefferson maintained a job on campus to defray the cost of his college expenses, which included $6.00 monthly for board and $1.50 for tuition. An additional $0.50 was charged for fuel and lights, and a fee of $0.50 per month was required of males who chose to have their laundry done by the institution.[38] During the summer months, John Jefferson returned to Rich Square and taught wherever and whomever he could.[39]

John Jefferson and his fellow Shaw students had to abide by stringent rules; failure to obey the rules could result in immediate expulsion. At all times, he and his classmates lived under supervision. When not in attendance for recitals, lectures, roll call, or divine worship, John Jefferson had to devote all of his time to his studies, with the exception of his work time. Given the school's strong emphasis on scholarly performance, John Jefferson and his classmates were instructed not to devote any time to trivial matters or frivolous conversation.[40] Neither was any male student allowed to call upon a young lady or converse or communicate with her in passing or on school grounds, with the exception of the first fifteen minutes after school, without permission from the school president. At all times, whether on campus or off, John Jefferson, as a student of Shaw University, was required to exercise healthy restraints and maintain high scholastic and moral standards.[41]

In May 1879, John Jefferson completed the four-year course of study in Shaw's classical (college) program and obtained the degree of AB. He then relocated to Halifax County, North Carolina, near Northampton County and his hometown of Rich Square. In Halifax, he resided in the Roseneath Township, where he taught school.[42] At night he spoke among other people of his race as he entered upon active Temperance work on various farms. His mission as a Temperance worker was to educate the Negroes about the effects of alcohol consumption and how its high rate of use attributed to many social ills, such as persistent poverty, immorality, crime, and unemployment. In his speeches, he emphasized the importance of complete abstinence from intoxicating liquors. Five years after John Jefferson began his Temperance work, there were 1,112 Temperance men, women, and children throughout the region, and peace reigned supreme as a result of his work.[43]

Little did John Jefferson know, his mother's slave husband, David Lawrence (Smallwood), lived very near him. David, who had been sold away from the Smallwood family at the same time as John Jefferson's brothers Tobias and Thomas were sold, was now living in Halifax County in the township of Palmyra, where he had moved in October 1870 to become a farm laborer.[44] Prior to moving to Palmyra, David had lived in the township of Deep Creek in Edgecombe County, North Carolina. He was now remarried and living with his wife and five children.[45]

It is quite possible that, during the five years that John Jefferson lived in Halifax County and provided Temperance work, David was one of the 1,112 Negroes to whom John Jefferson spoke. Interestingly, during the summer of 1875, when John Jefferson ran away from Rich Square to Southampton County in search of the man he called his "slave-born father," David was residing in the same vicinity. It is quite possible that John Jefferson crossed paths with David or could even have conversed with him without knowing who he was. Unfortunately for both of them, in the five years that John Jefferson taught in Halifax County, they were never able to come to know each other as father and son. If John Jefferson had known that David was his "slave-born father," he could perhaps have gotten information from him about his mother—even if nothing more than a description of her physical attributes, which would have been more than he already knew. It is unlikely that David would have known the whereabouts of John Jefferson's mother since he had been sold, together with John Jefferson's two brothers, even before John Jefferson was born.

In 1884, at twenty-one years of age and with five years of teaching experience behind him, John Jefferson left Halifax County. With a continued need to quench his insatiable thirst for knowledge, he traveled to Massachusetts to attend Wilbraham, known as Wesleyan Academy, to study under the tutelage of Dr. George M. Steele.[46] But despite these accomplishments, an empty void remained in John Jefferson's life. Although he knew he had to move forward with his life, he never lost the desire to find his mother.

CHAPTER SIX

UNQUENCHABLE THIRST:
WESLEYAN ACADEMY AT WILBRAHAM

When John Jefferson arrived on the campus of Wesleyan Academy in October 1884, he was one of 411 students enrolled and one of even fewer Negroes in attendance.[1] There were times during his tenure at Wesleyan Academy when he was, in fact, the only Negro student enrolled.[2] Not long after his arrival, he became acquainted with Drs. Loranus Crowell and George Steele personally. These two influential men would later become his friends and confidantes and would play an integral role in shaping his destiny.

At the time of John Jefferson's enrollment, Dr. Crowell was employed at Wesleyan Academy as a principal agent who secured funds for the academy, in addition to establishing an endowment for the school. Dr. Steele was principal of Wesleyan Academy and had been since 1879.[3] He was known to be a man of sound judgment and a successful disciplinarian who had a knack for school management. John Jefferson became particularly fond of Dr. Steele, who served as a sort of role model and mentor for him, and later emulated his conduct as an academician and his character as a person.[4] Dr. Steele, too, seemed to become fond of John Jefferson, whom he nurtured and guided. His positive influence inspired John Jefferson to reach for his highest potential.[5]

While under the tutelage of Dr. Steele, John Jefferson was introduced to the study of the English Bible, a method of study similar to that of classic literature. He admired Dr. Steele's method of teaching the English

Bible, though others had initially been skeptical that this kind of study would not be well received. Dr. Steele's method, which allowed students to gain a greater insight into and an intelligent view of the entire scheme of revelation, was one of many teaching methods that John Jefferson would later adopt and use in his career.[6] Under Dr. Steele, John Jefferson also studied Greek, Latin, and Hebrew,[7] in addition to several other courses for which his rigorous program of study at Shaw had well prepared him. In addition to Dr. Steele's classes, John Jefferson studied moral and mental science in his five years at Wesleyan (1884–1889).

Being one of few Negroes enrolled at Wesleyan and at times the only Negro student on campus, John Jefferson was constantly harassed by some of his white classmates. Though he made a considerable number of friends among the white students at Wesleyan—like Fred Estes, one of his most outspoken defenders—he was harassed, taunted, and called hateful and derogatory names by many white students who seemed to have a problem with his presence on campus. On more than one occasion, he had to contend with threats from classmates, and Fred often came to his rescue, many times refusing to remain a silent bystander when John Jefferson was mocked or ridiculed for his color.[8]

As the spring of 1889 approached, two promising events occurred that would set a precedent for the rest of John Jefferson's adult life. First, in early March, the United Literary and Lecturing Society of England sent the Honorable W. H. Bryan and General H. Clanton to America to meet with John Jefferson and offer him a contract to deliver lectures in Europe on race relations—"The Negro in America Politics" and "The Race Problem in America." The six-month contract, which was to begin in October of that year, stipulated that the literary association would cover all expenses, including the cost of secretarial services and an honorarium of $6,980.[9] John Jefferson accepted.

During that same month—six months before his twenty-sixth birthday and seven months before he left Massachusetts to deliver his lectures in Europe, where he would also study at Trinity College[10]—John Jefferson preached a sermon at a church in Lowell, Massachusetts. After his sermon, he stopped by the home of the Rev. W. T. Perrin and his wife. As he talked with Mrs. Perrin over dinner, she casually asked him about his family. This question was and had always been an emotional one for him. Although he was well versed in almost any subject that might be brought up, this particular topic was a matter about which he knew very little and one that continued to cause him a great deal of pain. As he desperately tried to conceal and control his emotion, he told her that, for nearly twenty-six years, he had lived without a family. After taking a deep breath and pausing for a moment, he explained that at a very young age he had been separated from his mother and that he knew very little, if anything, about her and the rest of his family. With great pain, he told Mrs. Perrin how he had prayed to God to see his family before he died. Mrs. Perrin comforted him and reassured him that that all things come to those who trust in the Lord. She further consoled him by reassuring him that God would make a way for him to find his family.[11] Mrs. Perrin understood John Jefferson's pain and felt compelled to do all she could to help him.

Not long after his conversation with Mrs. Perrin, John Jefferson discussed the matter of his family with Drs. Steele and Crowell. They both committed themselves to do all they could to help him find his mother and advised him on how to search for her. Dr. Crowell told him that, above all, he must trust God.[12] And that is exactly what John Jefferson did.

CHAPTER SEVEN

FINDING HIS MOTHER

This letter is presented in its entirety, as it was originally written by John Jefferson Smallwood. As the author of this book, I feel I would have committed a tremendous injustice had I attempted to tell this story in the words of anyone other than John Jefferson Smallwood himself. The letter itself was written and published in an unidentified newspaper in Franklin, Virginia, on August 27, 1889, and was provided to me through the kind courtesy of the Hampton University Archives in Hampton, Virginia.

The letter to follow was written by John Jefferson Smallwood a graduating student at Wilbraham. It is a thrilling, interesting and profoundly meaningful historical document that confirms the immense cruelty and barbarism of slavery that was imposed on the mind, body and soul of another human being; it was this dehumanizing system that once existed in the United States of America. Dr. G. M. Steele commends the writer and authenticates his tragic story. Dr. Steele in a personal letter says of the young man: "It is a little more than two and a half years since he entered the Academy, and he had never been at school in his life before. He is a natural orator, and will carry an audience anywhere. Last fall he stumped Indiana for Harrison[1] and was in the greatest demand everywhere. Harrison, Blaine,[2] Huston,[3] Gov. Hovey[4] and a great number of the Republican leaders took notice of him and treated him with great respect. We are trying to do what we can for him."

Franklin, Virginia, Aug. 27.

MR. EDITOR: Please let me thank the all-good and all-wise Father, our God, for His great blessings granted me. For nearly twenty-six years I have lived in this world without a mother or a sister. Last March, while at Lowell preaching, and while stopping in the home of that good brother, Rev. W. T. Perrin,[5] his excellent wife talked to me freely about my family. I told her that my mother, three sisters, and two brothers were sold before I was six months old. I told her how I had prayed that God might spare me to see my family before I should die. Sister Perrin[6] begged me not to despair, saying that God was just, and that all things worked for good to them that loved the Lord. She told me to seek the former master of my parents, and get the names of the parties that bought my people in 1863.

I commenced at once to make a new search for my mother and her children. Dr. Steele, of Wesleyan Academy at Wilbraham, told me to write to Mr. Johnson[7] in Alabama, who last sold my mother. Dr. Steele also told me not to show too much anxiety about the matter, that God would work the matter out in His own time. My dear friend and loving fatherly brother, Rev. Dr. Crowell, said to me early in the present year, "John, you must trust God for the finding of your mother." I did that, and early in May last I received a letter from Mr. Johnson in Alabama, telling me that he sold my mother in 1864 to a slave speculator down in Texas, and that he would find her for me if I would give him the sum of one hundred dollars. I did not have one hundred dollars, and I feared to speak to Dr. Steele about it, lest he should not approve of it. I could not tell it to my generous friend, Mrs. Vaughan,[8] because she had no confidence in Mr. Johnson.

But Mr. Johnson did find for me my aged mother,[9] in her 71st year, crippled and ignorant. I also found three sisters;[10] only one of them, however, was of the number that was sold from me, the other two having been born since 1863. I have not heard from my father[11] or my brothers,[12] only one of whom mother tells me has died.

While at Hamburg, in Germany, late in July, Mr. W. R. Crowell, of Jackson, Miss., cabled me to come on for my mother to New Orleans.[13] How happy I felt! My soul leaped for joy, and my heart praised the great God for His goodness. I left Europe early in August, but did not go to New Orleans, having received a telegram on my arrival at Norfolk to go to Birmingham. There in the house of Mr. J. K. Kelley I found an aged woman, yellow in complexion, her head perfectly white, stiff in her joints, half clothed and weeping copiously. Of course she did not know me. But when I had convinced her as to my identity, she exclaimed, "O my son, my younger son!" I could but put my arms about her and weep. Then we sat down, and my dear mother at once in her old plantation way commenced to tell me the same story that I have often told to the good people of Massachusetts.

I want to thank these people; they have done me great favors. When I was ignorant and degraded they put me in school at that good place, Wilbraham, and when I was without money, they would help me at any time, and that willingly. I can never forget their kindness. God bless them all! The one hundred dollars that a Christian brother at Springfield, Mass., loaned me, was one of the instrumentalities that enabled me to find my poor, aged mother. I thank all the people who have prayed for me so much, and who have done so much to help me in finding my family.

The story that my mother tells about her suffering for food and care, is indeed appalling. She and my sister are now in a home given them by a lady friend not far from this town. I thank God that I can say that I have a mother and two sisters living. Although ignorant and half clad, I love them. God be praised for all His goodness and loving kindness to the sons and daughters of men! I shall leave Virginia, Aug. 28 or 29, for New England. I shall go back to the Wesleyan Academy with a determination such as I never before entertained to study and to live alone for Jesus and His cause.

My earthly future looks dark and discouraging, but I am trusting God. I want to thank the good people also who showed so much interest in my trip to Europe. God has blessed me; and I want it forever understood that I am His servant. My life has been one of sadness and sorrow. I have prayed, for years, for the return of my mother, and now I promise those who have done so much for me, that they shall never regret it. I am determined to honor my God and my friends, and make myself a man.

JOHN J. SMALLWOOD

I toiled night and day to raise $7500.00 with which to buy this school-farm and to build this plain, wooden hall, pay debts and open school.

—*Dr. John J. Smallwood*
Letter to Rev. Dr. H. B. Frissell, Principal,
Hampton Normal Agricultural Institute
December 26, 1903

CHAPTER EIGHT

VISIONARY

At last, Dr. Smallwood had found his family—one that he had never ceased loving and one that he had desperately yearned and humbly prayed for all his life. He was no longer alone, and the weight of the world seemed to have been lifted from his shoulders. He moved his mother and sisters to North Carolina so he could be closer to them. His life was now complete—almost, at least.

Dr. Smallwood did not have to look far to see the suffering among his people. There was agony and hardship all around him, even within his own dear family. In the midst of all this misery, there was something profound that moved Dr. Smallwood—the humility of his people and their desire to be more than they were and had been.

As an accomplished and learned man, Dr. Smallwood had more opportunities available to him than many others of his race, yet he willingly cast aside his own personal needs to focus on the needs of his people. He saw the need to uplift them and impress upon them the need for self-respect, self-pride, and self-reliance. Dr. Smallwood believed that the only viable way this could be done was through education. He realized that if the people of his race were given the same educational opportunities he had been afforded, their newfound education would serve as a significant and potent weapon for addressing the problem of race in America. Deciding to devote his entire being to a cause that he deemed far greater than himself, he suppressed his own needs in order to serve the needs of his people. Making this commitment both to himself and to God, Dr. Smallwood became a visionary—one who had a clear, distinctive, and specific vision of the future for his race.

In 1890, Dr. Smallwood returned to Southampton County, Virginia, from Europe, where he had spent a year studying political science at Trinity College under the tutelage of one Dr. Baily, in addition to giving lectures for the United Literary and Lecturing Society of England.[1] He remained in America for only a brief period of time, however.[2] Within that same year, he departed again for Continental Europe, where he remained, traveling to France, Germany, and Great Britain, until the spring of 1891, when he returned to the United States.[3]

Upon his return to America, Dr. Smallwood was on a mission, with a clear vision and a precise plan to better his race through education. On August 11, 1891, for the sum of $1,800, he purchased 271 acres, more or less, of land from H. J. Arrington of Surry County, Virginia.[4] The property was next to the "hotel lot" on the edge of Claremont, Virginia, near Spring Grove, where John Jefferson resided,[5] and was the perfect place to make his vision a reality. Situated on a high bluff on the south bank of the historic James River, ten miles above Jamestown, Virginia,[6] Claremont had been an Indian town when English settlers first reached it on May 5, 1607.[7] With its rich history, mild climate, beautiful scenery, inexpensive land, and fertile soil,[8] Claremont was, by all accounts, a progressive and successful town. It was situated in a unique location on the James River, midway between the cities of Richmond and Norfolk, Virginia. The James was the primary route for the export and import of goods and supplies to points along the river, and Claremont was one of the towns where ships and steamers stopped at the wharf to load and unload cargo and passengers.[9] The town's various amenities and natural resources raised expectations that Claremont would become a major port city comparable to Norfolk,[10] and by 1885, a line of the Atlantic and Danville Railway leading inland from the James River was in operation at Claremont. In addition to its railroad, Claremont proudly boasted of a newspaper and several large businesses, including four hotels, a boardinghouse, two eateries, two bar rooms, a bakery, and ten merchants.[11] By the time Dr. Smallwood arrived in Claremont, the town had elected a mayor, five councilmen, and a recorder.[12] The town was progressive and prosperous, a place that Dr. Smallwood visualized as the perfect location for his school.[13]

On December 10, 1891, the twenty-eight-year-old Dr. Smallwood obtained a passport and traveled abroad, accompanied by a friend from Randolph, Massachusetts.[14] The exact length of time Dr. Smallwood and his friend remained abroad is unknown, but only ten months later he was again in Claremont, where, on October 12, 1892, he founded the Temperance Industrial and Collegiate Institute,[15] with less than ten pupils and less than fifty dollars in actual cash. Classes at Temperance were held in the old Parker Dining Hall on the 271-acre site that Smallwood had purchased the previous year.[16]

In founding the institute, the young and ambitious Dr. Smallwood had taken upon himself a tremendous responsibility that garnered skepticism from those who opposed his vision and censure from those who desired nothing more than to see him fail.[17] Many of his critics had initially believed that he would never purchase the land required to build his school; now that he had acquired land and built school facilities, they contended that he would establish a legitimate institution but would never have any students. Realizing that prospective students would have intense financial needs, Dr. Smallwood appealed to his friends and other supporters to assist with the operation of his school and the expenses needed to educate his people. Always in need of money, he preached and spoke at public affairs whenever and wherever he could in an attempt to solicit funds for his school and his students.[18]

Early in the spring of the 1892–1893 school year, the school's first year in operation, Dr. Smallwood surveyed the needs of his students and wrote to Mr. E. W. Fox, whom he had met at a three-day convention in London, England, in 1889. In his letter to Fox, he requested funds on behalf of his school and his students.[19] It is unknown whether Fox donated money to support Dr. Smallwood's enterprise, but regardless, the institution remained in continual need of assistance, and on November 11, 1893, Dr. Smallwood wrote to yet another acquaintance, Elizabeth Cady Stanton.[20] Mrs. Stanton had been the driving force behind the organization of the United States' first women's rights convention in June of 1848[21] and had worked closely with Susan B. Anthony to advocate for women's suffrage.[22] Dr. Smallwood's letters to Mr. Fox and Mrs. Stanton, in which he advocates on behalf of his students and the operation of his school, are preserved below.[23]

February 27, 1893

Mr. E. W. Fox
Milton [?] New Hampshire

My Dear Bro.

You will doubtless remember me as the young Negro Minister who went to the World and S. S. Convention held in London, England, July 2nd to the 5th 1889. We cross[ed] the Atlantic Ocean in the brave old s. ship, The <u>Bothmia</u>.

I am now engaged in the building of the institution named above. We opened the first term of the institution October 31st 1892. Our students come from the "rural districts" of Virginia and North Carolina. They are too poor to pay us six dollars per month. We have to beg for them.

Our object is to teach the Negro youth all the trades of the "American Industry"—shorthand, typewriting and bookkeeping will be studied. Housekeeping and all kinds of industry will carry on as a part of the regular course of study here.

Our race must be taught the trades. They must be made working men and women by becoming skilled in their labor. We must also impress the Negro that he must have "Race Pride" and "Self-Reliance" and "Self-Respect." We must teach the Negro that nothing like the color of the skin makes a man or gentleman, but real true character makes the gentleman.

My race is a poor, [?] and a badly treated race. They are shot down, hanged and [as in] two cases here in the South, they are tied to the stake and burned alive. Many of our young men are working for four dollars per month. We are treated like brutes in many sections of this fair southland. Education, temperance, skilled labor, morality, industry, wealth, and religion are the only instruments that can be used in the great conflicts here in the so-called "Race Problem."

We write, dear friend, to ask you to help us. We shall thank you for any amount that you may see fit to send us for the school. We need money and we need friends. We need sewing machines, washing machines, cooking utensils, carpenter and blacksmith tools. We need everything used in a young school like ours. We need good books, newspapers, desks, a church, and school furniture.

Our school is non-sectarian, non-political, but strictly industrial and religious. Please Help us.

I am yours truly,

John J Smallwood, President
Celestine Brown, Private Secretary

REV.JOHN J.SMALLWOOD,PRESIDENT AND GENERAL FINANCIAL AGENT   REV. P. V. HAZEL, PROFESSOR ENGLISH BRANCHES
MISS E. CELESTINE BROWN, SECRETARY AND FINANCIAL, AGENT   FIRST TERM OPENED OCTOBER 31, 1892; CLOSES MAY 31, 1893
MISS MARY E. LOCKLEY, {LADY TEACHERS AND FINANCIAL, AGENTS   FALL TERM OPENS OCTOBER 13, 1893; CLOSES, MAY 26, 1894
MISS ELLA C. HARRIS,

"BAGLEY HALL"

TEMPERANCE, INDUSTRIAL AND COLLEGIATE INSTITUTE
Claremont, Va., Nov. 11th 1893

Mrs. Elizabeth Cady Stanton
26 W. 61 St.
New York, N.Y.

My Dear Madam:

Our humble institution above named opened its doors and commenced upon its second years [sic] work October 12th 1893. The institution has gradually grown in the public's favor and in number and work from the first day it opened to the present. Our students come from North Carolina and Virginia mostly. They are poor and in many cases are unable to pay us six ($6) dollars a month which is all we charge them. In some cases we are compelled to clothe and feed them. They are all worthy young men and women. Every one is a total abstainer and purely religious. Our institution is non-sectarian and non-political but strictly religious, moral and industrial. The Negro youth is taught to have a high conception of what morality and industry is and to practice the same. The Negro must be taught a trade. He must be taught the art of all the trades and be a skilled laborer. He must also be taught race pride, self-reliance, self-respect and economy. We prefer here to teach telegraphing, photographing, cooking, washing, ironing and the higher pursuits of agriculture. Blacksmithing, house building and general house cleaning and work will be made a specialty. Two sewing machines have been purchased for the ladies industrial department. A steam engine and saw mill has just been purchased and we are now trying to buy a planing machine. We mite [sic] to *ask you to give us a contribution. We all are Negroes here trying to help ourselves. We shall thank you for any amount of money you may see fit to send us. Let me beg you please to send us some help in the midst of these hard times. We need so many things here. Send all money to us please by P.O. order or bank check to P.O. Box 75 Claremont, Va. Whatever you may see fit to send us will be most graciously received and readily acknowledged.*

I am, dear Madam
Yours Truly;
John J. Smallwood
Per, E. Celestine Brown, Priv. Sect'y.

P.S. Dear Madam

Wednesday morning, of last week, we were compelled here to eat boiled beans for our breakfast, without meat, having cooked them with salt and peper [sic]. Wednesday night, we had no sugar upon our table, and Thursday our sugar gave out. We need help soon. Won't you please send us something? We shall certainly feel grateful for all that you may see fit to send us. We are passing now through a great trial. Help us please my dear Madam. I am truly yours, for our Race, and Humanity.

J. J. Smallwood

As the 1893–1894 school year came to a close, Dr. Smallwood also wrote to Frederick Douglass and invited him to speak at the second annual commencement exercise. The commencement was to be held at the Temperance, Industrial and Collegiate Institute on June 6, 1894.[24] Mr. Douglass, born a slave in February 1818 in Talbot County, Maryland, was an American abolitionist, editor, orator, author, reformer, and statesman. Dr. Smallwood had great respect and admiration for Mr. Douglass and his work.[25] What follows is his letter of invitation to Mr. Douglass.

First Term opened October 31, 1892. **OFFICE OF**
Spring Term closed May 31, 1893. *Rev. John J. Smallwood,*
Fall Term opened October 13, 1893. **PRESIDENTANDGENERAL**
Spring term closes June 7, 1894. **FINANCIAL AGENT**

OF THE

Temperance,—Industrial—and—Collegiate—Institute,

Beautifully located in a most beautiful locality *BAGLEY HALL*
Work upon new building will be commenced
during summer vacation,

We need $50,000 by June, 1894. *Claremont, Va.,* March 24, 1894
  65,000 feet of lumber now ordered.

Hon. Fred. Douglass,
Washington, D.C.

My dear Sir.

It would be indeed be inspiring, to our teachers, to our pupils and to myself, to have you speak for us, June the Six, at our Annual Commencement. I therefore take great pleasure, Mr. Douglass, in asking you to come to historic Claremont, Va., and speak, if you please before the students of our poor humble institution, June, 6th. Our students are all poor, too poor to pay us the sum of Six ($6) dollars. Our school is strictly non-sectarian and non-political, but real moral, industrial and religious. Our teachers are all poor. They are not getting a cent for their labors. I have never received a penny for my time, nor my labors. I looked around. I see in no Negro, what I see in you. Let me beg you to come to us, and speak for us, if you can.

I am, my dear Mr. Douglass, honored to be your young friend

John J. Smallwood

P. S.

This will be our second annual commencement. You will find us poor, but earnest, young but sincere, Negroes, but believers in work. I do pray and trust that you will consent to come to us and speak for us June 6th.

J. J. Smallwood

It is not known whether Mr. Douglass honored Dr. Smallwood's request to be his guest speaker at the institute's second annual commencement exercise, but Dr. Smallwood continually strove to attract high-profile Negro speakers like Mr. Douglass to provide an inspiration to the students and teachers at Temperance, as well as himself. It does appear, based on Dr. Smallwood's invitation to Mr. Douglass, that he deeply admired and respected him and was honored to have made his acquaintance. Because of Dr. Smallwood's desire to educate the people of his race, it was only appropriate that he extended an invitation to such a man as Mr. Douglass, one who had for many years advocated on behalf of the Negro race. Dr. Smallwood, like many other Negroes, was a beneficiary of Mr. Douglass's hard work. Therefore, it was with great gratitude and appreciation that Dr. Smallwood would have welcomed Mr. Douglass to his campus. There is no doubt that the establishment of Dr. Smallwood's institute and Mr. Douglass's visit to its campus would have been an equally proud moment for both men.

The ideological framework of Dr. Smallwood's school represented a culmination of all the experiences and knowledge he had acquired during his keen observation of both the managerial skills required to operate a school and the character and style of influential men such as Drs. Armstrong, Tupper, Steele, and Baily. In keeping with the motto of his first alma mater, Hampton Normal and Agricultural Institute,[26] Dr. Smallwood's desire was to "gather" what he had learned under the tutelage of these great men and "scatter" this knowledge among his people, the same kind of people among whom he had once lived—poor, yet worthy of the opportunity for a good education.

Very seldom, if ever, did Dr. Smallwood ask for assistance for himself; instead, his pleas, as he traveled across the United States and abroad, were on behalf of his students. Because of his own personal experiences, he had a deep affinity for the poor, who had grown to an excessive number in the two decades following the Civil War, around the time Dr. Smallwood founded his school. At only thirty years old, he was one of only a few Negroes to embark upon such an audacious venture, for a noble and worthy cause—a cause so enormous that it would become his life's work and, ultimately, his life.

I vividly remember one day Uncle John coming home [to Rich Square, North Carolina]. It was an exciting time when he came home because he always gave me a couple of pennies. I don't remember exactly how old I was but I must have been around five or six years old. On this particular day, I remember Uncle John as he sat at the dinner table preparing to eat his dinner and my mother asked him, "John, why are you working so hard?" He replied, "I am trying to build a school so every Negro child can have an opportunity to get a good education."

—Mrs. Willie L. Lassiter
Niece of Dr. John J. Smallwood
June 9, 2007

CHAPTER NINE

TEMPERANCE, INDUSTRIAL AND COLLEGIATE INSTITUTE

On April 24, 1895, a year after the second annual commencement exercise was held at Temperance, Industrial and Collegiate Institute, Dr. Smallwood purchased additional thirty-six acres, more or less, with all buildings and appurtenances, including a wharf, from Hattie S. Chesbro and her husband, Hale Hiram Chesbro, of Nansemond, Virginia.[1] The property containing the Chesbro farm and wharf, which the Chesbros had purchased from J. Frank and Lillie Mancha in 1885, had previously been known as the Old Claremont Wharf property[2] or simply the Claremont and Wharf Property. Located on the scenic front of the James River in Claremont, Virginia, it was in close proximity to Old Jamestown and was the same site where America's first cargo of slaves had landed in 1620.[3] Temperance, Industrial and Collegiate Institute would soon be moved to and built on the very spot where the first Negroes had been sold at auction on October 12–13, 1621. Ironically, the institute opened 171 years later, to the date, on October 12, 1892, founded by a man who had himself been born into slavery.[4]

Dr. Smallwood's vision was to build a school to educate the young men and women of his race. The mission of the institute was to "give its students a thorough mental, moral, industrial and religious training,"[5] in order to strengthen their advancement in all efforts, both industrially and religiously.[6] Dr. Smallwood desired not only to build an institution that would teach his race all the trades of the "American Industry" but also to impress upon his race a sense of self-reliance, self-pride, and self-respect and to teach them "that nothing like the color of the skin makes a man or gentleman, but real true character makes the gentleman."[7] His institution was both nonsectarian and nonpolitical and was strictly industrial and religious. The curriculum encompassed housekeeping, shorthand, typewriting, bookkeeping,[8] religion, racial pride, morality, economy, sewing, cooking, laundering, farming, and carpentry. Strong emphasis was placed on religion, with the Bible as one of the textbooks required by the curriculum. The institute relied heavily upon faith in God[9] and the charitable donations solicited by Dr. Smallwood, who collected donations on behalf of the institute as he traveled to various states on speaking engagements. He also solicited donations from friends, patrons, and community resources and made sure to recognize the individuals who made donations to his school in the bimonthly school newspaper, the *Monthly Advocate*. In the *Advocate*—whose motto was "Temperance and morality, industry and economy, intelligence and race pride: Love for the home and country makes a nation its own controlling power"—he printed donors' names and places of residence, in addition to the amount of donations received from his friends on the East Coast. He also listed the amounts of money received and expenditures made.[10] Dr. Smallwood spent every dollar of money given to his school on feeding, housing, and educating his students.

The students themselves numbered fewer than ten when the first school term opened on October 31, 1892.[11] But by the 1895–1896 school year, the enrollment had increased significantly, with a total of 150 applications for admission. Even so, Dr. Smallwood accepted only the number of students he knew he could accommodate,[12] and he was proud of the fact that, in the first four years of its operation, his institute fed and schooled more than 150 students who had been too poor to pay for their own food and education.[13]

In its curriculum, the Temperance, Industrial and Collegiate Institute was similar to that of other facilities for Negro education around the turn of the century, and it emulated Tuskegee's model, with its strict reliance on agricultural and industrial education.[14] Dr. Smallwood's curriculum also shared commonalities with the programs at Hampton, Shaw, and Wesleyan, as it had a rigorous preparatory department integrated with classical, vocational, and religious courses. Temperance, Industrial Collegiate Institute forged a unique model of education by integrating distinct combinations of academic, religious, and industrial training.[15]

Soon after Dr. Smallwood purchased the additional thirty-six acres, plans were under way to build a dormitory to accommodate the institute's steadily increasing enrollment. The first building built by Dr. Smallwood and his students was Sawyer Hall, in 1895.[16] It was a girls' dormitory with spacious rooms and was named in honor of Philetus Sawyer, a United States senator from Wisconsin, because of his generous monetary contributions and strong interest in Dr. Smallwood's work.[17] Dr. Smallwood modestly referred to Sawyer Hall as a "plain, wooden hall."[18]

During the summer of 1895, Dr. Smallwood borrowed an unspecified sum of money from Emily Howland of Sherwood, New York.[19] Born in 1827, Ms. Howland was a Quaker humanitarian, philanthropist, abolitionist, educator, and activist for women's suffrage. She had long been a strong financial contributor to the advancement of Negroes and Negro education:[20] before the Civil War, she offered up her home as a station for the Underground Railroad;[21] after the war, disappointed that the government had reneged on its promise to give freedmen "forty acres and a mule," she purchased land and allowed Negroes to settle there.[22] Before, during, and after the war, Ms. Howland devoted her life to assisting the Negro people in whatever capacity she could, including teaching Negroes to read and write, and providing monetary support for the education of the Negro people. She was also a major supporter of Booker T. Washington, who had founded Tuskegee Normal and Industrial Institute in Tuskegee, Alabama, in 1881. The funds she donated to Dr. Smallwood's institute, in addition to allaying the overall expenses of operation, were perhaps used to purchase furniture and other personal property for the school. In appreciation for Ms. Howland's moral support and her financial contribution to his school, Dr. Smallwood named a building on his campus Howland Hall in her honor.[23]

In the fall of 1895, on September 12, Dr. Smallwood received a loan for the operation of his school from John W. Patterson and Catherine Peterson of Buffalo, New York, and from his own nephew, seventeen-year-old Marcus W. Smallwood,[24] who was a student at Temperance, Industrial and Collegiate Institute, and who shared a name with Dr. Smallwood's former slave master.[25] Mrs. Henry H. Cook of Lenox, Massachusetts, also loaned Dr. Smallwood money during the early formation of his school.[26]

By June 1896, Dr. Smallwood had traveled over ten thousand miles and had made over 250 speeches on behalf of the institution and race relations. He was most proud of the fact that, despite the naysayers who had criticized his work from the outset, he was able to keep his school open for four years and had paid out all expenses for lumber, land, buildings, and the boarding and schooling of his pupils. In addition to these accomplishments, Temperance's enrollment had increased almost monthly, with over 150 students having applied for admission during the 1895–1896 school year.

Although Dr. Smallwood's vision had begun to become a reality, he was still regularly criticized by his opponents and was often subjected to verbal slander because of his school's success, which his staunchest critics condemned. Part of the reason Dr. Smallwood received unyielding criticism was undoubtedly because, at the time, he was one of very few Negro men who had founded a school to educate Negroes; most other schools for Negroes, including Shaw, Howard, and Hampton, had been founded by white men. The widespread animosity of Dr. Smallwood's critics toward the work that he believed he was called to do exposed him to questions not only of the legitimacy of his work and faith but also of character. He was often referred to as an immoralist, a thief, a drunkard, a fraud, and a liar, and was accused of obtaining the money for his school under false pretenses. Dr. Smallwood reacted to these harsh critiques by relying deeply upon his faith. Certainly he felt discouraged at times—especially when he thought about how hard he had worked, day and night, without any money for compensation, once even selling all his valuables to carry on his work—but he knew he had to persevere, because his mission was much greater than himself. Many times he felt imposed upon, rebuked, and misrepresented, but he never questioned whether his efforts were worthwhile. He knew that the people he desired to serve were a poor but worthy race, deserving of the same opportunities and privileges as anyone else.[27]

Because of his diligent commitment to God as well as his fellow man, Dr. Smallwood often recounted his experiences by stating that he was determined to "fulfill every obligation to God and man," regardless of slanderous words of accusations.[28] He strove to serve God and to do the Lord's will while, at the same time, making sure that he honored any human obligations, including those to his creditors. Dr. Smallwood never denied the fact that he had borrowed large sums of money that resulted in debt. He openly admitted having made mistakes and even some outright blunders in his business dealings, but even so, he felt that the eyes of his enemies looked more frequently at his errors than at all the good that he had done. Although he had aimed, in founding his institution, to uplift his race by offering his students the best possible opportunities for a good education, the accusations of his enemies, nonetheless, disheartened him and made him feel that his opponents had "underlying selfish motives to impeach [his] reputation."[29] He reacted by saying, "I have done more to help the cause of Christ; to solve the so called Race Problem in a single year, here in Virginia than the man who now seeks to kill my influence, and to ruin my life and to cast me to the cold world, has ever done."[30] He challenged his enemies to commit themselves to helping the race problem and to serving God and dared them to make their sneaking statements about his character before an unprejudiced public audience on Virginia soil or anywhere else of their choosing.[31]

Because Dr. Smallwood relied heavily on his faith, he never gave up, though he occasionally became discouraged. From a young age, he had often witnessed or heard of attacks made by both whites and coloreds against Negroes who had tried to better their race, even under the most trying of circumstances. Often they, like himself, had gone half clad, hungry, or penniless and yet had endured accusations of immorality, dishonesty, and ignorance. Though he himself had advanced far beyond his initial means, the difficulties he faced in the management of his school enabled him to begin to see just how difficult it really was for a young man to launch out in life, without a dollar and without friends, with the goal of creating something, but finding his success subject to the jealousy and prejudice of others. Faced with the bigotry and intolerance of his critics, Dr. Smallwood came to understand that the Negro, regardless of his station, was in a precarious situation. Regardless of how ambitious a black man might be, he was often mistrusted and misjudged on every hand: when he was unmotivated, he was placed on a level with the rest of his race; when he did nothing, he was called a man of ignorance and of disrespect. But whether he founded a college, managed a store, preached the gospel, bettered himself through education, or made great sacrifices for his race, the Negro gained very little respect. And Dr. Smallwood was beginning to realize that, no matter how driven he was, he would not command any more respect than the Negro who did nothing to help his race.

In addition to brooking the disapproval of many whites, Dr. Smallwood also garnered criticism from Booker T. Washington, one of the most powerful Negroes in America at the turn of the twentieth century. Mr. Washington and Dr. Smallwood shared many commonalities. Both had attended Hampton Normal and Agricultural Institute, with Mr. Washington graduating in 1875, and both had a desire to uplift their race by building institutions of higher learning. Just as Dr. Smallwood had founded his institute, Mr. Washington had served, in 1881, as the first principal of the newly founded Tuskegee Institute, a school for Negroes in Tuskegee, Alabama.[32] But although the men agreed on the need for education and economic development in the Negro community, they appear to have had significant differences of opinion regarding the best philosophical, social, educational, and political approaches to achieving these goals. The specific points on which they differed are not known. Nor is it known whether the two men ever met, but for many years, Mr. Washington warned his supporters in the North against aiding Smallwood, whom he accused of "Fraud, Immorality, and Unfaithlessness."[33] In a letter to Emily Howland dated October 13, 1901, Washington stated, "I hardly know what to say about Smallwood. I presume the only thing is to let him run his course, of course exposing him whenever we can. I do not believe that anything that is not right will permanently continue to exist."[34] His open criticism of Dr. Smallwood prompted a response from at least one of Smallwood's supporters, South Carolina legislator Daniel Augustus Straker, who, in 1896, wrote a letter to Mr. Washington in defense of the work that Dr. Smallwood was attempting at Claremont:[35]

Detroit, November 19th 1896

My dear friend: The mail brings me to day your published report of "Tuskegee Normal and Industrial Institute." It is a grand showing and reflects much credit on you for the noble work you have done.

You have done more than raise money for the work the past year. You have uplifted the Negro race in America, aye, the World over. Your plan of Negro Advancement has met with general approval. There is but one thing more in my humble opinion to make the trestle board complete, and let the laborers go to work, and that is—Like opportunity for the Negro to work with his fellow white citizen; but I recognize that the work you are doing is necessarily preparatory. Go on, and God will bless you, and protect you in all your doings. It seems that God's protection is especially needed, when I tell you that Rev. J. J. Smallwood, President of Claremont, Va., Temperance Institute has been publicly denounced as a fraud and a cheat in the Detroit Journal. I hope he can make a complete defense. If not, what a mill stone will be around your neck. I am glad to see you spoken of for a Cabinet place in President Elect McKinley's Cabinet . . .

D Augustus Straker

In addition to such public condemnation as Straker's letter mentions, Dr. Smallwood also received a near-constant stream of letters attacking his work, his faith, and his character. Often he would respond to these attacks in his semimonthly campus newspaper, the *Monthly Advocate.* One critic, for example, objected to the work that Smallwood was doing on grounds that he was not married. Dr. Smallwood candidly addressed this critic, whom he described as his "enemy," by setting aside a section in his paper to explain the reasons he had not chosen to marry at that point in his life. In a piece titled "My Getting Married," Dr. Smallwood responded as follows:

One of the enemies of this school object[s] to the work that I am now doing and to me as a man, because I am an unmarried man. I want to be exceedingly plain and frank upon this point. I know that a married life is an honorable life and in many cases a happy life, when the vows there made are faithfully kept. I honor the married and the true women of our land. If I have a high regard for any living thing upon earth, it is the women of this world. They are the safe, the moral, and the pure ships that sail upon the great seas of life. Good women always have exercised an influence upon men that can never be made known with the credit for good which is justly due it. I respect women, and I hope never to be instrumental by word, act or unmanly deed to bring sorrow to any one of them, but ladies and gentlemen, I am not to be hurried in this life time matter, of selecting for myself a wife. I must make the condition of a lady, as well at least, if not better, than when she became mine. I am to obey the laws of God, but I am unwilling to be pushed by [a] man who knows nothing at all of my life, nor of my business; of my great obligations, that I shall get up and marry just to make a false impression upon the public. There are hundreds of white men and women all over the country and world, who are blessing the name of Jesus who are doing some real good and a practical work, yet they are not married. Men who cry about my not being married, forget that many of the leading and some of the most prominent ministers and school teachers that ever lived—lived unmarried lives. They gave their talents and money freely to the uplifting of humanity and the making of their fellows better. I shall never marry until I am able to feed and clothe my wife—until I can take her into my home and provide for her in every way that is honorable and husband-like. When I have a home; when I am able to place my

wife in such a position that will enable her to be very helpful
to me; when I can set by example what I am daily preaching to
our young men, then I shall marry me a wife, and one I trust
with such sympathy and disposition, that shall be a blessing to
my life and work.[36]

Even after all the work he had done during his institution's first four
years of operation, and all the personal sacrifices he had made on behalf
of the young men and women of his race, Dr. Smallwood was still being
watched, talked about, misrepresented, and misunderstood. He was subjected
to envy and ridicule by those who slandered his name and character and
accused him of immorality and theft. He often questioned how people who
did not know him and who had never offered to contribute to his institute
or to the work that he was doing could say cruel things about him and his
students. These people had never visited his school, nor given so much as a
piece of bread, nor bowed with him and his students in prayer, nor bid him
God's speed, yet they were his strongest critics. He often pondered how he
could be considered immoral when he had founded an institute without even
$100 in cash and in the face of opposition and had accumulated $15,000
in property with a little over $4,000 in debt within four years' time. How
could he be considered immoral, when he had organized temperance work
among his people, built one of the finest academic facilities in the county,
taken young Negro men and women from the rural districts of Virginia and
other states and provided them with a quality education, and given them
some idea of true woman—and manhood?[37]

As if attacks on Dr. Smallwood himself were not enough, rumors
circulated about his students' being drunkards, mean, arrogant, offensive,
and impolite. In defense of himself and his students, Dr. Smallwood
vehemently declared that "there is not a Democrat in all of Surry County,
who could not say of us, that our pupils are the cleanest or as clean, polite
and modest[ly] reserved, faithful to their duties and intelligent, as are
found in any school in this State be it white or colored."[38]

Yet even despite vicious accusations against himself, his school, and
his students, Dr. Smallwood felt no malice and often prayed to God to
pardon his enemies for their prejudices and forgive him for any mistakes
or wrongs that he might have committed against others. He felt that he

was doing the work that he had been called to do by an higher power, for he believed that it was not within his own power to create an institution for his race, but rather it was within the power of the Almighty God to do so. Moreover, he trusted that God was the source that made all his accomplishments possible for he knew he had had nothing more than a hundred dollars and a heart to do good when he arrived in Claremont. Humbly acknowledging the influence of the Almighty, he gave credit to God and willingly accepted the fact that he was simply a servant of the Lord, a vessel for carrying forth His will.[39]

Early in his career, Dr. Smallwood realized that if he took the time to answer every negative letter, comment, and accusation about his work, he would never have time to go about the business of educating his people. Therefore, he wrote in the *Monthly Advocate*, he had nothing to say "about any other Negro Institution in this state. I want to see them all succeed. I have no ill-will towards any black man or white man who is trying to build up the Negro race. They can best work upon their own plans and lines. I know nothing of them, so it is with me. I must work as I see my possibilities and my way back to work here. No other man must undertake to make me work upon his line. The Temperance, Industrial and Collegiate Institute is my first thought and my first line of operation in every respect."[40]

With the urge to respond to his critics behind him, Dr. Smallwood devoted the majority of his time and energy over the next sixteen years to his institute and to his speeches that he occasionally gave concerning the race problem in America. No stranger to hard work, he kept a rigorously demanding schedule every day. Much like in his days as a youngster in North Carolina, when he plowed fields and chopped and picked cotton "on one of the largest cotton farms in the Roanoke Valley,"[41] he typically began his days at the institute around 6:00 a.m. with plowing or other hard labor on the school farm, where he would generally work until ten o'clock. From 11:00 a.m. to 3:00 p.m., he would devote his time to the management of his school and then resume his labor on the farm until 6:00 or 8:00 p.m. He would then return to his office to work until midnight and sometimes until 1:00 or 2:00 a.m.[42]

In 1896, as Dr. Smallwood was enjoying the fruits of his labors, the United States Supreme Court legitimized the principle of separate but equal in its ruling *Plessy v. Ferguson*. This ruling opened the floodgates to a profusion of Jim Crow laws whose ultimate mission was to disenfranchise the Negro politically, socially, psychologically, and economically. With this ruling, as time progressed, "separate became more and more separate and less and less equal."[43] The new laws were so stringent that, as historian C. Vann Woodward had stated, "Even under slavery, the two races had not been [as] divided as they were under the Jim Crow laws of the 1890's."[44]

With the Supreme Court ruling, Dr. Smallwood realized that he had broader issues to address than just the education of his race. He would now have to address issues concerning race relations in America as a whole. He knew that even though the Negro race was making strides in terms of education, the ruling in the *Plessy v. Ferguson* case would ultimately cripple the entire race, bringing its recently acquired progress to a complete halt. The court's ruling confirmed the fact that Dr. Smallwood did not have time to answer each letter or respond to every critic who did not like the work he was doing, because there was much more work to be done.

The results of the *Plessy* case ushered in a period known as the Terrible Nineties, marked by ever more stringent Jim Crow laws and frequent lynchings. By some estimates, a Negro was lynched in the United States about every two days during this time. Lynchings had long occurred in the United States but were at their peak at the turn of the twentieth century—so much so that lynching actually became a popular photographic sport.[45] Pictures of brutalized and mutilated bodies burned at the stake or hanging from a tress were often sent in the form of postcards.[46] Lynchings were also considered an eventful occasion, with people traveling from great distances to witness them. Many times, the event was even advertised in advance in the newspaper.[47] Reasons for lynching a Negro varied, from accusations of rape, to talking too much, failing to address a white man as "mister," being too prosperous,[48] and even wanting to drink soda water.[49]

Even during this dark period in American history, Dr. Smallwood continued to remain optimistic about the future of his school and his race of people. Dauntless and devoted, he had initiated a dangerous and daring mission, one that could easily have been used as justification for a lynching. But Dr. Smallwood continued to pursue his dream, his passion to educate the young men and women of his race, even in the face of very real danger and against seemingly insurmountable odds. As a matter of fact, his school continued to grow, and the next sixteen years were, for the most part, years of great prosperity.

*Ladies and Gentleman, I am more determined to
give my life to this work. If I die, if I am crippled by
the enemy; if I suffer disgrace at my enemies' hands,
money or no money, I am determined to go on in this
work just as I am called to do.*

—*Dr. John J. Smallwood,
President and Founder of the Temperance,
Industrial and Collegiate Institute
June 13, 1896*

CHAPTER TEN

YEARS OF GROWTH

T hings were going quite well for Dr. Smallwood and his school
until Temperance, Industrial and Collegiate Institute suffered a
major setback. In 1897, its sawmill, planing mill, and mattress factory
were destroyed by fire.[1] These three facilities on the thirty-six acre
campus enabled male students to learn how to use and to care for tools
as well as ascertain planing, sawing, chiseling, and other practical skills
for constructing and repairing buildings on the campus grounds.[2] The
destruction of these factories, which struck a tremendous blow to Dr.
Smallwood's overall mission, devastated him. The grave disappointment
he felt at the burning of the factories only temporarily distracted him
from his goals, however; Dr. Smallwood's characteristic optimism soon
returned. He would surmount this obstacle as he had others in his life and
continued to pour all of himself into his students and his school.

One of Dr. Smallwood's goals was to teach his students self-reliance
and to instill in them the necessity of self-respect and self-pride.[3] He
believed that these qualities were the key to assisting his race of people
in becoming self-sufficient and, ultimately, independent. Dr. Smallwood,
fired up with ambition and filled with optimism, also hoped to impress
upon his students the need for them to play an active role in their country.

He believed that, in order to be taken seriously by others, one must be "true in [his] motive, earnest in his plan, judicious in [his] purpose and effectual in [his] influence upon the general public, so much so that regardless of one's prejudices, one could plainly see that you are worthy of citizenship."[4]

Dr. Smallwood urged the people of his race to think beyond the whipping post or the past 250 years of enslavement and exhorted them not to clamor over the past. Instead, he encouraged them to become intelligent men and women, and to act accordingly, by building colleges, establishing banks and bank accounts, and owning and operating smithies, carriage shops, and trains. He urged them to utilize the idle fields of the South, to become inventors and cultivators, to buy fine horses and carriages, to become presidents of their own colleges and historians of their own race. Additionally, he pressed them to teach their sisters and wives and daughters to become shrewd businesswomen, who would serve as faithful advocates in the communities where they lived, buying land and building factories and schools. Dr. Smallwood believed that his race could accomplish these things and many more, and he felt compelled to assist the Negro people in accomplishing these endeavors.[5]

By the time the seventh annual commencement exercise was held in June 1899, 393 students had attended and graduated from the institute, including 34 schoolteachers, 54 temperance workers, and 61 young men who pursued careers in farming.[6] The seventh annual commencement exercise began on Sunday, June 11, 1899, and continued through Wednesday, June 14. All exercises were held on the college grounds. Faculty members in attendance included Dr. John J. Smallwood, founder, president, and professor of history and science; Ms. Eleanor D. Owens, the lady principal and instructor in English and elocution; Ms. Fannie E. Smallwood, niece of Dr. Smallwood, secretary and instructor in Advanced Mathematics and Higher English;[7] Mrs. M. W. Gordon, director of the music and primary branches; and Mrs. S. L. Jones, the matron.[8]

The four-day commencement began on Sunday with an anthem, scripture lesson, musical solo, and prayer. The baccalaureate sermon commenced at 10:30 a.m., with the Rev. D. Webster Davis, AM, of Richmond, Virginia, as the speaker. The benediction was held at 2:30

p.m. in the chapel. The commencement exercises continued throughout the day with recitations and singing.[9]

On Monday, June 12, recitations, scripture reading, and singing began at 7:30 p.m. Ms. Hattie M. Lassiter, niece of Dr. Smallwood and native of Rich Square, North Carolina, gave the welcoming address.[10] On the following day, from 10:00 a.m. to 12:00 p.m., a reunion for former students was held in the chapel, in addition to a book reception, with Ms. Margaret E. Threatt presiding. The object of the reunion was "to learn of each other, what has been and is, the occupation, duties and successes of active, business, industrial, moral and religious life as they have learned and lead [sic] by actual contact with the outside world."[11] Of a similar purpose as the reunion, a Farmers' Congress comprised the afternoon services on the thirteenth, beginning at 2:30 p.m. The object of the congress was to bring colored landowners and farmers together so that the Negro farmers could more effectually work for the advancement of the home and the community in which they lived. Every local farmer and landowner was requested to be present and to take part in the deliberations of the congress. The Rev. W. L. Taylor gave the address, and P. Emmett Ellis of Scotland, Virginia, and Archer Williams of Providence Forge, Virginia, gave remarks, with the Honorable A. Q. Franklin of Ruthville, Virginia, presiding.[12]

Tuesday evening's services commenced at 7:30 p.m., with a public recognition of the contestants for the Gatling prize gold medal, an award honoring the best recital. Among the contestants were three of Dr. Smallwood's nieces, Ms. Lizzie E. Josey, Ms. Hattie M. Lassiter, and Ms. Lucille A. Smallwood, all of Rich Square, North Carolina. The other contestants were Ms. Rhoda E. Graves of Sturgeon Point, Virginia, and Ms. Fannie E. Proctor of Norfolk, Virginia. Ms. Gracie T. Ellis of Scotland, Virginia, addressed the contestants and those in attendance with opening remarks and the agenda for the evening. A prayer opened the ceremony, with intermittent singing between recitals. Ms. Lizzie Josey recited "The Story of Aunt Jemima's Courtship," followed by "The Raven" by Ms. Rhoda E. Graves. Other recitals included "The Song of Selma," by Ms. Hattie M. Lassiter; "The Frenchman and the Flea Powder," by Ms. Fannie E. Proctor; and "Toussaint L'ouverture," by Ms. Lucy A. Smallwood. The evening concluded with the awarding of the prize and a dumbbell drill led by Ms. E. D. Owens and Ms. M. E. Threatt.[13]

Wednesday, June 14, marked the last day of the commencement exercises. The day began with an address from President Smallwood, followed by a prayer and a three o'clock meeting of the trustee board in the president's office. Ms. Margaret E. Threatt of Norfolk, Virginia, and Mr. Marcus W. Smallwood of Rich Square, North Carolina, were awarded the Williams prize gold medal for the best original oration. Both students were also part of the graduating class of '99. The commencement exercises concluded that evening, with Mr. Marcus W. Smallwood reading the class history and Ms. Rhoda E. Graves of Sturgeon Point, Virginia, and Ms. Margaret E. Threatt of Norfolk, Virginia, reading an address to the class of '99. Ms. Threatt, the class valedictorian, also delivered a speech on "The Negro as an American Citizen." Dr. R. Emmett Jones of Richmond, Virginia, delivered the commencement address and presented the diplomas to the graduates of the class of '99.[14]

That year, Dr. Smallwood received endorsements from the Honorable P. B. Dolittle, former state senator of North Carolina, as well as the *Richmond Times* and the *Norfolk Landmark*. All three commended Dr. Smallwood for his hard work, commitment to his race, and dedication to solving the race problem.[15] Dr. Smallwood's work had come at a high financial cost, however: the institute's total financial expenditures for the 1898–1899 academic year far exceeded the amount of revenues generated by the school, with debt services for the year amounting to $2,645.17. The total amount spent on boarding and teachers' salaries was $1,275.90. Other expenses included $197.95 for books, $389.12 for farm supplies and equipment, $100 in general repairs on farm and buildings, $315.40 in railroad expenses, $145.98 for printing, and $596.94 for and stamps and stationery.

Total expenditures for the school year amounted to $5,675.46.[16] By comparison, the school's overall revenue for the year was $3,805.15, including the $1,000.00 paid to the institution by students. Friends donated $2,192.25, and $612.90 was raised by the school farm, but the institute still incurred a deficit of $1,870.31 at the end of the school year.[17]

Despite the institute's fiscal problems, plans commenced to enlarge the school. Dr. Smallwood solicited funds from his friends in the North to build a hall to accommodate students and patrons who attended the institute. He sought a sum of $20,000 to break ground for the expansion.[18] Supporters from New York, New Jersey, New Hampshire, Connecticut, Maine, Massachusetts, Virginia, Pennsylvania, Michigan, Wisconsin, North Carolina, Minnesota, Washington DC, Oregon, and Illinois all responded to his plea and made donations ranging from $1 to as much as $300.[19] Frederick Cooper Hewitt of New York bequeathed $3,000 to Temperance, Industrial and Collegiate Institute.[20]

Dr. Smallwood received so much financial support from his Northern donors that he often traveled to New York to render a financial accounting to those who had contributed money for the overall operation of his school. He understood that any money given him was given solely for school purposes, with the distinct understanding that it was not to be spent for his personal use. To that end, he was very cautious about how donors' money was used and maintained meticulous records of expenditures so that he could return exact reports to people who had given him money.[21] Letters from his personal correspondence show not only that Dr. Smallwood had friends who were strong supporters of his work, but also that he was well aware of his accountability to them. In a letter to his attorney, for example, he stated that he "was handed your letter of this date just as I was leaving Claremont for New York[;] I am bound to go to New York to take in my report to the money givers."[22] In another letter to his lawyer, Dr. Smallwood wrote, "I had exceeded my appropriation given to me by my friends, and I wanted to take time to confer with them . . . I have written to my friends that I would not need to trouble them about money until the last of August."[23]

By the end of 1899, letters of commendation had poured in from all over the United States, congratulating Dr. Smallwood on his noble work and his zeal for the education of his race. In these letters, in addition to newspaper articles, he was repeatedly described as a man of high moral character and one who was respected by many.[24] Widely commended for the success of his school, Dr. Smallwood could not have been prouder as the Temperance, Industrial and Collegiate Institute continued to grow, boasting a faculty of five and a matriculation record of several hundred students by the turn of the century.[25]

What made him perhaps even more proud was the fact that, in 1865, at the time of the emancipation, only "about one in every twenty Negroes could read and write," but by 1900, "thirty-five years later, more than one out of every two [Negroes] could read and write."[26] Dr. Smallwood's school had contributed significantly to this greatly enhanced number—proof that his vision was bringing about a real and positive change. The reasons why he had purchased land, built facilities to accommodate his students, and advocated earnestly on behalf of their needs were the same as the reason he rose each morning before dawn and plowed his school farm, often working until 2:00 a.m.: he wanted his people to become an intelligent race of people who could, ultimately, become leaders and prominent community figures in America.

Now that Dr. Smallwood was beginning to see some of the positive effects of his labors, he was finally in a position to provide for a wife in an honorable, responsible, and husbandlike way, as he had described in the *Monthly Advocate*. On September 20, 1900, a day after his thirty-seventh birthday, Dr. Smallwood married twenty-one-year-old year old Rosa E. Banks, the daughter of Mat and Phyllis Banks of Richmond, Virginia.[27]

Even after marrying, Dr. Smallwood spent much of his time on his school's 36-acre farm, as well as the additional 271 acres of farmland that he had purchased from H. J. Arrington in 1891. The larger of these tracts was considered some of the best farmland in Surry County and was used by the institute's agricultural department strictly for school purposes. But he also continued to spend a lot of his time teaching moral and mental science, traveling and speaking to solicit funds for his school, and conducting the overall operation of the ever-expanding institute.[28] The school, however, was not the only thing growing. On November 23, 1901, a little over a year after their marriage, Dr. and Mrs. Smallwood welcomed the birth of a baby girl named Thelma, the first addition to their growing family.[29]

Willie L. Lassiter (1900-), niece of Dr. John J. Smallwood, with John F. Street, mayor of Philadelphia (2000–2008), honoring her one hundredth birthday. (Courtesy of Willie L. Lassiter).

William Smallwood, cousin of Marcus W. Smallwood, John J. Smallwood's former slave owner, was a Revolutionary War officer and friend of President George Washington. He served as governor of Maryland from 1785 until 1788. (Courtesy of the Library of Congress)

General Benjamin F. Butler, a Massachusetts politician and Union officer who had been sent to fight in Virginia during the Civil War where at the time he served as commander of the Union Forces at Fortress Monroe, which was the most powerful fort of the United States during the Civil War. The Butler School was founded in 1861 and named in his honor. (Courtesy of Hampton University Archives)

This is a picture of the Butler School children ca. 1870. Dr. Smallwood was a very young seven-year-old when he arrived in October 1870. Students ranged in ages from five to twenty-four. He is perhaps one among the many students in this photograph. Note the Emancipation Oak in the background. (Courtesy of Hampton University Archives)

The Butler School was built by the United States government for newly freed slaves. (Courtesy of Hampton University Archives)

General Samuel Chapman Armstrong was founder and first principal of Hampton, Normal and Agricultural Institute in 1868. (Courtesy of Hampton University Archives)

Dr. Henry M. Tupper (1831–1893) was founder and first principal of Shaw University, the first historically black college of the south, from 1865–1893. (Courtesy of Shaw University Archives and Special Collections)

Shaw Hall, a male dormitory, was opened in 1872 and named in honor of Mr. Elijah Shaw. (Courtesy of Shaw University Archives and Special Collections)

Dr. Nicholas Franklin Roberts (1849–1934), a native of Seaboard, Northampton County, North Carolina, entered Shaw University in October 1871 and was one of the first graduates of the college department of Shaw University. Upon graduation in 1878, he was made professor of mathematics in the university. He later was named acting president immediately after Dr. Tupper's death and served from November 1893 to March 1894. He also served as vice president of the university. (Courtesy of Shaw University Archives and Special Collections)

A young John Jefferson Smallwood, born in Rich Square, Northampton County, North Carolina in 1863, was an 1879 graduate of Shaw University, Raleigh, North Carolina. (Courtesy of Flora Tann-Chambliss)

Dr. Manassa T. Pope, ca. 1900, born in Rich Square, Northampton County, North Carolina, in 1858. In 1874, he attended Shaw University and later studied at the Leonard School of Medicine at Shaw, the first four-year medical college in the state of North Carolina (black or white). He graduated in 1886. He became the first African American to receive a medical license in North Carolina. In 1919, he ran unsuccessfully for mayor in Raleigh, North Carolina. He died in 1934. (Courtesy of Shaw University Archives and Special Collections)

John J. Smallwood, ca. 1887, sixth from right, standing in front of Rich Hall with his classmates on the campus of Wesleyan Academy. (Courtesy of Archives Department, Wilbraham and Monson Academy, Wilbraham, Massachusetts)

Dr. George M. Steele (1823–1901), principal of Wesleyan Academy, Wilbraham, Massachusetts and a friend and confidante of Dr. Smallwood. (Courtesy of Archives Department, Wilbraham and Monson Academy, Wilbraham, Massachusetts)

Dr. Loranus Crowell (1815–1889), principal financial agent, Wesleyan Academy at Wilbraham, Massachusetts and a friend and confidante of Dr. Smallwood. (Courtesy of Archives Department, Wilbraham & Monson Academy, Wilbraham, Massachusetts)

Faculty, Wesleyan Academy, ca. 1886. Dr. Steele is seated in the first row, third from left. (Courtesy of Archives Department, Wilbraham and Monson Academy, Wilbraham, Massachusetts)

Dr. Smallwood, ca. 1886, first row, fourth from left, while a student at Wesleyan Academy. (Courtesy of Archives Department, Wilbraham and Monson Academy, Wilbraham, Massachusetts)

John J. Smallwood, ca. 1887, top left (standing), a student at Wesleyan Academy. (Courtesy of Department Archives, Wilbraham & Monson Academy, Wilbraham, Massachusetts).

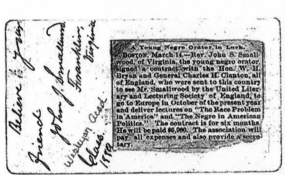

An unidentified newspaper clipping. Rev. John J. Smallwood was paid the sum of $6,980 to travel to Europe to deliver lectures on "The Race Problem in America" and "The Negro in American Politics." (Courtesy of Department Archives, Wilbraham & Monson Academy, Wilbraham, Massachusetts)

John J. Smallwood, ca. 1889, a student at Wesleyan Academy. (Courtesy of Department Archives, Wilbraham & Monson Academy, Wilbraham, Massachusetts)

Elizabeth "Betty" Smallwood (1858–1940). Dr. Smallwood's older sister. (Courtesy of Flora Tann-Chambliss)

Mary Eliza Smallwood-Lassiter (1865–1938), youngest sister of Dr. Smallwood, and her husband, John T. Lassiter (1858–1944). (Courtesy of Willie L. Lassiter)

Rev. Dr. John J. Smallwood. (Image used by permission of M. D. Harrison)

Sawyer Hall was the first building built by Dr. Smallwood and his students in 1895. It was a girl's dormitory and was named in honor of Philetus Sawyer, United States senator from Wisconsin. Dr. Smallwood modestly referred to Sawyer Hall as a "plain, wooden hall." (Courtesy of Hampton University Archives)

Rare copy of Dr. Smallwood's semi-monthly campus paper, the Monthly Advocate. (Courtesy of the Surry County Historical Society, Surry, Virginia)

Fannie Smallwood (1875–1914), third row, second from right, niece of Dr. Smallwood, enrolled in a school in New England as a teenager (ca. 1889). Ms. Smallwood later attended Temperance, Industrial and Collegiate Institute. After graduation, she served as secretary and instructor in Advanced Mathematics and Higher English at the institute. (Courtesy of Flora Tann-Chambliss)

Four unidentified female graduates of Temperance, Industrial and Collegiate Institute. (Courtesy of Hampton University Archives)

CHAPTER ELEVEN

COURSE OF STUDY

Not long after Dr. Smallwood had chartered the Temperance, Industrial and Collegiate Institute, students were traveling from far and near to attend, with the majority of students coming from Virginia. Other students traveled from New Jersey, New York, North Carolina, Delaware, and Washington DC.[1] Their most common modes of transportation to the institute were by way of the steamer *Pocahontas* or the railway at Union Depot, both of which departed from Richmond. Students traveling from the North first made their way to Richmond and then boarded the steamer or train for Claremont. Once students from the North arrived in Richmond, accommodations were available for them at the home of a Mrs. Leftwich. Students coming from North Carolina traveled by train from Weldon, North Carolina, to Bellfield, Virginia, then onto Claremont via the Southern Railway.[2] And the school continued to grow.

In 1902, the institute had a nine-member board of trustees and a thirteen-member prudential committee;[3] there were five faculty members on staff. The course of study included a normal preparatory and a college preparatory curriculum. The normal preparatory program included a four-year course of study: normal preparatory, junior normal, middle year normal, and senior normal. Students in the normal preparatory program studied courses such as arithmetic, geography (map drawing), English grammar, orthography, reading, physiology (primary), history of Virginia, penmanship, and Bible. In the junior normal program, students completed all the courses offered in the normal preparatory program, with the addition of civil government and agriculture.[4]

During the middle year normal, courses such as algebra, history of the Negro race, rhetoric, Latin, word analysis, political economy, ancient history, bookkeeping, and Bible were taught. Senior normal classes were more advanced and included courses such as plane geometry, moral science, psychology, chemistry, physics, botany, pedagogy, Latin (Caesar's *Commentaries on the Gallic Wars*), philosophy, and Bible. Physical culture, elocution, and vocal and instrumental music were also taught throughout the course.[5]

The college course of study was a four-year program with a rigorous curriculum that began with college preparatory courses that included Latin grammar and composition, Caesar's *Commentaries on the Gallic Wars,* Greek grammar and composition, algebra, outlines of general history, plane and solid geometry, ethics, physics, and Bible. Once students mastered these courses, they enrolled in more advanced courses. During the freshman year, students were required to study Greek (Xenophon's *Anabasis*), Latin (Virgil), natural philosophy, English literature, Roman history, geometry, and rhetoric. Sophomores were required to study mythology, chemistry, Greek (Homer's *Iliad*), Latin (Cicero and Horace), analytical geometry, and history of Greece. Juniors studied French, astronomy, Latin, Pericles's *Oration*, logic, philosophy, trigonometry, international law, geology, zoology, Greek (Xenophon's *Memorabilia*), and mythology. Fourth-year students studied composition throughout their senior year, in addition to moral philosophy, astronomy, advanced chemistry, review of languages, Latin, Greek, and English. A degree of AB was awarded to students who completed the entire program of study across the curriculum.[6]

In addition to the normal and college preparatory courses of study, the institute had two other departments—industrial and theological. In the industrial department, girls were taught sewing, cooking, needlework, housecleaning, laundry, and other industrial skills, and boys learned shoemaking and farming. Dr. Smallwood intended to increase the vocations taught in these departments as the institute's financial situation improved.[7]

Every Tuesday and Wednesday evenings, students were expected to attend prayer meetings held at seven o'clock. Chapel services were also mandatory, every day at 9:15 a.m. and 2:45 p.m. Bible reading was held at 7:45 a.m., and Bible congregational reading was at 3:00 p.m. Students were required to be in their seats five minutes after the bell rang and to show respect toward one another. Gossip was not tolerated; neither the president nor the faculty would hear any gossip from students.[8]

The monthly cost for tuition was $1.50, with an additional $5.00 per month for room and board. Students who chose to room alone paid an extra fee. All students were expected to keep their rooms clean, and all rooms were inspected each morning by the matron. Association between males and females was allowed only by permission of the faculty, but under no circumstances were young men and women allowed to write one another. The grading scale included grades of 70 as passing, 80 as fair, and 90 as good. A grade of 95 was considered excellent. If students violated any of the rules and regulations of the school, they were reprimanded with a private reproof from the administration for the first three offenses; the fourth reprimand entailed a public reproof, and a fifth resulted in suspension or expulsion.[9]

By November 1903, Dr. Smallwood had overcome the obstacle created by the fire of 1897: the institute was preparing to reopen its mattress factory and the administration hoped "to rebuild the saw mill on the property that was destroyed by fire."[10] Dr. Smallwood knew that the mattress factory, in particular, was necessary as a means of providing his students with opportunities not only for employment but also for paying their way through school, the typical method of financing education at industrial training schools around the turn of the century. The factory would help to pay for the institution and would, at the same time, provide students with the unique opportunity to learn the skill of mattress making.[11] In order to help more students defray the costs of their education, as well as the school's operation, Dr. Smallwood really needed all three of the factories that had been destroyed in 1897, the planing and saw mills in addition to the mattress factory.[12]

According to P. Emmett Ellis, the institute's treasurer, the sawmill would also give young men and boys opportunities for work. It would enable them to pay their way through school and, at the same time, teach them how to saw their own lumber and build their own buildings. Ultimately, this would enable them to become self-reliant, one of Dr. Smallwood's goals. Along with Mr. Ellis, Dr. Smallwood hoped that any lumber and mattresses made at the institute could be sold and that the monies earned could be used to cover the cost of operational expenses, as well as pay off institutional debt. He hoped that, in addition to learning a trade and obtaining an education, the young men on his campus would use the valuable skills they had acquired to build their own homes on the land he encouraged them to purchase once they left the institute's campus. If Negroes became land—and homeowners, Dr. Smallwood believed, they would gain a significant advantage in their fight to become self-sustaining.[13]

By 1903, the board of trustees of the Temperance, Industrial and Collegiate Institute still boasted nine members, despite some changes to the staff. Two new members, Dr. W. T. Johnson and Mr. A. S. West, were seated on the board, in place of the Honorable W. W. Lawrence and Mr. Willis R. Wright. The board met twice each school year on the twelfth of February (the anniversary of Abraham Lincoln's birth) and on the first day of June.[14]

Dr. Smallwood carefully selected his board members. Among them were Professors J. H. Blackwell and R. Kelser, both of whom had been engaged in educational work among the Negro race for over twenty years. Professor Kelser was a renowned scholar, and two other members, the Rev. Drs. W. T. Johnson and W. F. Graham, were pastors of the two largest Baptist churches in Richmond, Virginia. Mr. P. Emmett Ellis was a businessman who owned his own home; he had been involved in the advancement of the Negro race for quite some time. Joseph N. Gray was from the rural South and was a well-educated, careful, and sympathetic man. Mr. A. S. West was a businessman who employed a number of people in his three stores in eastern Virginia and was considered one of the largest merchants in that area. Mr. John W. Peterson, business manager for Temperance, had loaned Dr. Smallwood money during the formative stages of his school and was known for his accurate assessment of others' character.[15]

In 1903, a little over a decade since the school first opened its doors, a total of 497 students had passed in and out of the institute.[16] That same year, according to Mr. Ellis, graduates of Temperance, Industrial and Collegiate Institute included "fifty-nine men [who] have brought farms, seven have become ministers, four blacksmiths, twelve school teachers, one a lawyer, two doctors and three carpenters, eight hotel waiters, two temperance lecturers, seventeen tradesmen of various kinds and nine home owners in cities in North Carolina, Virginia and Maryland, New Jersey and Pennsylvania."[17]

Dr. Smallwood was, of course, proud of his students, but he was discontented, in a sense, despite these successes, because he desired much more for his students. He wanted to expand the departments on his campus and offer more trades. And he knew that if he did so, the resulting influx of students into Temperance, Industrial and Collegiate Institute would require more space to accommodate the growing population. Dormitories were needed for both girls and boys, teaching departments were in need of supplies, and a laundry, cooking, and housekeeping department was needed to teach girls these skills.[18]

On the plus side, Dr. Smallwood was very pleased that the sewing and dressmaking department was well under way and was able to pay for its own operating costs. The farming department was also flourishing, with abundant crops of corn, potatoes, and vegetables. Enough corn had been produced, in fact, for both stock and bread. There were also several orchards on the campus grounds, and students at the institute preserved the fruits by canning them. Scientific farming was a project in the making and was considered a priority for the 1903–1904 school year.[19]

Meanwhile, the 1902–1903 school year ended with commencement exercises that began on Sunday, May 31, 1903, in Claremont, Virginia, and extending through the night of Tuesday, June 2. On Sunday morning, the Rev. A. C. Skinner, BD, of Hampton, Virginia, delivered an eloquent baccalaureate sermon to an enthusiastic audience of an estimated five hundred to eight hundred people, both colored and white.[20] In the sermon, Reverend Skinner provided his audience with a complete history of the circumstances that led to his choice of text for the morning, Nehemiah 6:3—"And I sent messengers unto them, saying, I am doing a great work, so that I cannot come down: why should the work cease, whilst I leave it, and come down to you?" The Word of God electrified the audience, both white and colored.

Later that evening, Professor R. Kelser of Charlottesville, Virginia, addressed an audience of both colored and white people from nearby towns. He delivered a stern message on the urgent need for the Negro to reject all alcoholic beverages—King Alcohol, as he referred to it—and other stimulants. He reminded his listeners that the institute was strictly a temperance institution upon which the principles of temperance abounded.[21] The next evening, Monday, June 1, at 2:30 p.m., Dr. Smallwood met with the Annual Farmers and Landowners Congress, an organization he had founded to bring colored farmers and landowners together to discuss ways in which they could improve their homes and communities. Both colored and white farmers attended this congress in large numbers.[22]

The day's events ended with a keynote address by Professor Lafayette Hershaw, registrar of the U.S. Treasury, Washington DC. After a brief introduction by President Smallwood, Hershaw spoke before a large crowd on the fundamental principles of all systems of philosophy and religion, whether Pagan or Christian, and discussed the manhood and unity of mankind. He believed that man should be developed and elevated, the principle behind civilization and (essentially) the philosophy of Jesus. In order for mankind to become truly civilized, he said, people must be educated mentally, ethically, and industrially, at one and the same time. Hershaw emphasized that, throughout the history of the world, all truly advanced races have employed these three kinds of education simultaneously. The recorded experiences of four civilizations, in particular—Egyptian, Greek, Roman, and Anglo-Saxon—indicated the path that the Negro race should now walk. According to Professor Hershaw, all four civilizations "show that similar, if not identical studies were pursued in order to produce given effects in mental development. And yet in the face of these plain examples, men go to and from and up and down asking, 'What sort of education should the Negro be given?' The plain and correct answer is, the same sort of education that gave to the world an Egyptian, a Greek, a Roman and Anglo-Saxon civilization. The Negro is a man, therefore, whatever has helped other men, will help him."[23] Hershaw asserted that the Negro race, too, should be given the opportunity to gain a complete education because, contrary to many of the stereotypical portrayals of Negroes popular at the time, the Negro has a mind, one that should be trained and developed. Hershaw concluded his speech by stating that "the man who would differentiate between people living in the same climatic conditions and under the same flag, with an equal allegiance to the government, in matters of education and other civil and political privileges is an enemy not only to the race against whom he would discriminate, but to human progress and enlightenment."[24] He encouraged his audience that this "fad of proscription and discrimination" would soon fade away and that "men will return to rational methods of thought and be guided by the plain teachings of history."[25] Although the times seemed difficult, he reminded his captivated audience that "in spite of adverse conditions and encircling gloom, a bright day is sure to come."[26] The morning after Hershaw's speech, on Tuesday, June 2, 1903, the eleventh annual commencement services ended, with the conferring of degrees and peerless orations by four female graduates to the hundreds of people who continued to swarm the campus, hall, and chapel during the last of the three-day exercises.[27]

Throughout his career, Dr. Smallwood sincerely believed that, contrary to popular belief, the Negro could take care of himself if left alone.[28] That is, he could make great strides if divested of the crippling effects of America's pandemic Jim Crowism. While most Negroes around the year 1900 were living at subsistence level, they were advancing rapidly in terms of personal progress; literacy rates, for example, had risen dramatically. After the institution of Jim Crow laws,[29] however, Dr. Smallwood knew that Negroes' small yet momentous advances would soon be extinguished. In order to protect and continue their progress, he wrote extensively to various newspapers, vehemently expressing his concerns about race relations in America and its system that perpetuated and encouraged hatred, inequality, and disenfranchisement. He shared with his readers his views on the long-term and detrimental effects that these social ills would have upon an entire race of people. In one article published in the *Southern Workman*, Dr. Smallwood attested to the great advancements that Negroes had made within a short period of time and described his fears that Jim Crowism would bring their progress to a complete halt:

People say that the Negro is lazy. They said that he would do nothing after the war but steal chickens. I solemnly affirm that

I never stole a chicken in my life. But we did rest after the war. We had been working 250 years and we were tired. In 1865 the Negro paid taxes on $12,000 worth of property south of Mason & Dixon's line; there were no Negro lawyers nor doctors, and but two Negro editors, Douglas[s] and Langston;[30] they had no schools and colleges. In 1890, the Negroes owned $263,000,000 worth of taxable property south of Mason & Dixon's line; there were 892 Negro lawyers and 749 doctors; there were seven colleges, 17 academies and 49 high schools, all with Negro faculties; there were 995 Negro college graduates who were preaching the gospel, and 225 educated Negro women who were teaching. In South Carolina the Negroes own $31,000,000 worth of taxable property, and in Mississippi, $22,000,000. The finest church in Mississippi is a Negro church. In Florida there are 7,000 more black men who can read and write than there are white men and the same is true with Missouri.[31]

Frederick Douglass, whom Dr. Smallwood deeply admired and whom he had invited to speak at Temperance's second annual commencement exercise, had expressed similar sentiments when the question of what to do with the Negro surfaced after the Civil War. Mr. Douglass answered as follows:

[D]o nothing with [him] . . . Your *doing* with [Negroes] is their greatest misfortune . . . If you see him plowing in the open field, leveling the forest, at work with a spade, a rake, a hoe, a pick-axe, or a bill—let him alone; he has a right to work. If you see him on his way to school, with spelling book, geography and arithmetic in his hands—let him *alone* . . . If he has a ballot in his hand, and is on his way to the ballot-box to deposit his vote for the man whom he thinks will most justly and wisely administer the Government which has the power of life and death over him, as well as others . . . let him alone.[32]

Dr. Smallwood's vision was to teach his students to become entrepreneurs, thinkers, and doers. He believed that, rather than talking about the past injustices they had endured, they should instead focus their energies and attention on becoming self-reliant; they should become advocates for their own families and the communities in which they lived.[33] Dr. Smallwood also continuously emphasized to his fellow Negroes that they would not be equipped for the great challenges and opportunities of life unless they educated themselves, contrary to popular arguments about the Negro's intelligence—that he could not learn, that the Negro race was incapable of taking care of itself. Dr. Smallwood realized that this type of comment, common among those prejudiced against Negro advancement, could psychologically paralyze an already-fragile race of people and bring their recently acquired progress to a complete halt, and he vehemently warned Negroes not to fall victim to the rhetorical ploys of those who wished them ill. Always an optimist, Dr. Smallwood believed that Negroes did, in fact, possess the mental capabilities necessary for overcoming the overwhelmingly negative force of opposition, but only if they lived in accordance with the principles of temperance—self-discipline, self-control, self-restraint, and freedom from mind-altering stimulants.[34]

Mary of Bethany who, with her sister Martha,
pleaded with Jesus to raise their brother Lazarus
from the dead. Their grief was so great that Jesus
wept at the sight of it (John 11: 28–35).

—*Verse from the Negro spiritual "Oh Mary,*
Don't You Weep," which originated before the
American Civil War

CHAPTER TWELVE

MARY, DON'T YOU WEEP

D r. Smallwood had a twofold task at the turn of the twentieth
century. In addition to operating his school, he felt a sense of
obligation to speak out about expressions of white supremacy, whether
blatant or subtle, that were used to terrorize and disenfranchise Negroes.
He was a superb orator, and there was always a great demand for him to
speak on the race problem throughout the United States. Even with his
rigorous schedule at the institute, Dr. Smallwood continued to deliver
poignant speeches at various churches and public events. By 1904, he
had already traveled over twenty thousand miles and had made hundreds
of speeches.[1] Temperance, Industrial and Collegiate Institute, however,
remained his foremost responsibility.

While preparing to go and speak at a local Virginia church in 1904,
Dr. Smallwood received some sad news: his dear mother had died. He
had traveled from Claremont to her home in Rich Square, North Carolina,
several times over the past few years and was well aware of her declining
health. Though saddened by his loss, Dr. Smallwood, now forty-one years
old, was able to find solace and strength in the fact that he had gotten the
chance to know his mother for fifteen years.

After finding his mother, Dr. Smallwood wanted to provide for her in
the best way he could. Realizing that she had endured countless hardships
throughout her years as a slave, he tried in every way he could to make her

life better than it had been. She had spent a lifetime concealing her true identity as the daughter of Nat Turner, for fear of reprisal, and harbored painful and horrible memories of the slave trade, slave life, suffering, and humiliation. She had also witnessed the sale of her sister, brother, and husband, and ten of her children, in addition to the torture and beating of her mother and the execution of her father. Dr. Smallwood realized he could not undo the past injustices and wrongs that had been inflicted on her; neither could he make up for all the lost time that had elapsed in their nearly twenty-six years of separation. But one thing he could do was to make all attempts to compensate her for her losses and her pain and suffering by showering her with the unconditional love that she so earnestly deserved.

Dr. Smallwood made a point of impressing upon the merchants in Rich Square to provide his mother with whatever she desired or needed—he would pay all expenses. He took care of his mother financially, while three of his sisters looked after her physical well-being. He visited Rich Square frequently and would require his nieces and nephews, her grandchildren, to refrain from making excessive noise, as it would disturb her while she was resting. Little did he know, his mother welcomed the sounds of the tiny feet of all her grandchildren as they pranced across the hardwood floors. Although she had suffered the loss of her sight and could not physically see them, she enjoyed knowing that they were near as the last days of her life approached. For many years she had been continually robbed of her relatives and friends, and all her life she had yearned for the chance to have a real family. As her days came to an end, she did not die alone, but surrounded by four of her fourteen children—ten of whom she had never seen again after they were sold from her—and many grandchildren.

As Dr. Smallwood said good-bye to his mother, a thousand memories entered his mind. One in particular stood out more than the others: how profusely she was weeping when he laid eyes on her, still at a distance, for the first time in his adult life. The image of his mother weeping remained etched in his mind for many years. But as Dr. Smallwood and his sisters laid their mother to rest in Willow Oak Cemetery in Rich Square, North Carolina, the Smallwood family was at peace. They found consolation and solace in knowing that though her grief had been great and her life's journey exhausting and inconceivably unjust, Mary Eliza, their mother, did not have to weep anymore.[2]

Soon after his mother's funeral, Dr. Smallwood returned to Claremont to find that the enrollment at his institute had increased tremendously—so much, in fact, that he saw fit to expand two of its vocational programs. It had always been his desire to expand the range of training programs offered at the institute, and in keeping with this vision, he and his wife decided to acquire more land for the school. The next year, on September 9, 1905, Mrs. Smallwood purchased 99½ acres of land from James and Susan Boyce in Surry County, Virginia. It was a portion of land known as Claremont Estate, located on the north side of the Cabin Point Road.[3] Added to the 271 acres purchased in 1891, the newly acquired acreage was a tremendous asset to the industrial and agricultural departments at Temperance.

The 1905–1906 scholastic year began on October 5, with Professor R. R. Holmes appointed as the newly elected vice president of the industrial department. The course of study in 1905–1906 was similar to the curriculum in 1903, with a few exceptions. The department had now increased the number of vocations to include carpentry, with emphasis placed on the repair and maintenance of buildings and grounds, as well as general and practical applications to construction made from drawings. Boys were required to work one hour daily without compensation. Training in horseshoeing and blacksmithing would be added in the near future.[4]

Mr. T. H. Hepler was the superintendent in charge of agriculture at Temperance. His intentions were to have a model farm managed scientifically on 165 acres of the best farmland in Surry County. Future plans were to add new features such as horticulture and dairying. Vocational training for women at Temperance included courses in sewing, domestic science, and cooking,[5] all taught by Mrs. Mary B. Owen, matron and supervisor of the sewing department.

Students had the option to participate in a work program that compensated them with a wage of $1.50 to $2.00 per month that could only be credited to their bill. Tuition and board remained the same as it had been in 1903: $5.00 per month for board and $1.50 per month for tuition. A one-month advance charge was requested for board and tuition prior to a student's enrollment in the school, with all remaining payments due at the end of each month. Boys were charged an extra fee of $1.00 for laundry, and girls were responsible for doing their own laundry.[6]

By the 1906–1907 school year, the board of trustees had increased to ten members from its original nine. The fall term began Monday, September 24, and closed December 24, with Christmas vacation extending from December 25, 1906, to January 1, 1907. The winter term began January 2, 1907, and closed Saturday, March 2. Spring term began only two days later, on Monday, March 4, and ended June 6.[7]

The school year began with several changes authorized by the board. The preparatory course of study now required three years of study instead of four, while the college course of study remained at four years. Programs in the industrial and collegiate departments also remained at four years. It is not clear whether the faculty and board of trustees intended to emphasize one department more heavily than the other, but it is fair to assume that the industrial and agricultural departments were considered an integral part of the curriculum.[8]

The staff also increased significantly from five faculty members to thirteen, including Dr. Smallwood. Apart from him, only one other faculty member had earned a Ph.D.—Dr. L. B. Tallman, who taught history, Latin, carpentry, and pedagogy at the Institute. Dr. Smallwood's wife, Mrs. Rosa Smallwood, was assigned to teach English literature and rhetoric, and his niece, Ms. Reddie E. Josey, a graduate of the institute, taught vocal and instrumental music and preparatory studies. Dr. Smallwood himself taught economics and psychology, in addition to biblical history and moral and mental science.[9] The newly expanded staff of the institute also included a twelve-member prudential committee and a nine-member financial committee, with the Honorable J. Thomas Newsome of Newport News, Virginia, serving as Dr. Smallwood's attorney.[10]

School officials clearly intended to prepare students for advanced graduate studies upon completion of their rigorous programs. Graduate programs at Temperance were based on the robust collegiate curriculum offered by Dr. Smallwood and his colleagues during the required four years of coursework.[11] Some students who graduated from Temperance enrolled directly in graduate degree programs at other schools because of their ample scholarly preparation.[12]

Dr. Smallwood and his trustees propounded a holistic approach to education, in keeping with the name of the school—the Temperance, Industrial and Collegiate Institute. Dr. Smallwood wanted to offer an education that would provide "its students a thorough mental, moral, industrial and religious training," rather than solely to produce teachers for the Negro community at large, as was the purpose of most normal schools. The fact that Dr. Smallwood did not want exclusively to train teachers was perhaps the reason that he chose to exclude the word "normal" from the title of his school. Because of the lack of professional opportunities for Negroes in the early twentieth century, however, many Temperance graduates probably did assume teaching positions in the community.[13]

Throughout its first fifteen years of operation, from 1892 to 1907, Dr. Smallwood's institute offered Negro students an excellent opportunity to secure a quality education. It was an exceptionally good offer for the expense of only $6.50 per month, tuition and room and board included. This cost had increased only once, by $0.50, since the school first opened its doors in October 1892.[14]

CHAPTER THIRTEEN

THE RACE PROBLEM

E ven with his demanding schedule, Dr. Smallwood continued to speak on the issue of the race problem in America and its crippling effects on his people. As Jim Crowism grew more intense, so did the need to address these concerns. In the summer of 1906, Dr. Smallwood received an invitation to speak in St. Luke parish on the subject of the recent race war that had occurred in Texas and his position on the race problem in America. After graciously thanking those in attendance for the invitation, he opened his lecture, entitled "The American Negro, His Past, Present and Future Education," by paying tribute to ex-president Grover Cleveland, whom he described as a "writer, statesman and a Christian."[1]

Dr. Smallwood then spoke briefly about the race wars in Texas, where several groups of Negroes had recently been accused of murder and some of them killed. The first race war that Dr. Smallwood discussed occurred on Monday, March 28, 1904, in the town of Silsbee, Texas, a small settlement seventy miles north of Beaumont. On that night, a white man named Sidney Stewart had been fatally shot, and two of his companions wounded, reportedly by Negroes. This incident rapidly precipitated a race war that threatened the extermination of Negroes in East Texas.[2] Within ten days of the incident, five more white men were killed, and in each case Negroes were blamed for the murders. In retaliation, four Negro men were killed by a posse of whites and several others were charged with robbery and arson for allegedly attempting to destroy the oil fields of Sour Lake, Batson, and Saratoga, resulting in the destruction of over $150,000's worth of property.[3]

As terror reigned throughout the small town of Silsbee and its neighboring communities, white citizens began ordering more guns and ammunition from Houston, Beaumont, and other places; upon hearing this news, black residents followed suit and began to gather arms themselves. Negroes were ordered out of Silsbee and a number of other oil and lumber camps, where several hundred of them had been employed as laborers. But instead of leaving Silsbee, unconfirmed reports stated, over a hundred well-armed Negroes defied the order and took refuge in the woods nearby.[4] Their discharge from the mills and oil fields was said to be the underlying cause of the race war.

The second race war in Texas occurred near Brownsville during the summer of 1906, on the night of August 13, when black soldiers of the Twenty-fifth Regiment, stationed at Fort Brown, were accused of murdering a white bartender and wounding a white police officer. Despite the fact that all of the white commanders at Fort Brown confirmed that the black soldiers had been in their barracks at the time of the shootings, their testimony was not enough to convince the white citizens of Brownsville of the soldiers' innocence. President Theodore Roosevelt ordered an investigation, during which the soldiers suspected of committing the offenses were at no time presumed innocent or provided legal representation. Despite all indications of the men's innocence, the investigators assumed their guilt and simply sought to prove their involvement.

Because the identities of the alleged perpetrators were unknown, all the black soldiers in the Brownsville area were pressured to name the twelve men who had supposedly committed the crimes. The soldiers not only maintained their innocence, insisting that they had no idea who was responsible for the offenses, but also contended that, since their arrival in town, they had been subjected to racial discrimination.[5] As a result of what was considered a conspiracy of silence on the part of the black soldiers, 167 Negro soldiers from the Twenty-fifth Regiment—which included soldiers from three separate companies—were dishonorably discharged by President Roosevelt on November 5, 1906, and barred from holding any future governmental positions.[6]

Addressing the race wars, Dr. Smallwood stated that, in both Silsbee and Brownsville, the law did not have any proof that Negroes had committed the crimes of which they were accused. Rather, the actions of the white posse in Silsbee were a prime example of society's all-too-common rush to pronounce judgment and take the law into its own hands. Furthermore, he stated, it was very likely that politics had brought on the Silsbee and Brownsville race wars, because certain local political factions may have desired to bring about civil strife in order to obtain their own political gains.[7]

As Dr. Smallwood continued his speech on the "Past, Present and Future of the Negro," he spoke eloquently about his pride in being both a Southerner and a Negro. He cautioned the audience not to fall victim to past myths that freedom was an unfortunate state for the Negro and that they were first cousin to the baboon. On the contrary, he told the audience, there had been Negro scholars from the time that blacks had first landed on American shores in 1620, and even throughout the period of the Civil War. He went on to say that, counter to popular beliefs and propaganda, the Negro possessed the "mental capacity to do more than just sing, dance a jig, eat and go to bed."[8]

Dr. Smallwood also spoke about the Negro's present situation, which appeared promising, despite the fact that political and social inequalities were daily being instituted to disenfranchise the race. At the present time, Negroes owned 72 colleges in the South, 18 banks, and $397,000,000 in taxable property. There was even a Negro merchant in Richmond who employed seventy-five clerks, and in South Carolina alone, Negroes owned taxable property amounting to $28,000,000.[9] Ironically, this state was the home of Benjamin "Pitchfork" Tillman, one of the most outspoken advocates for white supremacy in the early 1900s. Filled with a deep hatred for the Negro race, Tillman was viewed as a champion of the Southern white poor and did all in his power to disenfranchise Negroes as they moved toward political, economic, and social independence.[10] Tillman's call for a state constitutional convention in 1895 had been a major factor in the institution of the Jim Crow laws and the disenfranchisement of most of South Carolina's Negro men. Tillman himself made no apologizes for his actions, and he proudly and unapologetically proclaimed in 1900, "We have done our level best [to prevent blacks from voting] . . . we have scratched our heads to find out how we could eliminate the last one of them. We stuffed ballot boxes. We shot them [Negroes]. We are not ashamed of it."[11]

In Dr. Smallwood's view, Tillman, with his racist rhetoric and continuous campaign for Negro disenfranchisement, was rather presumptuous. Tillman's beliefs that a Negro should not get the same for his fifty cents as a white man and that any white who sat down to the same table as a Negro would be tainted by Negro blood prompted Dr. Smallwood to respond that any decent Negro certainly would not care to sit at table with Tillman or his kind. Instead of focusing on the "privilege" of sitting with or next to whites, Smallwood stressed, Negroes were more interested in obtaining the right to cast their own ballots and have them counted individually—one man, one vote. All the Negro wanted, Dr. Smallwood stated, was fair treatment and equal opportunities; however, he did not feel confident that the Negro would ever get his rights or even deserved them, for "[b]y not having the courage to stand up like a man and permitting the ward heelers to lead him by the nose, the Negro inadvertently retards his own progress." He proceeded by saying that in his congressional district there were four Negroes to every white man with a right to vote; yet it was impossible for them to elect their own representative to Congress. The Negro can tolerate this "for a season," Dr. Smallwood told his captivated audience, "but rottenness always rots out its own hole." Dr. Smallwood concluded his speech by stating that the future of the Negro race was hopeful, and that he was aware of the unpleasant conditions that many of them had to endure. Yet, he encouraged them to be patient for a little while longer and assured them that their situations would eventually change in their favor. In closing, he shared with his audience that he believed, in spite of all the atrocities that the Negro had been subjected to, in their best interest, they should remain in the South.[12]

Dr. Smallwood emphasized the importance and the need for the Negro to remain in the South in many more of his speeches. At the turn of the twentieth century, "nine out of every ten Negroes lived in the south,"[13] but a great number of them did not share Dr. Smallwood's views about remaining there, for many obvious reasons.[14] Included among these reasons was the South's long history of disenfranchisement, racism, and discrimination that had begun in the decades immediately after the Civil War.

During the postwar Reconstruction period, Negroes had actually held elective offices in the South and were quickly learning to adapt to a new way of life. But the presidential election of 1876 and the resulting compromise of 1877 drastically changed things. In 1876, Republican presidential candidate Rutherford B. Hayes received 165 electoral votes, and Democrat Samuel J. Tilden 184, but 20 votes were left uncounted, resulting in a bitter dispute. Resolution of this dispute fell to Congress, which set up a special electoral commission with an equal number of Democrats and Republicans, to award the disputed votes. In the end, Hayes was granted the victory, possibly because of an agreement known as the Compromise of 1877.

The compromise came about after Democrats in the Senate tried to prevent the specially appointed electoral commission from reporting by threatening a filibuster. Republicans then negotiated for abandonment of the proposed filibuster and came to terms with the Democrats: in exchange for the election of their candidate, Hayes, Republicans promised to withdraw all federal troops from the South, to appoint at least one Southern Democrat to Hayes's cabinet, to build another transcontinental railroad using the Texas and Pacific in the South and to legislate for industrialization of the South. Unfortunately, withdrawal of federal troops meant that Republicans essentially abandoned the enforcement of racial equality in the South. As a result, the compromise not only returned power to Southern Democrats—resulting in further disenfranchisement legislation, more Jim Crow laws, an increase in lynchings, and the subjection of Negroes to the mercy of their former slave owners—but also brought an end to the period of Reconstruction following the Civil War.[15]

Following the compromise, "a succession of weak presidents between 1877 and 1901 facilitated the consolidation of white supremacy in the South and Northern acceptance of victory for 'The Lost Cause.'"[16] As a result, Southern state legislatures passed laws to disenfranchise Negroes socially, politically, educationally, and economically. From the 1870s on into the twentieth century, the South's economy became increasingly unstable and unpredictable, and this period of instability, in turn, tremendously affected both white and black Southerners.

Negroes, however, bore the brunt of the ill affects of the unstable Southern economy. With the exception of the brief period of Reconstruction, conditions for them had steadily worsened since the institution, in 1865, of Black Codes, special laws designed to inhibit the freedom of ex-slaves on local and state levels by limiting their movements, activities, and labor. These codes controlled almost every aspect of Negroes' lives and varied from state to state, although most imposed the same kinds of restrictions. In addition to Black Codes, Southern Negroes endured the rise of the Ku Klux Klan (founded in 1866), a dramatic increase in lynchings, and the birth of Jim Crow legislation in the 1890s.[17] By the turn of the twentieth century, the position of the Negro in the South had reached its lowest point since the introduction of Black Codes. Faced with deplorable and impoverished conditions, racism, and even (in many cases) death,[18] Negroes began to leave the South in massive numbers, seeking a better life elsewhere.

Despite the actions of lynch mobs in the South and other hallmark implements of white supremacy, which aimed at terrorizing and disenfranchising the Negro race,[19] Dr. Smallwood continued to emphasize how important it was for the Negro to remain in the South. He believed that the South presented the best opportunities for Negroes to acquire land and home ownership. As more and more Negroes sought refuge in the large cities of the North, however, his plea for them to remain in the South seemed to fall on deaf ears.[20]

CHAPTER FOURTEEN

REMAINING ON SOUTHERN SOIL

D espite all that was going on around him, Dr. Smallwood continued to remain focused on his goal of providing his students with a quality education—so much so, in fact, that during the 1907–1908 school year, he rebuilt Old Bagley Hall,[1] with the assistance of his students. Old Bagley was first built in 1622 and was part of the corps of buildings and appurtenances that came with the original thirty-six acres of land purchased by Dr. Smallwood in 1895. It occupied the site of the old slave pen where Dr. Smallwood's great-grandparents had possibly been housed when they arrived in bondage on American soil.[2] On the institute's campus, Old Bagley was located a hundred yards from Sawyer Hall and had been the president's house before the construction of the new presidential cottage.[3]

At a cost of $10,000, Old Bagley Hall was rebuilt with the best lumber available from Virginia, North Carolina, and Georgia.[4] Once renovated, "New Bagley Hall" had seventeen rooms, spacious and well arranged, with every sanitary provision. It was used as a dormitory for boys. Mississippi journalist Charles T. McDaniels described New Bagley in an article in the *Journal and Guide* as "beyond the shadow of doubt the finest and the most substantially [sic] wooden structure in Eastern Virginia."[5] McDaniels further noted that the construction of Bagley Hall was as much to the credit of the white people of the community of Claremont as it was an honor to the Negro race.[6]

In December 1908, in addition to his obligations at the institute, Dr. Smallwood continued to speak on the subject of race relations and the importance of Negroes' remaining in the South. As the guest speaker of Dr. James E. Harlan, president of Cornell College, Dr. Smallwood delivered an exceptional speech on the subject of the race problem at the ME Church in Mount Vernon, New York. One attendee later described the talk as the "most eloquent and substantial address ever heard in that section by any speaker upon that all-important subject." Descriptions of Dr. Smallwood himself characterized him as a natural-born orator who possessed a mellifluous voice and an unassuming demeanor and as an exceptionally bright and knowledgeable man who was well versed in most subject areas.[7]

By now, Dr. Smallwood's face had become very familiar in many of the halls and cities of the east, as he continued to travel throughout the United States, speaking on the subject of the race problem. He was well learned on the subject, having studied under the tutelage of the late Rev. Dr. Loranus Crowell, an elder of the ME Church of the Lynn, Massachusetts, district; the late Phillip Brooks; and Dr. Daniel Dorchester, Indian commissioner under President Benjamin Harrison.[8]

After speaking at Cornell College, Dr. Smallwood traveled to Cedar Rapids, Iowa, to address an anxiously awaiting audience. In this speech, he reiterated that Negroes wanted a fair chance in life and the right to be citizens, as well as to be treated fairly. He underscored the importance of racial pride, self-respect, and the pursuit of a practical trade and emphasized the essential need for the Negro race to remain in the South to become a "substantial producer" and a "commercial benefactor." In spite of the "political proscription, the social ostracism" met daily by Negroes in the South, Dr. Smallwood wholeheartedly believed that the South was the best place for the Negro, and he quickly exclaimed that "Mr. Tillman does not represent the best white people in the South."[9]

When asked by an audience member if he had found racial prejudice more pervasive in the North than the South, Dr. Smallwood answered that he had but that "it is upon a different scale." He elaborated on the difference between racial prejudice in the South versus that in the North by stating, "At the South we do not expect anything from the white man, except the good old will that was placed in his heart by the faithfulness of the Negro to his family and services during his long years of human slavery and plantation life. But the white man at the North seems to hate a more intense hatred for the Negro, upon his lack of a more accurate knowledge of the Negro as a man." In continuing, Dr. Smallwood stated that a higher and better class of whites should teach Southern as well as Northern whites that Negroes of the present day were not the same as the Negroes of the 1850s or 1860s; indeed, Negroes now possessed the ability to think freely, and unlike their forefathers in the mid-1800s, each had the potential to become "a lawyer, a banker, a merchant, a college president and a professor, a scientific farmer, a skilled mechanic, a learned doctor, a land owner, a peanut and cotton planter, and a government official."[10]

Dr. Smallwood concluded his speech by reiterating that Negroes wanted a fair chance in life, that they wanted to be treated like human beings and like men, and that they wanted to be able to express their political opinions by casting their own votes. The people of the Negro race, he said, "would like to be allowed to stay in your hotels as he travels from city and state seeking lodging. He does not want to be turned away or told that same 'old gag' that 'we have no rooms available'; yet he sees his white counterpart being accommodated with lodging."[11]

Dr. Smallwood remained in Cedar Rapids for several nights after his speech and then headed northwest into the Dakotas for his next speaking engagement.[12] As he traveled and spoke to various audiences across the country, his intention was threefold: to speak on behalf of the race problem, to emphasize the importance of Negroes' remaining on Southern soil, and to raise money for his school so that he could continue to educate the people of his race.[13]

In between speaking engagements and his work at the institute, Dr. Smallwood spent time with his family. He lived with his wife and eight-year-old daughter, Thelma, in Claremont, Surry County, Virginia, on Cabin Point Road. Mrs. Smallwood had given birth to two other children since Thelma's birth in 1901, but both died in infancy. Their deaths affected Dr. Smallwood tremendously. He had always yearned for a family—undoubtedly because he had been without one for much of his life—and the loss of two of his children, added to the fact that he still missed the earthly presence of his mother, continued to weigh heavily on his heart. But Dr. Smallwood would not falter from his mission. He still had a lot of work left to do.[14]

Uncle John really loved his family. I guess you could say he had that kind of spiritual love in that he loved everybody. He went throughout the south teaching and preaching so that colored people could get a good education so they could take care of themselves.

—Mrs. Willie L. Lassiter
Niece of Dr. John J. Smallwood
February 3, 2010

CHAPTER FIFTEEN

PRAYED JUST AS HARD AS HE WORKED

In January 1911, Dr. Smallwood had a plan that he had discussed with only a few people. His vision for the Temperance, Industrial and Collegiate Institute had become even greater and would require a significant expansion of the campus. Since September 28, the beginning of the fall term, 144 students had already applied for positions in the school's work-study program. Fees had increased slightly to a rate of $8.50 per month for room, board, tuition, fuel, and use of reading materials and the library, but students in the work-study program, who were allowed to enter school ten days before the official start of the term and remain ten days after its close, paid only $35.00 for the entire school year.[1]

Dr. Smallwood was ecstatic about the growth of his school. During a visit to his hometown of Rich Square, North Carolina, he told his sister that he wanted to build a school so that every child could be afforded the opportunity to get a *good* education.[2] He had worked tirelessly for most of his adult life so that this vision could become a reality, and now, thanks to the school's constant growth, he was finally reaping the harvest of his labors. Dr. Smallwood had achieved his life's dream, but even so, at forty-eight years of age, full of ambition and determination, he was just getting started.

He knew that a *good* education was the best way for the Negro race to free itself from the bonds of oppression and devaluation. But he wanted his people to receive an education on a nice, spacious, and beautiful campus, one that would help them to develop a sense of pride and self-worth. He knew that many of his students were poor but that they deserved to learn in a state-of-the-art facility just as much as any other students. And so Dr. Smallwood realized that, as his school grew, he would need to find a way to accommodate all his students comfortably. The only way to do so was to acquire more land on which he could build more facilities for his growing student population.[3]

In February 1911, Dr. Smallwood put Mr. W. Stanley Burt on retainer as his legal counsel. Burt's duties were to attend specifically to Dr. Smallwood's legal work in connection with building operations, property, and other matters pertaining to the funds of Temperance, Industrial and Collegiate Institute.[4] Mr. Burt, a white man, had been a slave owner and was known as a true Southerner. He was considered one of Virginia's wealthiest lawyers and was quite possibly the largest landowner in Surry County. He was a lifelong Democrat and a close friend of Dr. Smallwood.[5]

After examining records pertaining to the establishment of the institute, Mr. Burt informed Dr. Smallwood that the school had no charter. It had been Dr. Smallwood's understanding that a charter was issued in 1892 at the time of the school's opening by the presiding official, Judge Hancock, but this was not the case. According to Mr. Burt, a charter was indeed granted to the Temperance, Industrial and Collegiate Institute, but the necessary formalities required to put that charter into effect were never executed. Dr. Smallwood was flabbergasted to learn that his school did not have a charter, after nearly twenty years of operation, and requested that Mr. Burt procure a charter as soon as possible. With great haste, Burt began immediately, and a charter was secured early in the spring of 1911.[6]

By 1911, there were already several buildings on campus, besides Bagley Hall and Sawyer Hall. The chapel, within a few yards of Sawyer Hall, was the place where religious services were held and was named in honor of Mr. D. Wilson Moore. Mr. Moore, a constant friend and supporter of Dr. Smallwood, had come to Smallwood's rescue in 1892, 1896, and again 1898, when he was ostracized, criticized, and characterized as a mere dreamer for working to establish a school for his race.[7]

There were also several barns on campus that Dr. Smallwood used to house the school's horses, pigs, and other animals. One of the barns, the Moore-Farm Barn, was also named after his friend Mr. Moore.[8] In addition to this structure, there were three other farms encompassing about 148 acres on the institute's campus. These 148 acres were perhaps part of the 271-acre tract that Dr. Smallwood had originally purchased from H. J. Arrington in 1891.[9] Alternatively, they could have been part of the 99½ acres that Mrs. Smallwood purchased from James and Susan Boyce on September 9, 1905.[10] Dr. Smallwood called this acreage, located on "old historic Cabin Point Road," the James Boyce Farm. In any case, of the several farms on the institute's grounds, one was used to cultivate peanuts, corn, and cowpeas; another was designated for the cultivation of cabbage, sweet and white potatoes, beans, peas, and general garden products.[11] To manage production on these farms, Dr. Smallwood appointed Mr. W. G. Vincent as farm manager, Mr. S. B. Johnson as head of the carpenter's department, and Mr. William H. Baker as general manager, responsible for the wharf, barns, stables, stock, and general school interests.

One white visitor, Mr. Charles Thomas McDaniels of Mississippi, was sent incognito to Temperance, Industrial and Collegiate Institute at the request of some white friends in New York and Massachusetts. He toured the school to make an assessment of how things were being managed and was very surprised at what he found. He reported to his friends that he was quite impressed with everything and everyone he had seen on campus. The institute's grounds were immaculate and its students respectful, polite, and industrious.[12] He was also astounded that everyone at the institute worked, including Dr. Smallwood. It was not usual to see Smallwood in his overalls, plowing, chopping, and driving the teams, and he had worked relentlessly and tirelessly right along with his students since the school opened. Even as the president of the institute, he kept to the same work schedule that he had followed as a young field hand.[13] Journalist Charles McDaniels's assessment of the school, printed in the *Journal and Guide,* stated, "There was never a more polite, cleaner, more religious and actively industrious set of pupils in all of this country than the girls and boys found at Claremont, under the instruction of John J. Smallwood."[14]

Dr. Smallwood was now well-known throughout the North and South as a devoted man and a hard worker. His devotion, however, was not limited to his work alone; he was equally devoted to prayer. He relied heavily on his faith and was a true believer in the power of prayer. He prayed not only for himself, his enterprises, and his friends, but also for his enemies. He prayed for the individuals who tried to kill his commitment to God and to mankind, and he prayed for those whose hearts were filled with spiteful jealousy. Throughout his quest to found his institute, he had endured trying and embarrassing circumstances, including hunger and a near-complete lack of strength and spirit and, in the midst of sacrificing for his students, often did not know where his next meal would come from. Even so, he was still committed to doing whatever he felt was God's will.[15]

Before 1911, the wharf on the campus of the Temperance, Industrial and Collegiate Institute had been deemed out of service because of its dilapidated condition. First built in 1624, the Old Claremont Wharf, as it was called, was located at the very site where the second cargo of slaves to be imported to America had landed on May 12, 1622. (Ironically, this same site was now owned by a Negro who was himself born into slavery, and it had been converted into a place where ex-slaves and the descendants of slaves were receiving an education and obtaining meaningful employment.)[16] Later restorations of the wharf had occurred in 1733, 1812, 1854, and 1865, but by 1911, its state of disrepair was such that the renovations required to restore it to its full capacity would cost the institute $1,500.

In an effort to raise the money needed to rebuild the Old Claremont Wharf, Dr. Smallwood and his treasurer, P. Emmitt Ellis, solicited friends for donations.[17] The monetary assistance provided by these friends enabled Dr. Smallwood to break ground on the construction in 1911, and he commissioned T. L. and W. F. Tennis of Hampton, Virginia, to rebuild the wharf and its accompanying bridge. The Tennises built a new wharf and a commodious warehouse and pulled up all the old piles still left on the site. At the time, the project, as described in McDaniels's article, was the "most daring and determined manifestation of Negro will and labor."[18] T. L. and W. F. Tennis would later describe Dr. Smallwood as one of the most positive men they had ever met and one of few men with whom they had done business who would not make a business commitment that he could not keep.[19]

On January 23, 1911, Dr. Smallwood purchased an additional 16¼ acres of land from Mr. Frederick Maglott and his wife, Eva Maglott, in the town of Claremont, Virginia. The land was located on the east side of the Spring Grove Road.[20] Later that same year, he purchased from Daniel and Maria Stone another 13⅓ acres, more or less, located north of Schaffer Avenue in Claremont,[21] and a second tract measuring just 7,500 square feet, more or less.[22] With these additions, the Temperance, Industrial and Collegiate Institute was now in possession of a 65¾-acre, more or less, spread of land along the James River, in addition to the 271 acres purchased by Dr. Smallwood in 1891, and the 99½ acres purchased by Mrs. Smallwood in 1905.

As Dr. Smallwood surveyed his recent accomplishments, he beamed with joy. He was now in a position to move forward with his mission to secure proper housing to accommodate the influx of students enrolling in his school. He was also in a position to unveil his major expansion—the construction of Lincoln Memorial Hall.

Ladies and Gentlemen, Mr. Lincoln expected great things of us. We must honor that man who has honored us.

—John J. Smallwood
On the fifty-first birthday of Lincoln
The Monthly Advocate, June 13, 1896

CHAPTER SIXTEEN

LINCOLN MEMORIAL HALL
IN HONOR OF THE GREAT EMANCIPATOR

L incoln Memorial Hall would be named in honor of Abraham Lincoln, "the Great Emancipator." Dr. Smallwood had often spoken highly of Lincoln and had long cherished the freedom that the former president had conferred on him and others of his race, and he felt it was only fitting that he honor his benefactor by naming for him the most magnificent edifice on his campus. The building was to be 133½ feet by 49½ feet long, with 4½ stories, and was to be built of stone and brick. It would have large, spacious rooms and all the modern conveniences, including electric lights, steam heat, and hot and cold water. The hall would house private and public offices for Dr. Smallwood, additional offices for secretaries and bookkeepers, a kitchen, and several dining rooms. The "guest chambers," which were to be furnished by a wealthy Northern friend of Dr. Smallwood's, would contain a bedroom and reception rooms.[1] Once completed, Lincoln Memorial Hall would front both the James River and the Old Claremont Wharf Road and would be the greatest brick and stone building in Surry County, Virginia.[2] Cost of construction would amount to $37,800, and modernization and general improvements would cost an additional $15,000–$20,000.[3]

The hall was to be erected less than two hundred yards from Sawyer Hall and New Bagley Hall. It would be the first building erected on Southern soil in honor and memory of the great statesman Lincoln. It was also the first building of its kind erected by the individual efforts of a Negro, and it would stand on lands owned by a Negro. It gave Dr. Smallwood tremendous pride to know that, once the hall was erected, it would be on the very spot where some of the first slaves had landed after crossing the Atlantic.[4]

John Milton Hay, a longtime friend and confidante of Dr. Smallwood's, was one of many financial contributors to the institute. An American statesman and author, Hay served as assistant and private secretary to President Lincoln until Lincoln's death in 1865. In 1878, Hay was appointed assistant secretary of state and moved to Washington DC. Together with John G. Nicolay, he published the biography of Abraham Lincoln. In March 1897, President McKinley appointed Mr. Hay Ambassador to Great Britain, and from September 20, 1897, until his death on July 1, 1905, Hay served as secretary of state under both McKinley and his successor, Theodore Roosevelt. He was responsible for the implementation of the 1899 Open Door policy in the United States' dealings with China.[5]

Mr. Hay assisted Dr. Smallwood many times over a number of years, often in secret. It was Hay who had given Smallwood his first start in school, and he continued to provide him with financial help as he traveled through Europe in pursuit of a higher education. Journalist Charles McDaniels stated that nearly all of Dr. Smallwood's successes came from Mr. and Mrs. Hay, but it was said that Dr. Smallwood never mentioned Mr. Hay's name to a living soul and that Mr. Hay never mentioned to anyone that he had assisted Dr. Smallwood.[6]

A firm friend nonetheless, Mr. Hay, according to Mr. McDaniels, often spoke very highly of Dr. Smallwood and considered him to be one of the great men unto whom the Negro must look as an example of race pride, self-reliance, self-respect, practical industry, and higher education. Even after Hay's death in 1905, his wife, Clara, continued to support Dr. Smallwood in whatever way she could.[7] In honor of his friend, Dr. Smallwood named the wharf facility the John Hay Wharf.[8]

Once it was completed, Lincoln Memorial Hall would contain a hall of fame. Statues of President Abraham Lincoln and the Honorable John Hay would be placed in the main Hall of Fame to honor the two men, for whom Dr. Smallwood had great admiration and respect and whom he felt assisted him in more ways than one.[9] The architect selected for this project was

Mr. Carl Ruehrmund, a gentleman educated in Germany who had worked for the United States government for several years. He had previously completed projects in Richmond, Washington, New York, and Berlin. In Claremont, he drew the plans for Lincoln Memorial Hall and acted as the general superintendent of its construction.[10] Mr. D. J. Farrar of Richmond, Virginia, was the contractor and builder. Farrar was instructed to complete the basement and first and second stories and to cover Lincoln Memorial Hall by October 12, 1911, at which time the dedication would take place.[11]

Attendees expected to be present at the dedication included Dr. M. W. Stryker, president of Hamilton College in New York; the Honorable W. Burke Cockran of New York; former governor George W. Gatling; the Honorable Claude Kitchin, MC, of North Carolina; the Rev. Dr. B. Henry, of Scranton, Pennsylvania; the Rev. Dr. David Jones, also of Scranton, Pennsylvania; U.S. senator Thomas H. Martin, Esq., of Virginia; and former governor Claude W. Swanson, who was now a Virginia senator. On October 8 and 13, seven of the best Negro educators in the country would be present to speak at the hall's dedication.[12]

Months before the completion of Lincoln Memorial Hall, in March 1911, George C. McMahon, an ex-judge from Minnesota, acknowledged the singularity and significance of its construction before a large audience of white citizens, to whom he was introducing Dr. Smallwood as a guest speaker:

> It is not any longer a dream that a Negro is to build upon Virginia soil a useful monument to the life and worth of Mr. Lincoln, but now it is a real fact, and for this independent effort of Dr. John J. Smallwood, a brave, worthy Negro, his work should receive the highest commendation of the American people. It is free from any political pull, and he has no special religious creed attached to his work, nor the institution. This alone proves Dr. Smallwood's superior manhood and individual courage. The people, white and black, who are honestly interested in the practical development of a higher citizenship of the Negro will be only too glad to help and to encourage this brave, manly black man, who comes to us with a work worthy of our consideration.[13]

In response, Dr. Smallwood thanked Mr. McMahon for his kind words and the audience for their attendance and paid tribute to Lincoln, "the Great Emancipator," by including in his lecture an excerpt from a speech that he had delivered many times before to commemorate the birthday of Lincoln. Speaking to a very excited audience, he said the following:

> Let us do our duty. We cannot honor Mr. Lincoln, however, not even by the accumulation of the property just named; we are compelled to go back to the fields of industry and commencement anew. The busy hum of the factory wheels can be heard when it belongs to the negro; the train laden with its cargo of human souls drawn through this world at almost lightning speed, the whistle upon that train must belong to the negro; the electricity that is being discovered and so generally used, the great natural facilities of these idle fields of the south must be taken up by the black man and utilized. The negro must become President of his own college, the historian of his own race, and, by continual arguments upon the line of intelligence, by constant accumulation of property, by a strong and wonderful moral line drawn between the Judases and Isaiahs of the race, we must honor that man who has honored us. Again, ladies and gentlemen, Mr. Lincoln expected of us great things. It has been said in history that we cannot learn, that we possessed such incapabilities that we were unable to take care of ourselves. It has been said by the historian that there was no mental capacity in the race to fit it for the great duties and chances of life and when Mr. Lincoln made it possible by the issuing of the Emancipation Proclamation for the Negro to become a freed man, he then expected the greatest thing possible of us.[14]

Two months after Dr. Smallwood delivered this speech, in May 1911, Governor William Hodges Mann of Virginia also alluded to the significance of Lincoln Memorial Hall in an address to the graduating class of 1911 at the Temperance, Industrial and Collegiate Institute's

nineteenth annual commencement exercise. In his speech, delivered in
New Bagley Hall, he stated as follows:

> Professor Smallwood is doing a GREAT, GOOD WORK for his
> race and for Virginia, at Claremont, and should be encouraged
> by all good citizens. How many WHITE MEN under similar
> conditions, would have accumulated one hundred and fifty
> thousand dollars of school property, erected CREDITABLE
> wooden and brick buildings, bought farm lands, improved them
> and at the same time kept an IGNORANT people upon the best
> terms with the best white people. Dr. Smallwood's race should
> feel proud of him as a man who believes in the highest and
> best CITIZENSHIP, active and a practical MORALITY and
> RELIGION. The future of the Negro depends entirely upon
> his practical Education. Let every good man in this Grand Old
> COMMONWEALTH encourage The Negro who tries to benefit
> and uplift the masses of his people in this Commonwealth. This
> Negro educator has already given NINETEEN OF THE BEST
> YEARS OF HIS LIFE in establishing this institution. Now,
> let all good citizens encourage him, as HIS BURDENS and
> RESPONSIBILITIES are increased. I look upon Dr. Smallwood
> as being a most useful citizen.[15]

Soon after commencement services, as the completion of Lincoln
Memorial Hall drew near, plans were made to invite Vice President
James S. Sherman to Claremont to speak at the hall's dedication. A
delegation of Dr. Smallwood's Negro friends, headed by Dr. P. B. Ramsey,
of Richmond, Virginia, traveled to Washington DC to personally invite
Sherman to attend.[16] In addition, United States senator Thomas S. Martin,
who headed the Virginia congressional delegation to invite Sherman,
and the Honorable Claude Swanson both submitted letters in May 1911,
requesting that Sherman speak at the dedication services, to be held on
October 12. Their sentiments were endorsed by Congressman Holland
of Suffolk, Virginia, who was serving as congressman from the Second
District, and Judge Tumber, who served as congressman from the Fourth
District of Virginia.[17]

WHAT THE LEADING VIRGINIANS
SAY ABOUT DR. SMALLWOOD
AND THE BUILDING OF
LINCOLN HALL

May 24, 1911

Mr. President, we the citizens of Virginia call upon you, to invite
you to attend the dedication of the Abraham Lincoln Memorial Hall
now being built by Dr. John J. Smallwood, Founder and President
of the Temperance, Industrial and Collegiate Institute, at Claremont,
Virginia for the education of the Negro youth. Dr. Smallwood is a most
worthy citizen and a learned scholar and deserves the encouragement
and confidence of the American public. We, the Virginia Senators and
Congressmen agree with the Honorable W. Stanley Burt of Claremont,
when we say, Mr. Sherman that we want you to be at Claremont and
be The Speaker at the dedication of Lincoln Hall.

Thomas S. Martin

U.S. Senator

SENATOR SWANSON:—When I was Governor of Virginia,
President Smallwood was a frequent visitor to my office, and I
talked with him upon the subject of "Negro Education." I have
always found Prof. Smallwood sound with good common sense,
manly and certainly very plucky. Mr. President, every white man
in Virginia wants you to go to Claremont, and make the Speech at
the dedication of the Lincoln Memorial Hall. This Hall is 133½
by 49½ feet long. Four and one-half stories high. It is to have
every modern improvement and when actually completed will
cost at least $55,000.00. Hon. W. Stanley Burt of Claremont is
doing all that he can to help Prof. Smallwood. Smallwood is a
practical Negro citizen. We want you to come to Claremont.

Hon. Claude A. Swanson

U.S. Senator from Virginia

Of great concern to Dr. Smallwood was the fact that he had not received any recognition from leaders among his own race, despite the frequent recognition he was receiving from whites. He had done a great deal of good for his race and the lack of respectful consideration from fellow Negro leaders caused him a measure of despair, although he tried to overcome these feelings with his faith. At times, however, he still found it difficult to conceal his dejection, which was quite noticeable to some of his closest friends and associates.

Those who knew Dr. Smallwood best often described him as a modest and practical man possessed of an unassuming demeanor. He neither imposed himself on others nor went where he believed he was not wanted, even though his presence was often an inspiration to those in the places where he traveled. A man of a rather quiet nature, he did not yearn for recognition or desire to be in the limelight, but he felt ostracized and isolated nonetheless by the lack of recognition and moral support from leaders among his own race.[18]

The rigorous tasks of managing the institute and ensuring that the construction of Lincoln Memorial Hall was completed on time eventually took their toll on Dr. Smallwood. Physically, mentally, and emotionally exhausted, he became ill on August 30, 1911, less than two months before the scheduled dedication of Lincoln Memorial Hall. From his hospital bed, Dr. Smallwood wrote a letter to his attorney, Mr. Burt, in which he specifically asked him to take care of the institute's business matters should he die.[19] With Dr. Smallwood ill and the dedication date of October 12 fast approaching, the institute sent out the following letter, announcing a delay of the dedication services:[20]

> *We regret very much to have to inform you that the Dedication of Lincoln Hall at the Temperance, Industrial and Collegiate Institute could not be held on October 12, 1911, as intended.*
>
> *Several unfortunate circumstances have worked to cause the Dedication of this building to be postponed until some later date, the exact time of which you will be advised later on.*

In addition to the Contractor having trouble in obtaining the necessary material and labor with which to erect this building, the President of the School, Rev. John J. Smallwood, was stricken with appendicitis about the time the building was gotten under way and it was necessary to remove him to the Memorial Hospital in Richmond, Virginia, to be operated upon, which of course, delayed matters.

While Professor Smallwood has not yet entirely recovered from the effects of his illness and operation, he is now able to be out and to give some attention to matters pertaining to the Institute and we trust that his recovery will now be rapid and complete and that he will soon be attending to the affairs of the School with his accustomed push and energy.

We regret very much that this delay has been made necessary by circumstances which were beyond our control, however, all matters are now progressing satisfactorily and you will be given ample notice of the date set for the Dedication of Lincoln Hall.

Respectfully,

TEMPERANCE, INDUSTRIAL
& COLLEGIATE INSTITUTE

CHAPTER SEVENTEEN

DEDICATION OF LINCOLN MEMORIAL HALL

On Sunday, May 19, 1912, around 8:00 a.m., a party of visitors boarded the steamer *Pocahontas* at Richmond's Old Dominion Wharf and sailed down the James River to attend the dedication services for Lincoln Memorial Hall on the campus of Temperance, Industrial and Collegiate Institute.[1] Among the party were Governor William H. Mann of Virginia; W. Stanley Burt, attorney for Temperance, Industrial and Collegiate Institute; Rev. Charles S. Morris, pastor of the Bank Street Baptist Church in Norfolk, Virginia; John Mitchell, junior editor of the *Richmond Planet;* H. R. Pollard, city attorney of Richmond; U.S. senator Thomas H. Martin,; Governor Claude W. Swanson (now a U.S. senator); Dr. M. W. Stryker, president of Hamilton College, New York; W. Burke Cockran, of New York; Claude Kitchin, MC, of North Carolina; former governor George W. Gatling; the Rev. Fred Estes of Boston, a former Wilbraham classmate of Dr. Smallwood's; a host of other prominent educators, ministers, and dignitaries; and a large contingent of Richmond residents.[2] According to an article printed in the *Richmond Planet* on May 25, 1912, it was the consensus of the attendees that the dedication of Lincoln Memorial Hall was one of the most enjoyable and memorable trips that they could ever recall having.[3] There was a substantial crowd waiting to greet the visitors and escort them to campus once the *Pocahontas* put in at John Hay Wharf.[4]

The new Lincoln Memorial Hall commanded a splendid view of the James River and could be seen by the Richmond contingent long before they reached the campus. The buildings of the school, seen from a distance as the party docked, were elevated some fifty feet above the level of the river and sprawled over 65¾ acres of land along the James. In the James itself, the resourceful Dr. Smallwood had found a number of large granite blocks, dumped by Confederate forces to impede the progress of the Union army during the Civil War. With the help of his students, he had raised the blocks for use in the foundation of Lincoln Memorial's main hall. Mrs. Clara S. Hay, wife of the late John Hay, contributed much of the $43,370 spent on the total construction of the facility.[5] The imposing and magnificently built brick-and-stone structure was four and one half stories high with an open roof garden and a penthouse.[6] The hall housed a chapel, a reception hall, a spacious dining hall, storage rooms, and a kitchen assembly room. The new building also contained the president's office, administrative offices, a library, and domestic and science rooms. A parlor, guest chamber, laundry room, and fifty additional rooms for the accommodation of teachers and pupils were all included in the facility.[7] The third and fourth floors above housed female students.[8] There was also an auditorium wing.[9]

The magnificence of Lincoln Memorial Hall far surpassed that of the other buildings on campus, even though they, too, were immaculately kept and their walkways well maintained. The plain wooden constructions of Sawyer and Bagley halls stood nearby, and the campus also boasted three faculty houses, including Mayflower Cottage, Sunnyside Cottage, and Roslyn Cottage. Other facilities included a pavilion, a pump house, an artesian well, a framed chapel, the president's house, several barns, and the John Hay Wharf.[10] Additional improvements included underground cables, transformers, poles, twelve streetlights, seven interphones, and twenty-five meters for houses in the town of Claremont.[11] A cannery manned by students assisted in raising funds to defray the cost of some of the institute's financial obligations.[12]

Apart from Lincoln Memorial Hall, of interest to many of the visitors from Richmond was the brick powerhouse that was located on the 65¾-acre tract along the James. The powerhouse was said to have cost between $15,000 and $20,000 and had been installed by the Westinghouse Electric Company. It furnished steam and electricity to the institute.[13] The electric power generated by the powerhouse furnished residents of the school as well as the town of Claremont with their first electricity[14] and the sale of electricity from the plant generated revenue for the town of Claremont.[15]

As more visitors arrived, the Rev. Charles S. Morris, DD, pastor of the Bank Street Baptist Church of Norfolk, delivered an able discourse in the institute's chapel. In the audience were several of Dr. Smallwood's white friends from Massachusetts who had come to participate in the dedicatory services.[16] Dr. Smallwood himself, only nine months after his most recent hospitalization, was busily trying to make sure that all his guests were taken care of and that events were going according to plan. Many of those in attendance, wanting a further glimpse of the magnificent campus, strolled along the grounds outside the chapel during Rev. Morris's speech. They complimented the great work that Dr. Smallwood had done and spoke admiringly of the accomplishments he had achieved in such a short period of time.[17]

Around 10:00 a.m. that morning, consecration services, led by Dr. Smallwood, were held in Lincoln Memorial Hall, with general services beginning at ten forty-five. Dr. Smallwood then delivered a stirring sermon. Many of those in attendance had heard or read about his skill at speaking, but this was, for some of the guests, their first opportunity to witness his oratorical prowess firsthand. It was the consensus of the various groups in attendance that hearing him speak was one of the highlights of the dedication ceremony.[18]

The next event on the agenda for the dedication was a tour of the campus. The party from Richmond was significantly impressed, pleasantly surprised, and completely awed by what they saw as they strolled around the grounds, enjoying the scenic beauty of the campus. Not only did they witness the dedication of Lincoln Memorial Hall, but they also learned about the school, its founder, and all it had to offer. Equally impressive with the campus, in the opinions of the group from Richmond, was the gracefulness and politeness of the young men and women who attended the institute. It was mutually agreed by all the visitors in attendance that they had not seen anything quite like this before.[19]

Even so, the party from Richmond noted, there were whispers and grumblings from Dr. Smallwood's neighbors about his successes and accomplishments in his efforts to build a magnificent school for the benefit of his people. Dr. Smallwood appeared unaffected by this obvious criticism, however, and he continued to greet guests in a warmly hospitable manner, although it was clear to nearly everyone in attendance that a degree of envy and resentment toward Dr. Smallwood still hung in the air.[20]

Later that afternoon, lunch and dinner were served in the dining facilities of Lincoln Memorial Hall, and a crowd gathered at the chapel to hear the guest speaker, the Rev. Fred M. Estes of Boston. But because the chapel was not large enough to accommodate the sizeable crowd, services were held outside. Before Reverend Estes began his speech, Dr. Smallwood took a few moments to share an anecdote about an incident that occurred when he was the only Negro student in attendance at Wilbraham at Wesleyan Academy, traditionally an all-white school. He told the enthusiastic crowd that, at Wesleyan, he had been threatened on account of his color by one of his white classmates and that the Rev. Estes had acted as his most outspoken and ardent defender. The audience responded with a thunder of applause commending Rev. Estes's actions, which had been courageously performed at a time when demonstrations of brotherly love across racial lines were unpopular.[21]

Reverend Estes's sermon was followed by brief remarks from John Mitchell Jr. who, having realized that the hour was late and the steamer was preparing to leave, shortened his speech. After an entire day of scheduled activities, the party from Richmond regrettably departed Temperance, Collegiate and Industrial Institute's campus at 5:30 p.m. aboard the *Pocahontas*. As they traveled up the James, they agreed that they had thoroughly enjoyed the hospitality they had received. The campus was breathtaking, the students simply phenomenal, and the course of study second to none. The consensus of the group was that the overall experience was simply awesome; they could hardly wait to tell others about Temperance, Industrial and Collegiate Institute and the great work that Dr. Smallwood was doing. As they conversed and enjoyed the relaxing ride back to the Old Dominion Wharf, the lights of the city of Richmond came into view at 10:15 p.m.[22]

The next day, on Monday, May 20, Governor Mann presided over the dedication services for Lincoln Memorial Hall, the electric plant, and the John Hay Wharf. The services were followed by opening remarks from Dr. Smallwood, who warmly greeted and welcomed his audience. W. Stanley Burt, attorney for the school, also gave an address, followed by a captivating speech by Governor Mann. Mann's message, directed primarily at the colored people in the audience, was full of optimism, which was a source of pleasure and gratification both to coloreds and whites who had the honor of hearing him speak. Dr. Smallwood stood by, beaming with delight.[23]

In July 1912, only a couple of months after the dedication of Lincoln Memorial Hall, the institute's board of directors held its first meeting under the school's new charter, which empowered Dr. Smallwood and the board to "establish and maintain an institution of learning for the purpose of education, both mental and manual, of the colored youth, male and female, of the State of Virginia or any other State or foreign country."[24] Also incorporated into the charter was a list of the names and addresses of the nine members of the board of trustees and a summary of their responsibilities in managing the institute's affairs and upholding its purpose. Members of the board had the power to employ and terminate teachers, staff, and officers, and determine salaries for employees based on their respective duties. Other powers bestowed upon board members included the authority to make rules and regulations governing the institute, grant diplomas upon recommendation of the president and faculty, confer honorary degrees, make contracts on behalf of the institute, and arrange work-study for students who had difficulty paying their bills.[25] Dr. Smallwood's salary was also determined at this time.[26]

The annual board meetings were held each year on the last day of the final exercises of the term. Other meetings could be called at the discretion of the majority of the board after a ten-day advanced notice.[27] Board members included Dr. John J. Smallwood, president and trustee (Claremont, Virginia); William Dillard, secretary and trustee (Claremont, Virginia); H. W. Clark, trustee (Claremont, Virginia); P. B. Ramsey, trustee (Richmond, Virginia); A. D. Price, trustee (Richmond, Virginia); C. B. Henry, trustee (Binghamton, New York); David Jones, trustee (Scranton, Pennsylvania); Fred M. Estes, trustee (Woburn, Massachusetts); and Charles T. Davis, trustee (Roslindale, Massachusetts).[28]

That same month, Governor Mann appointed Dr. Smallwood to attend the annual convention for the National Negro Educational Association in

St. Paul, Minnesota. Dr. Smallwood delivered such a stirring speech there that it was unanimously decided to hold the convention in Claremont the following year.[29]

Needless to say, Dr. Smallwood was pleased with the way things were going; he was, however, still in poor health. And because his illness had significantly reduced his strength, he knew that he needed to transfer the burden of managing the institute to someone else. He had hoped to have a successor by this time but had not met anyone with the same amount of zeal that he himself possessed—the amount necessary to continue the challenging demands of operating the institute. Until he found such a person, he would have to persist in managing the school as best he could, and despite his illness, he continued to shoulder the tremendous responsibility, with the assistance of his wife.[30]

I have fought the good fight, I have finished the race,
I have kept the faith.

—2 Timothy 4:7

Chapter Eighteen
"My Work Is Finished"

The 1912–1913 school year opened with more than 160 students in attendance at the Temperance, Industrial and Collegiate Institute.[1] Dr. Smallwood's desire to have Lincoln Memorial Hall erected and in operation by the beginning of the fall term had been accomplished. He now could accommodate all of his students and continue to provide a *good* education to the young Negro men and women of his race.

On September 11, 1912, Dr. Smallwood returned to Claremont after a visit to New York, on which he consulted with friends regarding the possibility of turning over the school's property to its board of trustees. He had pondered this decision for quite some time now and was still somewhat skeptical about it. His apprehension is evident in a February 10, 1912, letter to W. Stanley Burt, his lawyer, in which he stated, "I am bound to make up my list of Trustees to whom I am to deed this property, and I am being very solicitous about that class of men to whom I turn over $150,000 worth of property."[2] Unsure how best to handle the situation, he consulted with Burt and asked him whether he should turn the property over to the trustees with a remaining debt of $15,000 owed on the buildings and let the board arrange to pay the debts or wait until he had enough money to pay the $15,000 himself. Burt advised the latter course and suggested that he "pay off the entire indebtedness on the property and deliver it to the Board free from all encumbrances and with a cash surplus to go into the treasury of at least $5,000.00."[3]

On the same day as his return from New York, Dr. Smallwood wrote a letter to Mr. Burt, saying, "I have worked twenty years here, and have not received a dollar's compensation, and the Trustee Board has not voted one single dollar for past years' services, and, although I may require them to pay one thousand dollars a year and some back pay. I shall talk this matter over with you and Mr. Clarke, and I will tell you about this by and by."[4] In the same letter, Dr. Smallwood also stated, "I have ruined my health and my life trying to complete this work."[5] Three days later, on September 14, 1912, Dr. Smallwood put all matters pertaining to the school in the hands of the board.[6] On September 17, 1912, two of Dr. Smallwood's closest friends, Mr. J. R. Pollard and Dr. P. B. Ramsey, acted as witnesses to the execution of his last will and testament.[7] Two days later, on September 19, Dr. Smallwood celebrated his forty-ninth birthday. After another two days, on September 21, he drafted a second letter to Mr. Burt in which he stated that he planned to turn over all money in his possession to the treasurer of the institution by the first or twelfth of October 1912.[8]

Between September 21 and 29, Dr. Smallwood's health steadily declined, so much so that he was admitted to the Retreat for the Sick in Richmond, Virginia, where he had an operation, or perhaps a series of operations.[9] Around nine o'clock in the morning on Sunday, September 29, Mrs. Smallwood hitched up her horses and began the forty-mile drive from Claremont to Richmond to visit her husband. While she was still en route, Dr. Smallwood, having finished the work he felt he had been called to do, quietly and peacefully surrendered his earthly life in exchange for an eternal one. He passed away at ten forty-five that morning at the Retreat for the Sick in the city of Richmond. Mrs. Smallwood arrived at the Retreat later that afternoon.[10]

The contributory cause of Dr. Smallwood's death was adhesion from appendicitis, according to his official death certificate.[11] Some of the old residents of Claremont, however, put no stock in the medical cause of death,[12] believing instead that Dr. Smallwood had simply poured all of himself into his school. Dr. Smallwood's body was removed from the Retreat for the Sick and later carried to his residence in Richmond, Virginia, where a host of friends and sympathizers gathered to view the remains of a man whom many had loved and honored.[13]

The news of Dr. Smallwood's untimely death spread immediately, like wildfire. People came from near and far to show their respects and pay tribute to a man whom they cherished deeply. Dr. Smallwood was remembered not merely as an educational leader but as a man who had spent most of his own life trying to create a better life for others.[14] Many people remembered him as a man who had devoted his life to temperance work, who not only preached temperance but also lived it and required the same from others. He was so much an advocate for temperance work that he even put the word "temperance" in his school. Others remembered him as a warm, loving, and generous man who made tremendous sacrifices and who seemed to care more about the welfare of others than he did for himself.[15]

Everyone who knew him agreed that he was the type of man who neither cared for the limelight nor made any effort to seek it or be a part of it.[16] He was not one who boasted about his accomplishments, but rather one who felt compelled to do God's will and live his life as a servant unto the Lord. Many believed that Dr. Smallwood had lived to see his dream begin, only to die on the eve of its full realization. Others described his life as a brilliant career with a tragic ending.[17] Many also believed that Dr. Smallwood's humbling influence would live long in the hearts of those who were fortunate enough to have been in his presence.[18]

On the afternoon of Tuesday, October 1, 1912, at 3:00 p.m., funeral services for Dr. Smallwood were held in Richmond at the Third Street AME Church, with the Rev. C. S. Morris officiating. Many friends and sympathizers came to pay tribute to him. Among the most prominent attendees were George R. Hovey, president of Virginia Union University, and John Mitchell Jr., editor of the *Richmond Planet,* who both delivered eulogistic addresses.[19] Dr. Smallwood's longtime friend Dr. C. S. Brown was also in attendance and served as one of several honorary pallbearers.[20] Early the next morning, Dr. Smallwood's body was transported from the church to the steamer *Pocahontas* for its final trip to the Temperance, Industrial and Collegiate Institute. The steamer arrived at the John Hay Wharf in Claremont at 1:00 p.m., and funeral services on campus commenced an hour later, with Rev. C. S. Morris again officiating. After services ended at 5:00 p.m., Dr. Smallwood's body lay in state in the church to be viewed by the public until ten that night. Farmers and residents from near and far came to pay their last respects to a man who had spent the best years of his life in the interest of that section only to die when the fruit of his labors and the hope of a lifetime had been realized. Funeral Director A. D. Price had charge of the last interment and accompanied the remains to Claremont. Because Dr. Smallwood was a Mason and a member of the Mt. Hermon Masonic Lodge No. 50 of Burrowsville, Prince George County, Virginia, the Masonic Charity Lodge No. 35 consented to perform the funeral honors.[21] In charge of all arrangements was Dr. P. B. Ramsey, Dr. Smallwood's bosom friend.[22]

When news of the sudden death of a dear brother, uncle, neighbor, and friend reached Dr. Smallwood's hometown of Rich Square, North Carolina, family members and local residents alike were devastated. At first, they found the news completely shocking and totally unbelievable. Dr. Smallwood's 110-year-old-niece, Mrs. Willie L. Lassiter, vividly remembers the day she and her mother received the news. It was a day she says she will never forget and one that she recalls as one of the saddest days of her life:

> I will never forget that day. My mother and I were in the field that day working when this man rode up on a horse and wagon and told my mother that he had some sad news to tell her. My mother, sensing something was wrong and shyly making eye contact with this man, never responded. This man, regrettably having to be the bearer of bad news, told my mother that her brother had died. Upon hearing the news, I could not move. It seems like my knees buckled and I became paralyzed. The last thing I wanted to do was look my mother in the face because I could not take having to see her deep pain, though I felt it. It was such a sad time. My mother grieved for so long and when her sisters heard the news, they grieved just as hard and just as long. We did not go to his funeral because when we got the news he had already been buried I suppose.[23]

As time passed, Dr. Smallwood continued to be remembered by many. He remained in the hearts and on the minds of those who loved him and who were grateful for the work and the many acts of kindness he bestowed upon others. One in particular was Rev. W. Hubert George, a Surry County resident who shared with his congregation a story demonstrating the character and devotion of Dr. Smallwood. He told the story of how Reverend Harrison, another Surry County resident, "could hardly write his name" prior to entering Dr. Smallwood's school. Dr. Smallwood taught Reverend Harrison how to "read, write, and study the Bible." Years later, when the cornerstone was laid at Harrison Grove Church, Reverend Harrison invited Dr. Smallwood to be the principal speaker at his church's opening ceremonies. Dr. Smallwood accepted the invitation.[24]

This was the type of man Dr. Smallwood was and how he would be remembered by those who knew him or had the good fortune to be in his presence. He was known to many as a natural-born educator who loved his brethren more than himself and who saw the need for and importance of providing his race with an education—a *good* education, one that many of his forebears had been denied for centuries.[25]

On a high point overlooking the peaceful James River, "where the river lies calm and still and all nature is hushed and sleeping,"[26] Dr. Smallwood's remains were interred almost directly in front of Lincoln Memorial Hall.[27] His work was now finished. Friends and patrons later erected a monument in his honor. The inscription reads as follows: ·

JOHN J. SMALLWOOD
FOUNDER and PRESIDENT
TEMPERANCE, INDUSTRIAL AND COLLEGIATE INSTITUTE
BORN: SEPT. 19, 1863
DIED: SEPT. 29, 1912
AGE: 49

MY WORK IS FINISHED

"HE BUILDED WELL WHILE THE SUN WAS YET HIGH; AND WHEN EVENING CAME, HE LAY DOWN TO REST IN THE SHADE OF THE FRUITS OF HIS LABOR."

"HIS GREATEST MONUMENT IS THE INSTITUTION OF LEARNING AND CULTURE HE FOUNDED AND ERECTED UPON THE SOIL HIS SOUL NOW HALLOWS. HIS BEST EPITAPH IS WRITTEN IN THE HEARTS OF MANY WHO KNEW HIM AS SCHOLAR, EDUCATOR, FRIEND."

I have glorified You on earth. I have finished the work which you have given Me to do. And now, O Father, glorify Me together with Yourself, with the glory which I had with You before the world was.

—John 17:4–5

CHAPTER NINETEEN

SMALLWOOD MEMORIAL INSTITUTE

Soon after Dr. Smallwood's death, Mrs. Smallwood pledged to continue his legacy.[1] And so, on Thursday, December 12, 1912, approximately three months after her husband's death, Mrs. Smallwood, together with J. R. Pollard, her attorney, called a meeting of the board of trustees in New York to discuss several critically important issues. First, she desired to change the name of the Temperance, Industrial and Collegiate Institute to the Smallwood Memorial Institute in memory of her late husband and the work to which he had dedicated his life. The board of trustees fully endorsed the change of name. Second, Mrs. Smallwood, now acting president of the Smallwood Memorial Institute, requested that attorney J. R. Pollard make revisions to the existing charter and urged the board to execute the charter that her late husband had not yet put into effect.[2]

Mrs. Smallwood's new role as acting president entailed putting into effect many important changes to the charter. As part of these revisions, she added six new members to the existing nine-member board of trustees.[3] She also turned over to the board the deed to the school's property under the responsibility of the officially chartered corporation. Mrs. Smallwood further suggested that board members should write to Dr. C. S. Morris of Norfolk, Virginia, to ask if he would accept the position of president of Smallwood Memorial Institute. Mrs. Smallwood described Dr. Morris as highly qualified for the position and requested that his appointment to the presidency be made expeditiously. In the meantime, until confirmation of his acceptance of the position was officially received, she would continue to fill the role of acting president.[4]

The board of trustees unanimously agreed to endorse every request made by Mrs. Smallwood. Additionally, as a condition of surrendering the deed, the board agreed to pay her a comfortable salary for as long she desired to remain at the school. They also agreed to pay both her and her daughter a pension for the rest of their lives.[5]

On January 23, 1913, Smallwood Memorial Institute was incorporated, with a total of fifteen trustee members. Dr. Charles S. Morris, formerly of Norfolk, Virginia, was now residing in Claremont as the new president of the institute. Mr. J. R. Pollard served as secretary, treasurer, and trustee. Bylaws remained the same as originally formulated under the Temperance, Collegiate and Industrial Institute.[6] The former acting president, Mrs. Smallwood, remarried soon after Dr. Morris's appointment. She and her new husband, Mr. William H. Walton, resided in Richmond, Virginia.[7]

Later that year, during the 1913–1914 school year, J. R. Pollard replaced Dr. Morris as president. The institute, at the time of his replacement, employed seven colored teachers, including two males and five females. Their salaries ranged from $13 to $30 per month, with the average teacher's salary being $25 per month.[8] The total number of students in attendance was sixty-three. Fifteen of the pupils were in a normal course, which included some secondary subjects. The industrial work was basically confined to a little cooking and sewing. The study of agricultural theory comprised one hour per week.[9]

President Pollard inherited a huge debt. At the time of his appointment, the financial records for the 1913–1914 school year were so poorly managed that it was difficult to assess records accurately or obtain any concrete information pertaining to the actual income or expenditures of the institute. Since the death of Dr. Smallwood, the Smallwood Memorial Institute had incurred substantial debts within a very short period of time: as a result of bad management, the debt ranged from $15,000 to $40,000, including heavily mortgaged property.[10] The overall estimated value of the property, by contrast, totaled over $100,000. The estimated value of the electrical plant and machinery was assessed at approximately $5,000; the buildings at $50,000; the wharf at $3,000; the plant at $65,000; dormitory and classroom furniture at $3,000; and farm implements and livestock at $2,000.[11]

To make matters worse, Dr. Smallwood's debt on the original farm, the 271 acres of land purchased from H. J. Arrington in 1891, had come due, and additional money was owed for other expenses incurred on behalf of the institute, such as the legal fees created by litigation between Mrs. Smallwood and the board of trustees.[12] These proceedings, known as *D. J. Farrar* (plaintiff) *et al. v. Rosa E. Smallwood* (defendants), *Executrix, etc. et al.*, were conducted for the purpose of clarifying how the institute's property was to be distributed, as Dr. Smallwood's will had not provided specifics. Mrs. Smallwood had assumed, prior to Dr. Smallwood's death, that he had deeded the school property to the board of trustees, but this was not the case. As a result, a lawsuit was filed in the Chancery Court of the City of Richmond, Virginia, for the purpose of apportioning the institute's properties.[13] Litigation continued for two years, from 1913–1915.

Partly at issue in the suit were several large sums of money that were deposited into Dr. Smallwood's accounts by anonymous sources in October 1912, a month after his death. More than likely, these deposits were made by some of Dr. Smallwood's wealthy friends, who continued to support his efforts in the operation of his school, even after his death. The monies were perhaps meant to help cover the expenses that he had incurred prior to his death and to make sure that all his existing debts were paid in full, as Dr. Smallwood had stated in his will that he wished his wife, as executrix of his estate, to pay off all his just debts.[14] He also requested that she pay all debts resulting from his medical expenses, including payment to the nurses who cared for him during his illness.[15]

As the executrix of Dr. Smallwood's estate, Mrs. Smallwood was required to give an account for all the monies she had received. In compliance with the court and as requested by the institute's board of trustees, she provided financial documentation dating from October 1912 to July 1, 1913.[16] In the end, the court found that Mrs. Smallwood had successfully fulfilled her duties as executrix of her husband's estate. She had paid all bills as she was supposed to and had not squandered any funds for personal gains. The amount of money remaining in Dr. Smallwood's accounts totaled $1,825.36, and the debts amounted to $1,824.34. All that remained for Mrs. Smallwood after the court's ruling was $1.02 and an estranged relationship with some of the board members.[17]

CHAPTER TWENTY

LAWSUIT

Soon after Mrs. Smallwood settled the lawsuit with the members of the board of trustees, she found herself embroiled in another lawsuit, *Commonwealth ex rel. Moore, Auditor, et al. v. Smallwood Memorial Institute*. In this instance, the Smallwood Memorial Institute filed a suit against the Surry County treasurer, deputy treasurer, and commissioner of revenue in an effort to stop the treasurer from selling part of the institute's personal property. The Surry County deputy treasurer had taken possession of this property for the purpose of collecting taxes and levies for the year 1913 against Mrs. Smallwood in her capacities as trustee for her daughter, Thelma, an administratrix of the estate of John J. Smallwood, and also for the Smallwood Memorial Institute. The institute ultimately filed suit regarding 1914 taxes and levies as well, based on the same reasoning.[1]

In the first hearing of the case, a circuit court determined that the Smallwood Memorial Institute was exempt from paying taxes and levies on certain real estate and personal properties located within Surry County, Virginia,[2] on grounds that the properties in question belonged to a charitable institution. The court reasoned that, since the property was used as a school, it was exempt from taxation, making the Smallwood Memorial Institute not liable for the 1913 and 1914 taxes.[3] The court also reasoned that the farmland located on school grounds had been used in such a way as to defray the costs associated with operating the school. Even though the land itself was not strictly "school" property, it had been employed as such and was thus exempt from taxation.[4] The court made its rulings on the 1913 and 1914 taxes on the tenth and thirteenth of June 1915, respectively.[5]

The next year, on May 24, 1916, C. Lee Moore, auditor of public accounts of Virginia, asked the court to reconsider its opinion on the taxes and levies pertaining to the years 1913 and 1914.[6] After some deliberation, the court upheld its earlier verdicts and, on March 28, 1917, decided that its rulings had been appropriate. Moore, however, appealed this decision to Virginia's court of appeals,[7] arguing that the lower court should not have granted the Smallwood Memorial Institute a reprieve from taxation because the state did, in fact, have the right to tax the school. A state's intent to exempt an institution, Moore contested, must be "clear beyond a reasonable doubt" in order for a declaration of exemption to be valid, but the state of Virginia had not demonstrated clear intent in the case of the Smallwood Memorial Institute.[8]

The document containing the opinion of the Virginia Court of Appeals contains a full summary of Moore's arguments as well as the response given by the legal counsel of the Smallwood Memorial Institute. In his arguments, Moore conceded, in keeping with the Constitution of 1869 (Article X, Sec. 3), that "[t]he legislature may exempt all property used *exclusively* for State, county, municipal, benevolent, charitable, educational and religious purposes."[9] But, he argued, the Constitution did *not* extend exemption to "any lot or building, partially or wholly used for any *private* purpose, unless the profits arising from such use [were] applied to public, charitable, benevolent or literary purposes."[10] On the basis of this clause, he took issue with the court's findings on the institute's farmland, arguing that there was some question as to whether the land should be considered the (nontaxable) property of an "incorporated institute" used for charitable purposes (e.g., defraying the costs of attendance) or should be classified as (taxable) private property, the profits of which could not be used for public or charitable ends. Classification of the property as taxable or nontaxable, he argued, must be based on the use of the property itself rather than on the use of any of its profits, such as the income produced by the sale of the institute's crops.[11] If any one part of the institute's property could be shown to be liable to taxation, he contended, then, the remainder of the property must also be considered taxable.[12]

Moore further argued that not only had the institute not been classified under the proper category of exemption, but it had also not even been proven to be a school. Indeed, he maintained, it appeared that the school was not owned by the Smallwood Memorial Institute, but by the Temperance, Industrial and Collegiate Institute,[13] which had not been proven to be an educational institution as defined in the 1869 Constitution. Since Temperance had not been proven to be an exempt institution, he argued, the school currently run in the former institute's facilities could not receive exemption from taxation either.[14]

Apart from the farmland, Moore also took issue with several other pieces of the institute's property, including a 7½-acre tract of land that contained a house and a farm used for raising potatoes and corn. Moore presented evidence that this land and all buildings on it had been rented out to one William Holloway, who had promised to pay taxes on the property. Holloway himself conceded that he lived on the property and had negotiated the terms of his rental with Rosa Smallwood in September 1914, although he had already been living on the property for five or six years by that time.[15] Moore also declared that Dr. Smallwood had identified this land as his own personal property in his will, because he specified that either the land itself or the proceeds of its sale would go to Mrs. Smallwood and her daughter. Based on the evidence of Dr. Smallwood's will, Moore argued that it was never John J. Smallwood's intention to allow the 7½-acre tract to be a part of the school—and thus it should have been taxed.[16]

Moore also questioned the use of the 99½-acre property known as the Boyce tract because it was not directly adjacent to the school. Its lack of proximity to the school, he claimed, indicated that it was not used for educational purposes and was therefore not exempt from taxation. Moore alleged that, in 1913, parts of the Boyce property were clear-cut, and the debris hauled to the river, with no evidence that these improvements had been made for school purposes. Rather, he suggested, the clearing of the land indicated that the institute had intended to turn a profit by selling off the newly cleared portions of the Boyce place, making the proceeds from any sale of those portions of the property unrelated to school purposes.[17] Moore also cited one of John J. Smallwood's letters to argue that Smallwood himself had considered the Boyce place his personal property and had known that it was liable to taxation.[18]

Regarding the thirty-six-acre Old Wharf tract, which housed the John Hay Wharf, the former Howland Hall, and the electric powerhouse,[19] Moore stated that the property was held by Rosa E. Smallwood and J. R. Pollard as trustees for Thelma Smallwood, John J. Smallwood's daughter. If the property was owned by Smallwood's wife and daughter, he argued, it could not be considered tax-exempt property used for charitable, instead of private, purposes. He cited as evidence a deed stating that Rosa E. Smallwood was entitled *in her own right* to a three-fourths fee simple in the land on which the school buildings were located—i.e., the deed gave her outright ownership of the property without any conditions, as opposed to partial ownership in some type of trust for the Smallwood Memorial Institute. The other one-fourth interest passed to John J. Smallwood's daughter under the conditions of his will. The will did, however, state (and Moore conceded) that it was the intention of John J. Smallwood to exclude from his private estate any part of the property occupied by the institute for school purposes.[20]

In a further review of the deed, Moore showed that the Old Wharf property had been conveyed to John J. and Rosa Smallwood by D. Wilson Moore on February 23, 1909, while the Smallwood Memorial Institute did not acquire an interest in the property until June 19, 1914.[21] On this evidence, he argued that the property had not been owned by the school but by individuals until June 1914. As such, it had been private property from 1909–1914 and should not have been exempt from taxation under the status of an educational institution; rather, it should have been taxed.[22]

In his review of the court's opinion of March 28, 1917, Moore also examined the articles of personal property that were ruled exempt from taxation for the years in question. Two horses, one carriage, and furniture were assessed against Rosa Smallwood; and five horses, fifteen hogs, six carriages, four wagons, two pianos, and furniture were assessed against the Smallwood Memorial Institute and listed as articles of personal property.[23] Moore argued that there was neither allegation nor proof that the property was wholly devoted to educational purposes or that it belonged to and was actually and exclusively used by an educational institution pursuant to the definition given in the 1869 Constitution.[24]

Lastly, Moore reiterated the argument that the Smallwood Memorial Institute was not an "educational institution," under the stipulation that true educational institutions were not conducted for profit. He argued that the institute profited from the tuition charged for admittance and, furthermore, that the institute's claim that the sale of its agricultural produce was used to defray the costs of operation did not constitute a legitimate exemption from taxation.[25] Exemption, he argued, did not apply to industrial schools such as the Smallwood Memorial Institute, which was not state-owned and received compensation from students' labor and articles sold in the community.[26]

In response, the counsel for the Smallwood Memorial Institute stressed that, in the original suit decided in the lower circuit court, the institute had merely sought to stop the sale of personal properties levied to satisfy taxes. Moreover, Smallwood Memorial Institute was the successor to the property formerly held by Temperance, Industrial and Collegiate Institute, and both organizations were charitable industrial schools, not conducted for profit but maintained by donations of money made to John J. Smallwood, president of Temperance, Industrial and Collegiate Institute. All property was used exclusively for the purpose of running a charitably maintained industrial school, with the exception of the electric power plant, which produced current that was sold in the community outside the school.[27]

In addition to summaries of the arguments made by Moore and the institute's counsel, the opinion of the Virginia Court of Appeals includes several depositions, testimony given by witnesses under oath outside the courtroom. Among the witnesses to the case was W. Stanley Burt, the attorney retained by Dr. Smallwood to oversee building operations and other local matters at Temperance. Burt testified that he had never heard Dr. Smallwood say anything that would have led him to believe that Smallwood claimed personal ownership of any of the institute's real estate or property, except for a few items of personal property. Burt stated that he knew that a large portion of the money given to Dr. Smallwood for his school was given with the distinct understanding that it was not to be used as his own, personal funds. What was more, Burt said, Dr. Smallwood had never intended that the school should operate the power plant, despite its location on school grounds. Rather, Burt himself had applied to the Town of Claremont for a franchise to light the town streets and had personally paid for the franchise with his own money. Because he had not used school funds and did not act on behalf of the school in operating the plant, the institute was in no way connected to the enterprise. Even when Burt later forfeited the account for noncompliance, ownership of the plant did not revert to the Smallwood family or the institute, making it unnecessary for the institute to pay any taxes associated with the powerhouse.[28]

The testimony of J. R. Pollard, president of Smallwood Memorial Institute since May 1914,[29] was also provided in the documents of the opinion of the appellate court. Pollard attested to the fact that the Smallwood Memorial Institute succeeded the Temperance Industrial and Collegiate Institute. He stated that Dr. Smallwood had obtained funds for the property through gifts, particularly from Mr. and Mrs. John Hay. Pollard also testified that the institute was run as a charitable institution, with sales occurring only in exchange for labor. He stated that the wharf on school grounds was reserved for school purposes and operated for the sole purpose of advertising the school and its efficiency, without an eye toward profit. None of the land was rented out for profit by the school, and all personal property belonged to the school, including the farming implements, which were used to cultivate the farms located on school property. Pollard did concede that there were houses located on two tracts of land not used for school purposes but stated that he was not aware of whether the houses were occupied, except in the case of the house on the Boyce tract, which had not been occupied for some time and was designated for use as an industrial training facility. Pollard also stated that there was a charge of $8 per month at the school, but that students who were unable to pay that amount were allowed to trade labor as payment for their board and tuition; books could be purchased by extra employment on school premises.[30]

W. L. Gwaltney, deputy treasurer, also testified. Acting under the direction of A. W. Bohannan, treasurer, Gwaltney seized personal property of the Smallwood Memorial Institute. All the property levied upon, except one horse, was found on the premises. While on the property, Mr. Gwaltney confronted President Pollard and asked him to pay the taxes. Pollard informed Gwaltney that the taxes had been settled and that the school did not owe any further monies; Gwaltney replied that Pollard was mistaken.[31]

Various witnesses provided testimony on the subject of several properties owned by the institute. C. A. Santmyer, recorder and treasurer, testified to William Holloway's rental of the 7½-acre portion of the school's property.[32] In his own testimony, Holloway confirmed that he lived on the 7½ acres, which, he stated, were owned by Rosa Smallwood and declared that he paid rent by way of state taxes.[33] O. D. Belding, whose property adjoined the Smallwood Memorial Institute, testified that the school charged for the use of the wharf and that the resulting fee was paid to the institute's farming manager. Belding confirmed that students performed labor on the campus of the institute and stated that, to his knowledge, sewing, carpentry, industrial painting, and other trades had been taught at the school.[34] He also testified that wood had been cut the previous summer and during the fall of 1914 and used for running the electric plant on the school property. Rosa Smallwood gave a deposition in which she stated that the money raised by her husband for the construction of his school had been used solely for the purchase of land on which to build the school and for the construction of buildings and other improvements. While C. Lee Moore, the auditor, attempted to divide up the various pieces of land owned by the institute and identify certain portions of the school's holdings as taxable private property, Mrs. Smallwood believed that all property held by the institute was the property of a nontaxable educational institution that was to be held in trust until it was large enough to be turned over to a board of trustees.[35]

In the appellate court, Dr. Smallwood's last will and testament was also presented as evidence. In it, he bequeathed to his wife his residence in Richmond, Virginia, with all its furniture and the remainder of his belongings that were in the house and on the property. He also willed her, for life, the 99½-acre tract of farmland known as the James Boyce Farm, situated on Cabin Point Road in Surry County, Virginia, under condition that, should she and the board of trustees elect to sell the property, the proceeds would be divided equally between his wife and daughter. Mr. J. R. Pollard was to hold the title to all of Thelma Smallwood's interests until she became an adult. The 7½-acre tract known as the A. J. Holloway tract was to be held under similar conditions. The 4-acre plot adjoining the 32 acres on which Temperance was situated were to go to Dr. Smallwood's wife during her widowhood and, upon her death, to the institute, as reserved in a deed executed by Dr. Smallwood to the trustees of the Temperance, Industrial and Collegiate Institute. Dr. Smallwood's library, in addition to any residue of his property, was to be kept intact and shared jointly between his wife and daughter.[36]

In the course of the suit, an appraisal was made of the total value of Dr. Smallwood's property, including both his private residence and the grounds and facilities of the institute. Barns and sheds, including their contents—horses, mules, pigs, chickens, vehicles, farm wagons, farming implements, harnesses, grain, and hay—were assessed at $2,282.50 and growing crops at $200.00. Mayflower Cottage and its furniture, together with the furniture from the chapel, Sawyer Hall, and Bagley Hall, as well as the students' beds, a wash basin, and piano, were valued at $410.00. Lincoln Hall's furnishings—a piano, seats, office and dining room furniture, beds, typewriters, a sewing machine, a safe, rugs, and carpets—were judged to be worth $1,305.00. Prof. John J Smallwood's personal belongings (clothing, a watch, a ring, and his library) were appraised at $600.00. The farm and buildings on the institute's campus varied in value: the farm, $3,500.00; Lincoln Hall, $41,000.00; the power plant, $10,000.00; the pump house, $400.00; Bagley Hall, $6,000.00; the wharf, $2,000.00; the pavilion, $700.00; Mayflower Cottage, $1,200.00; Sawyer Hall, $1,000.00; Sunnyside Cottage, $400.00; Roslyn Cottage, $800.00; barns and sheds, $800.00; chapel, $100.00; and the power plant, $5,000.00. Dr. Smallwood's residence in Richmond had an appraised property value of $3,500.00, with an additional $500.00 for furniture, and the land at the Holloway Place was estimated at $1,450.00. At the time of his death, Dr. Smallwood had a combined total of $1,888.27 in four different bank accounts, plus other stocks and bonds. He had an overall appraised value of $50,670.99.[37]

Ultimately, the Virginia Court of Appeals sided only in part with the decision of the lower court. It ruled that the tracts of land measuring 7½ and 99½ acres, in addition to the power plant, had not been used solely for school purposes and were thus liable to taxation. The remainder of the institute's property, the court decided, was exempt from taxation.

Meanwhile, in 1917, while the case was still in litigation, the Smallwood Memorial Institute was in the midst of a financial crisis. Not only was the lawsuit against the school ongoing, but the institute's new president, Caleb G. Robinson,[38] also reported that the school had outstanding debts of about $36,000, despite the fact that the school's previous charter had limited the amount that the institute could have, at any one time, in outstanding notes or bonds to $25,000.[39] The Institute was unable to pay.

In May 1917, the board of trustees met in Richmond and unanimously agreed that it would be in the best interest of the institute to amend its charter to permit the borrowing of a sum sufficient to satisfy the institute's indebtedness. And so the existing charter—which had been adopted on January 23, 1913, and signed by Mrs. Rosa Smallwood, J. R. Pollard, and D. J. Farrar—was amended so that the board could increase the limit of the institute's outstanding notes and bonds to an amount not exceeding $50,000.[40] President Robinson signed the new certificate, and its corporate seal was attested by Secretary J. H. Blackwell on May 12, 1917.[41]

In an effort to defray some of the financial costs for the operation of the institute, the board of trustees partnered with other schools in the surrounding areas. The next year, on June 17, 1918, Virginia Normal and Industrial Institute held its summer school sessions at Smallwood Memorial Institute, and in an effort to recruit students and inform the public, a local newspaper, the *Claremont Herald,* advertised the courses offered.[42] Colored teachers from various parts of the state were allowed to take part in the classes, and total enrollment during the summer sessions consisted of 175 teachers.

Even after the ruling by the appellate court, the case against the Smallwood Memorial Institute was again appealed. It was finally decided in 1919 by the Virginia Supreme Court, the highest court in the state. Again, the issue was whether the institute could claim exemption from taxation under Section 183 of the Constitution, based on the argument that its properties were used for school purposes. The state supreme court determined that the three parcels of land adjoining the institute, along with the institute's furniture, furnishings, books, and farming equipment, constituted property exempt from taxation.[43] At the same time, however, the court's review of the 7½—and 99½-acre tracts determined that these portions of the institute's property, together with the electric light and power plant and the land on which it was located, were not used for school purposes.[44] The court reasoned that the 7½—and 99½-acre properties were never technically conveyed to the school and were therefore intended to benefit Dr. Smallwood's wife and daughter rather than the institute. As a consequence, the court declared, the original rulings of the circuit court had erroneously determined the property to be exempt from taxation. In the end, Mrs. Smallwood was required to pay taxes on these two tracts of land as her separate personal property; all other lands were judged to be owned by the institute and remained exempt from taxation—a decision by which Mrs. Rosa Smallwood would have to abide.

Prof. John J. Smallwood, Ph.D., founder and president of the Temperance, Industrial and Collegiate Institute, as he appeared while opening the exercises for the speech of the Hon. William Hodges Mann, governor of Virginia. Dr. Smallwood was noted as having made the greatest speech of his life. (Courtesy of Hampton University Archives)

President John J. Smallwood and his secretary. (Courtesy of Hampton University Archives)

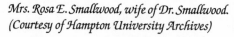

Mrs. Rosa E. Smallwood, wife of Dr. Smallwood. (Courtesy of Hampton University Archives)

Bagley Hall, on the campus of Temperance, Industrial and Collegiate Institute, first built in 1622, once occupied the site of the old slave pen where Negroes were once housed when they arrived in bondage upon American soil. Bagley Hall was renovated in 1906 by Dr. Smallwood and his students and was used as a dormitory for male students. (Courtesy of Jackson Davis Collection, Special Collection, University of Virginia Library)

Side view of Bagley Hall, ca. 1915. (Image used by permission of M. D. Harrison)

Lincoln Memorial Hall, on the campus of Temperance, Industrial and Collegiate Institute, built in 1911, was named in honor of President Abraham Lincoln and was the very spot where the first Negro was sold from an auction block, October 12 and 13, 1621. (Courtesy of Jackson Davis Collection, Special Collections, University of Virginia Library)

President's (Dr. Smallwood's) cottage (center building). On the left side is a barn where Dr. Smallwood housed his horses and carriages. (Courtesy of Jackson Davis Collection, Special Collections, University of Virginia Library)

Old Claremont Wharf was where the second cargo of slaves landed May 12, 1622. The wharf was rebuilt in 1911 by President Smallwood and renamed John Hay Wharf in honor of John Milton Hay. (Courtesy of Hampton University Archives)

Marcus W. Smallwood (1873–1935), nephew of Dr. Smallwood. He was an 1899 graduate of Temperance, Industrial and Collegiate Institute. (Courtesy of Flora Tann-Chambliss)

Hattie Lassiter-Spencer (1883–1968), niece of Dr. Smallwood. She attended Temperance, Industrial and Collegiate Institute. (Courtesy of Willie L. Lassiter)

Lucille Smallwood-Butler (1881–1974), niece of Dr. Smallwood. She attended Temperance, Industrial and Collegiate Institute. (Courtesy of Flora Tann-Chambliss)

Lizzie Josey (1875–1969), niece of Dr. Smallwood. She attended Temperance, Industrial and Collegiate Institute. (Courtesy of Dorothy Ruffin)

Vo. T

SEVENTH ANNUAL COMMENCEMENT

—OF THE—

TEMPERANCE, INDUSTRIAL

—AND—

COLLEGIATE INSTITUTE

at Claremont, Surry Co., Va.

COMMENCING SUNDAY, JUNE 11, 1899, AT 10.30 A. M.

AND CONTINUING THROUGH WEDNESDAY, JUNE 14TH

All exercises will be held upon the College Grounds.

FACULTY:

PROF. JOHN J. SMALLWOOD, Founder, President and instructor in History and Science.

MISS ELEANOR D. OWENS, Lady Principal and instructor in English and Elocution.

MISS FANNIE E. SMALLWOOD, Secretary and instructor in Advanced Mathematics and Higher English.

MRS. M. W. GORDON, Music and Primary Branches.

MRS. S. L. JONES, Matron.

YOU ARE INVITED TO BE PRESENT.

Compliments of Faculty.

WEDNESDAY, JUNE 14.

EDUCATIONAL CONGRESS, 2:30 P. M.

PRES. J. J. SMALLWOOD, Presiding.

PRAYER.

It is hoped that every school teacher and all persons interested in the educational welfare of the Negro race will lend their presence and efforts to make this Congress a success.

Address and essays by Miss E. D. Owens, [Lady Principal]

Other addresses by friends whose names will be announced at the Congress.

Meeting of Trustee Board in President's office 3 P. M.

1899.

Graduating Class of "99."

Miss Margaret Erminie Threatt, ... Norfolk, Va.

Mr. Marcus William Smallwood, . . Rich Square, N.C.

Williams' Prize, ... Gold Medal.

Awarded for the best Original Oration.

WEDNESDAY, JUNE 14th, 7.30 P. M.

COMMENCEMENT EXERCISES.

PRAYER.

CHORUS—"Graduating Song"

The address to the "Class of '99." . . . . Leslie

Miss Rhoda F. Graves, . . . Sturgeon Point, Va.

CLASS HISTORY.

Mr. Marcus William Smallwood, . . Rich Square, N.C.

CLASS POEM.

Miss Margaret Erminie Threatt, ... Norfolk, Va.

SOLO—"Only a Rose" . . . . . Wellington.

Miss Fannie E. Smallwood, Rich Square, N.C.

ORATION—"Incompatibility of the Times."

Mr. Marcus William Smallwood, Rich Square, N.C.

VALEDICTORY—Subject: "The Negro as an American Citizen."

Miss Margaret Erminie Threatt, . . . Norfolk, Va.

DUET—"Graduation Song."

Miss M. E. Threatt, Mr. M. W. Smallwood.

Presentation of Diplomas and the address to the Graduates by

Dr. R. Emmett Jones, Richmond, Va.

PRESENTATION OF PRIZES.

Program of the Seventh Annual Commencement Temperance, Industrial & Collegiate Institute. Commencement exercises were on Sunday, June 11, 1899. (From the copy in the Rare Book Collection, The University of North Carolina at Chapel Hill)

John Milton Hay served as President Lincoln's assistant private secretary until Lincoln's death in 1865. He served as Secretary of State under Presidents McKinley and Theodore Roosevelt's administration. He was a long time friend and confidante to Dr. Smallwood and was, along with his wife, Clara Hay, one of many financial contributors to his school. (Courtesy of the Library of Congress)

Dr. Hollis B. Frissell, second principal of Hampton Normal and Agricultural Institute from 1893-1918. (Courtesy of Hampton University Archives)

Temperance, Industrial and Collegiate Institute,

CLAREMONT, VIRGINIA.

For Both Sexes   Non-Sectarian.   Board and Tuition $6.50 Per Month.   Chartered July, 1902.

Prof. J. H. BLACKWELL, Sec. Trustee Board, Manchester, Va.   P. EMMETT ELLIS, Treas., Claremont, Va.

JOHN W. PETERSON, Business Manager.

OUR NEEDS:

ENDOWMENT.
GIRLS' HALL.
GENERAL IMPROVEMENTS.
HEATING PLANT.
SAW MILL.
SEWING MACHINES.
LAUNDRY FIXTURES.

HOME BUYING and FARMER'S CONGRESS,
January 4-5 and June 1-2 Each Year.

BOX 104, CLAREMONT, VA. _Dec 26_ 190 3.

... in the extreme. I was only twelve years of age when I ran away from my birthplace of Rich Square, N.C., worked all day and studied the old Webster Speller at night. I walked sixty miles from N.C. into the town of Franklin where my poor, slave-born father and mother once lived and where my great but misguided Grandfather was executed Aug. 1831. I speak of my Grandfather (Nat Turner) who led the Southampton insurrection in 1832 as being "great." I do not mean in a foolish, selfish way but as a fact. I returned to Rich Square in June '7. went a...

One of a four page letter to Dr. Hollis Frissell, principal, Hampton Normal and Agricultural Institute, Hampton, Virginia, written in the hand of Dr. Smallwood, December 26, 1903. Note where Dr. Smallwood speaks of his grandfather, Nat Turner. (Courtesy of Hampton University Archives)

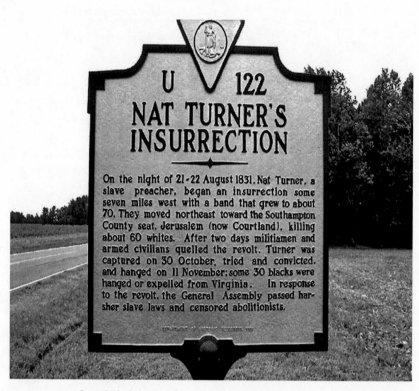

Commemorative Placard of the 1831 Slave Rebellion led by Nat Turner, Southampton County, Virginia. (Author's collection)

Emily Howland (1827-1929) was a philanthropist, humanitarian, abolitionist, educator, and activist for women suffrage. She was a strong financial contributor to the advancement of Negroes and Negro education. In appreciation of her moral support and financial contribution to his school, Dr. Smallwood named a building on his campus "Howland Hall" in her honor.

Frederick Douglass (1818-1895), was an American abolitionist, editor, orator, author, reformer, and statesman. Dr. Smallwood invited Mr. Douglass to speak at the Second Annual Commencement exercise at Temperance, Industrial and Collegiate Institute. (Courtesy of the Library of Congress)

Elizabeth Cady Stanton (1815-1902), was one of the forerunners, the driving force behind organizing the first women right's convention in June 1848 which was the first women right's movement in the United States. Dr. Smallwood wrote to Ms. Stanton advocating on behalf of his students and the operation of his school. (Courtesy of the Library of Congress)

Niagara Movement Leaders W.E.B. Du Bois (seated), and (left to right) J.R. Clifford, L. M. Hershaw and F.H. M. Murray at Harpers Ferry, August 1906. Mr. Hershaw was the guest speaker at Temperance, Industrial and Collegiate Institute's Eleventh Commencement exercise on June 1, 1903 in Claremont, Virginia. (Special Collections and University Archives, W.E.B. DuBois Library, University of Massachusetts Amherst)

JOHN J. SMALLWOOD DIES AFTER BRIEF ILLNESS.

Tragic Ending of a Brilliant Career—Orations Delivered Here and at Claremont.

REV. JOHN J. SMALLWOOD, Ph. D.

Dr. Smallwood succumbs to an untimely death at the age of 49. Richmond Planet, October 1, 1912. (Courtesy of Library of Virginia)

The late Rev. John J. Smallwood, Ph.D. (Courtesy of Willie L. Lassiter)

On a high point overlooking the peaceful James River, Dr. Smallwood's remains were interred almost directly in front of Lincoln Memorial Hall. (Courtesy of Barbara Hopper)

Lincoln Memorial Hall, ca. 1915. Dr. Smallwood's monument was erected on the right side of Lincoln Memorial Hall after his death. (Image used by permission of M. D. Harrison)

Front epitaph of Dr. Smallwood's monument. (Author's collection)

Full view of Dr. Smallwood's monument. His monument was moved from the campus of Temperance, Industrial and Collegiate Institute to Abundant Life Christian Church cemetery in Cabin Point, Virginia. (Author's collection)

Left side epitaph of Dr. Smallwood's monument. (Author's collection)

Right side epitaph of Dr. Smallwood's monument. (Author's collection)

Dr. Calvin S. Brown (1859-1936), a native of Salisbury, North Carolina and an 1886 graduate of Shaw University, Raleigh, North Carolina was Founder and Principal of Chowan Academy, in Winton, Hertford County, North Carolina from 1886-1893, which later changed its name to Waters Normal Institute in 1893. In 1937, the school was named Calvin Scott Brown High School in his honor. Dr. Brown was a close friend of Dr. Smallwood and served as an Honorary Pallbearer at his funeral. (Courtesy of Marvin T. Jones)

Rev. Dr. Charles H. Corey (1834-1899), served as "President of the first Negro Theological Seminary." Corey Memorial Institute, named in his honor in 1906, later merged with Smallwood Memorial Institute in 1921 to form Smallwood—Corey Memorial Industrial and Collegiate Institute. (Courtesy of Virginia Union University Archives)

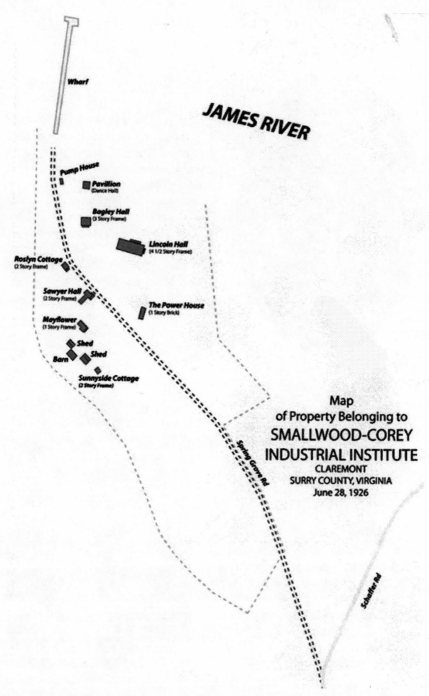

Map of Property belonging to Smallwood-Corey Industrial Institute, Claremont, Surry County Virginia. June 28, 1926. Map drawn by Tom Ludwig. Taken from the Negro World, 1926.

The Universal Negro Improvement Association (UNIA) purchased Smallwood-Corey Industrial Institute on June 19, 1926. The Negro World, July 31, 1926. (Bostock Library, Duke University, North Carolina)

T. (Timothy) Thomas Fortune (1856-1928) was a prominent nineteenth century and early twentieth century journalist and editor. Known as the "Negro Agitator," and an outspoken activist for racial equality, he was the first to advocate the use of the term Afro-American. From 1923 until his death in 1928, he served as editor of Marcus Garvey's Negro World. He was one of the speaker's at Dr. Smallwood's commencement.

Marcus Garvey (1887-1940), Founder of the Universal Negro Improvement Association (U.N.I.A.) in 1914, which purchased Smallwood-Corey Industrial Institute, formerly Temperance, Industrial and Collegiate Institute in 1926. Marcus Garvey was imprisoned at the time the U.N.I.A. purchased the Institute. The creation of a Negro educational Institute was one of the eight goals in the program of the U.N.I.A. and had been a dream of Garvey from the time he had become inspired by the work of Mr. Booker T. Washington. (Courtesy of the Library of Congress)

Robert L. Vann (1879-1940), a native of Ahoskie, Hertford County, North Carolina, was a lawyer and one of the founders of the Pittsburgh Courier. In 1925, while Marcus Garvey was imprisoned in an Atlanta Federal Penitentiary, Mr. Vann contacted Mrs. Garvey about the possibility of becoming her husband's counsel for a pardon appeal. In late 1927, Garvey was released from prison by President Coolidge's executive pardon. Two years later, in late 1929, while Garvey was exiled in Jamaica, Mr. Vann invited him to write weekly articles in the Courier. (Courtesy of Virginia Union University Archives)

Willie L. Lassiter (1900—), niece of Dr. John J. Smallwood, with actor Clifton Davis, whose desire it was to share the unrevealed story of her uncle's life's work. Her superb memory at 110 years of age undergrids every page of this book. (Courtesy of Willie L. Lassiter)

Russell Lassiter (1897-1994), nephew of Dr. Smallwood, and his wife Obelia Elizabeth Drew-Lassiter (1902-1996) ca. 1990, shared stories of his uncle who built a school for "colored people somewhere near Richmond, Virginia." (Courtesy of Dr. Genora Lassiter-Shaw)

Venus Josey-Barbee (1916-1946), a native of Rich Square, North Carolina, and great niece of Dr. Smallwood, desired to attend Temperance, Industrial and Collegiate Institute; however, the school had closed when she became of age to enroll. (Courtesy of Joyce Lawrence)

Eva Josey-Mangum (1918—), a native of Rich Square, North Carolina, and great niece of Dr. Smallwood shared oral family histories that had been passed down to her about her great uncle and the Smallwood family that contributed mightily to the creation of this story. (Courtesy of Joyce Lawrence)

Flora Tann Chambliss (1926-2009), a native of Rich Square, North Carolina and graduate of Howard University School of Pharmacy, and the great niece of Dr. Smallwood who, through her persistence and unyielding curiosity, inquired about her ancestral lineage, and therefore was able to pass on much of the family history to the next generation. (Courtesy of Flora Tann-Chambliss)

Clarence Lassiter (1923-   ), born in Rich Square, Northampton County, North Carolina, and great nephew of Dr. Smallwood, who served in World War II, provided a tour of Dr. Smallwood's birthplace and a wealth of valuable family history. (Courtesy of Clarence Lassiter).

CHAPTER TWENTY-ONE

SMALLWOOD-COREY MEMORIAL INDUSTRIAL AND COLLEGIATE INSTITUTE

In April 1865, soon after Confederate troops surrendered in Virginia, ending the Civil War, the Home Mission Society sent eleven teachers to Richmond. In November of that same year, the Rev. J. C. Binney, DD, former president of Columbian College (now George Washington University) in Washington DC, arrived in Richmond with the intention of starting a school to train freedmen in the ministry. Even without suitable accommodations, Dr. Binney somehow managed to start a school with twenty to twenty-five students who worked during the day and attended classes at night. About eight months after his arrival, Dr. Binney left Richmond.[1]

Two years later, in 1867, seventy-three-year-old Nathaniel Colver, DD, was invited to Richmond by the National Theological Institute and University, under the auspices of the American Baptist Home Mission Society, to open a school for training freedmen in the ministry. Dr. Colver, upon his arrival in Richmond, found himself in circumstances similar to those of Dr. Binney. His students showed promise, but a lack of adequate space for boarding and instruction was a major concern. One day, as Dr. Colver was considering the problem, he chanced to meet Mary Jane Lumpkin, the "fair-faced freedwoman, nearly white," the widow of a white slave owner and dealer.[2] She suggested that he consider using as a site for his school the Lumpkin Jail property, located on about half an acre of land between Franklin and Broad streets in the Shockoe section of Richmond.

This property, once owned by Mrs. Lumpkin's husband, consisted of four buildings, two of which had been used as slave pens, where slaves had been kept before auction, and a jail, where slaves had been imprisoned.[3] Dr. Colver agreed to lease the property from Mrs. Lumpkin for a period of three years.[4] By the end of that same year, enrollment in his school, now called the Richmond Institute, had increased to eighty-eight, with both day and night students.[5] Only a year later, however, in June 1868, Dr. Colver, stricken with grief over the recent death of his wife and dealing with his own health issues, discontinued his work with the institute. He died on September 25, 1870, in Chicago, Illinois.[6]

Colver's successor was a man well prepared for the task at hand. Dr. Charles Henry Corey was born in New Canaan, New Brunswick, on December 12, 1834, and received degrees from Acadia University, Nova Scotia, in 1858 and the Newton (Massachusetts) Theological Institution in 1861.[7] Prior to his appointment as president of the Richmond Institute, Dr. Corey served in several positions. After graduating from Newton, he worked as a pastor in Seabrook, New Hampshire, from 1861 to 1864, when he joined the Army Christian Commission and was stationed in Charleston, South Carolina, for the remainder of the Civil War.[8] In 1865, he entered upon service, as requested by the Home Mission Society, to engage in work with freedmen in Charleston, South Carolina.[9] Throughout his career, Dr. Corey was honored with numerous awards, and the degree of doctor of divinity was conferred upon him four times.[10]

In 1867, under the auspices of the National Theological Seminary, Dr. Corey traveled to Augusta, Georgia, where he was appointed principal of the Augusta Institute.[11] After serving there for only a year, Dr. Corey resigned to become president of the Richmond Institute in September 1868.[12] In January 1869, the Richmond Institute was renamed the Colver Institute in honor of Dr. Colver.[13]

The next year, after the terms of Colver's original lease had expired, the Home Mission Society (known also as the Freedmen's Bureau) deemed the Lumpkin Jail property an undesirable location for the Institute.[14] The society then purchased a four-story building on the corner of Nineteenth and Main streets known as the United States Hotel (formerly known, until 1853, as the Union Hotel), and the institute moved to this new location.[15]

On February 10, 1876, the school was incorporated as the Richmond Institute, with a nine-member board of trustees,[16] by the Virginia General Assembly. Ten years later, it was renamed Richmond Theological Seminary,[17] with Dr. Corey serving as the "president of the first Negro Theological Seminary."[18] Dr. Corey was compelled to resign from the presidency in 1898 after his health deteriorated,[19] but he continued the interests of the seminary by consolidating it with Wayland Seminary of Washington DC to form Virginia Union University in 1899.[20] Dr. Corey died on September 9, 1899.[21]

Seven years after Dr. Covey's death, in 1906, the Corey Memorial Institute was founded at Portsmouth in Norfolk County by the Norfolk Union Baptist Association, an affiliate of the Baptist General Association of Virginia (Colored). Corey Memorial Institute, a large three-story building, was built on eight city lots and contained classrooms, boarding and lodging facilities, and an office named in honor of the late Dr. Charles H. Corey.[22] The first principal of the institute was the Rev. Benjamin E. McWilliams, a native of Toledo, Ohio, and a graduate of Virginia Union University. He single-handedly organized the institute during its initial years, serving as both teacher and principal until he resigned in 1912 to accept a pastorate elsewhere. The Rev. J. Early Wright, another graduate of Virginia Union University, succeeded him.[23]

Rev. Wright remained at the Corey Memorial Institute until 1915, when the Rev. Charles H. Morton succeeded him. Reverend Morton was a native of Staunton, Virginia, and a graduate of Lincoln University in Oxford, Pennsylvania. Morton went to Corey Memorial Institute from Matthews County, Virginia, where he had been pastor of the Ebenezer and Antioch Baptist churches for three years. He had previously taught science, English, and Latin at Spiller Academy in Hampton, Virginia, in 1897 and was a strong advocate of education. He believed that it was through education that the black race would eventually elevate itself to a level of acceptance in society.

In 1918, the Rev. H. M. Henderson of Suffolk, Virginia, who had graduated with a Bachelors of Divinity[24] from Virginia Union University in 1902, succeeded Reverend Morton and became the fourth administrator of Corey Memorial Institute.[25] By 1919, under Reverend Henderson's leadership, the enrollment at the institute reached a point beyond which the school was not physically able to accommodate more students. The Norfolk Union Baptist Association became concerned about the matter and prevailed upon the Baptist General Association to render assistance in resolving it.

In response, the Baptist General Association purchased a 172-acre tract of land in Claremont, Virginia, in early 1920. The site, which had previously been occupied by the Smallwood Memorial Institute, contained nine large buildings that were ideally suited to the needs of Corey Memorial Institute. The total value of the property was estimated at more than a quarter of a million dollars when the Baptist General Association of Virginia (Colored) purchased the property in 1920.[26]

In May 1921, Corey Memorial Institute was relocated to Claremont, Virginia, and renamed the Smallwood-Corey Memorial Industrial and Collegiate Institute, according to the charter recorded at the Surry County Courthouse. The same document stated that the curriculum would include, in addition to the ordinary branches of education, instruction in industrial arts, agriculture, classical education, and theology.[27]

Two months prior to the move, on March 21, 1921, the Smallwood-Corey Memorial Industrial and Collegiate Institute, formerly Smallwood Memorial Institute, was incorporated. The principal office of the corporation was in the town of Claremont, Surry County, Virginia, and a proposed office was to be established in the city of Norfolk. The purposes for which the corporation was formed were to establish and maintain an institution of learning for the education, both mental and manual, of colored youth. Smallwood-Corey Memorial Industrial and Collegiate Institute was owned, maintained, and supported by the Baptist General Association (Colored) of Virginia, the Women's Baptist Missionary and Educational Association, the Baptist State Sunday School Convention of Virginia, the Baptist Young People's Union of Virginia, the Norfolk Union Baptist Association, the Rappahannock Union Baptist Sunday School Convention, the Women's Missionary and Educational Union of Tidewater, the Lebanon Baptist Association, and any other affiliated bodies that applied to become members of the corporation.[28]

The trustees of the corporation were fifty-three, five of whom were nominated and recommended by each of the affiliated bodies aforementioned, and twenty were elected by the other trustees and classified in three divisions. The board members had voting power as well as the power to fill all vacancies and elect other members. The board of trustees was also empowered, by the addition of a new bylaw to the school's charter, to invite the superintendent of public instruction or any other state official to inspect and make recommendations on the institute's course of study or any other matter deemed essential for the educational development of the institution.[29] At the time the charter was incorporated, the Rev. Robert J. Langston was secretary, W. H. Willis was treasurer, and F. W. Williams was acting principal.[30]

Soon after the new charter was put into effect, Reverend Langston was elected to become the first principal of the newly created Smallwood-Corey Memorial Industrial and Collegiate Institute, and he opened the school at Claremont in 1921.[31] He succeeded Reverend Henderson, who had been the principal of Corey Memorial before the merger.[32] During Langston's tenure, from 1921 to 1924, the Smallwood-Corey Memorial Industrial and Collegiate Institute experienced a significant increase in enrollment. Within one academic year, by September 1922, a hundred students were enrolled. Under Langston's leadership, the faculty also increased: it rose to nine, the largest number in the history of the school. Resident students comprised a larger percentage of the student body than at any prior time, under any of the institute's other incarnations.[33]

On April 21, 1923, the board of the Smallwood-Corey Memorial Industrial and Collegiate Institute held a meeting in Richmond, with two-thirds of its members present, to discuss amendments to the school's charter.[34] After a unanimous vote in favor of the proposed alterations, the name of the institution was shortened from Smallwood-Corey Memorial Industrial and Collegiate Institute to Smallwood-Corey Industrial Institute. The principal office of the corporation was also moved from the city of Richmond to the town of Claremont. The corporation would be run as a Baptist coeducational institution. The new charter was signed by F. W. Williams in the capacity of acting president, and the corporate seal was affixed and attested by J. H. Blackwell, secretary, on September 26, 1924.[35]

After the new charter was created, the Baptist General Association appointed Rev. H. M. Henderson—former president of Corey Memorial Institute (1918–1921)—principal of the newly named Smallwood-Corey Industrial Institute. Reverend Henderson remained principal through May

1926, when he resigned. The school suffered severe financial difficulties during the year of his resignation, and the board of trustees, forced to seek external sources of funding, looked to black nationalist leader Marcus Garvey for help.[36]

Smallwood, the distinguished Negro and founder of the institution, was sent as a forerunner to help prepare the way for the Hon. Marcus Garvey and his great movement.

—The Negro World
August 7, 1926

CHAPTER TWENTY-TWO

MARCUS GARVEY / UNIVERSAL LIBERTY UNIVERSITY

Born in St. Ann's Bay, Jamaica, in the British West Indies on August 17, 1887, Marcus Garvey was the eleventh child of Sarah and Marcus Garvey and was one of only two of their children to reach adulthood. As a child, Marcus, like his father, loved to read. At age fifteen, he left public school to work full-time as an apprentice in a small print shop owned by his godfather; he did not, however, leave behind his desire for learning. His schooling continued in the back room of the shop as he read books, magazines, newspapers, and any other publications that were available to him.[1] By age eighteen, he had advanced to master printer and foreman at one of the largest printing shops on the island, run by his uncle in Kingston, Jamaica. In his early twenties, Marcus started his own newspaper, called *Garvey's Watchman,* but the paper was short-lived, because Marcus felt a pressing need to do more to improve the status of Jamaican blacks. To that end, he became more involved in political activities and left Jamaica in 1910, at the age of twenty-three, for Costa Rica and Panama.[2]

In Costa Rica, Garvey worked as a timekeeper on a banana plantation, but he became despondent over the extremely poor working conditions to which many of the black West Indian workers were subjected. Disturbed by the apathy of the British consulate and the lack of organizational political involvement by the black laborers, Garvey left Costa Rica and traveled to Colombia, Venezuela, Nicaragua, and several other Latin American nations, only to find similar working conditions among the West Indian migrant workers there.[3]

After a brief return to Jamaica in 1912, Garvey traveled to England, where he took courses in law and philosophy at the Birkbeck College in London.[4] He then spent some time traveling through Western Europe and returned to England in late 1913, where he came across Booker T. Washington's *Up from Slavery*. Inspired by Mr. Washington, Garvey began to envision an organization that would help Negroes to help themselves. He believed he had found his purpose in life—to unite his race of people into one body and uplift them economically, educationally, politically, mentally, and socially, in order to develop within them a sense of racial pride, and give them the resources needed to establish their own government.[5] He dreamed of establishing a Jamaican Tuskegee Institute, modeled after the Tuskegee Institute that Booker T. Washington had founded in Alabama. With this goal in mind, Garvey returned to Jamaica on July 15, 1914, and formed an organization called the Universal Negro Improvement and Conservation Association and African Communities League, later renamed the Universal Negro Improvement Association.[6]

The UNIA struggled in Jamaica. When, by late 1915, there were only about a hundred members, Garvey came to realize that he had to look elsewhere to carry out his purpose.[7] On March 23, 1916, he arrived in the United States. His first stop was New York City, which soon became the headquarters of his Harlem-based movement. Housed in an auditorium at 114 West 138th Street, Liberty Hall became the center where Garvey often held his UNIA meetings, acting as president general.[8] The Harlem branch started out with just seventeen members, but by the spring of 1918, thanks to Garvey's strong advocacy of Negro economic and political independence, racial pride, and unity, UNIA branches, and divisions began to spring up in towns and cities across the United States and soon in other countries as well. In the same year, Garvey began publishing the UNIA newspaper, the *Negro World*.

By 1919, the UNIA had soared to prominence, with millions of members in various chapters around the globe. It served as a gateway to economic independence for the Negro race and provided employment opportunities through enterprises such as its Negro Factories Corporation.[9]

In Harlem alone, the UNIA owned restaurants, laundries, and a chain of grocery stores, in addition to several other businesses.[10] Nationally, the organization owned and operated the Black Star Line, a shipping company with its own fleet of ships.[11]

Garvey himself mesmerized Negroes worldwide with his messages of racial pride, conveyed through newspapers and speeches.[12] In August 1920, he organized the first Annual Convention of the Negro Peoples of the World, sponsored by the UNIA and designed to promote Negro unity through a gathering of delegates from the various Negro peoples of the world. At the convention, Garvey introduced a red-black-and-green flag that was chosen by delegates in attendance as the official colors of the African race[13] and composed the Declaration of Rights of the Negro Peoples of the World.[14] He also announced the proposed opening of Booker T. Washington University, which was to be located on the same site as the UNIA-operated Phyllis Wheatley Hotel. The university, used to train teachers, was ultimately short-lived, but Garvey and his organization continued to envision the establishment of a regular educational training institution—one of the eight goals of the UNIA program.[15]

Garvey's prominence brought him his share of legal troubles. In 1919, the United States Bureau of Investigation (later known as the FBI), under the direction of J. Edgar Hoover, began monitoring the activities of the UNIA. Hoover believed that charges should be brought against Garvey for fraudulent business dealings with the Black Star Line, and his investigation into Garvey's operations continued over the next five years.[16] Near the end of 1921, the postal department accused Garvey of illegally circulating false advertisements to raise money for the Black Star Line. He was arrested and charged with mail fraud in January 1922 but was soon released on bail. The next year, in June 1923, Garvey was convicted on charges of mail fraud and was sentenced to five years' imprisonment.[17] UNIA attorneys quickly filed an appeal, and Garvey was released on bail only three months later. In February 1925, his appeal was rejected, and he was assigned to the Atlanta Federal Penitentiary to serve his five-year term.[18] Membership in the UNIA declined between 1925 and 1927, after Garvey's incarceration.

When Garvey began serving his sentence in Atlanta, two prominent attorneys, James Cobb and Robert L. Vann, one of the founders of the

Pittsburgh Courier,[19] contacted Garvey's wife, Amy Jacques Garvey, about the possibility of becoming her husband's counsel for a pardon appeal. Mrs. Garvey sought her husband's advice, lobbied in Washington DC, and arranged for committees to meet with the attorney general and President Coolidge, but was advised to have her husband set his own grounds for a pardon. Therefore, she never hired Cobb and Vann.[20]

Meanwhile, in Claremont, Virginia, the board of trustees of the Smallwood-Corey Industrial Institute appealed to the UNIA for financial assistance. After a series of negotiations with the Executive Council of the UNIA, with the instruction and direction of the imprisoned Garvey, Smallwood-Corey Industrial Institute became the property of the UNIA on June 19, 1926.[21] Fred Toote, "acting as Trustee for and on behalf of a group of persons who propose to organize a corporation to take over, maintain, and operate a school for colored people at Claremont, Virginia," paid a total of $7,300 for the institute and assumed payment of its remaining debts.[22]

The purchase of the Smallwood-Corey Industrial Institute included not only the actual property but also all the buildings and appurtenances thereon, including the John Hay Wharf. At the time, there were twelve buildings on campus: Bagley, Sawyer, and Lincoln halls; Mayflower, Sunnyside, and Roslyn (or Roseland) cottages; and two sheds, a barn, a power house, a pump house, and a pavilion. Lincoln Hall, the main building on the campus, was estimated to be worth $100,000 and was later renamed Garvey Hall.[23]

At a local weekly mass meeting of the UNIA, held at the Commonwealth Auditorium in New York City on Sunday, July 18, 1926—less than a month after the UNIA acquired the Institute—an enthusiastic crowd cheered wildly over the purchase. Dr. J. G. St. Clair Drake, vice president of the institute and one of the key negotiators who assisted in securing the UNIA deal, addressed the audience. He spoke about the newly acquired property in Claremont as well as the organization's overall intent in purchasing the institute—to acquire schools, colleges, and universities for the training of the Negro race, in keeping with the overall objectives stated in the third section of the UNIA constitution. The property, worth an estimated $250,000, according to Dr. Drake, "was practically a gift to the organization, there being only $53,000 debt on it in mortgage and judgments" that the association would assume.[24]

Another negotiator instrumental in securing the institute was Caleb G. Robinson, a graduate of the Hampton Institute and member of the UNIA. Mr. Robinson had previously served as president of the Smallwood Memorial Institute in 1916,[25] before the merger with Corey Memorial Institute. After the merger, Robinson was reappointed president of the Smallwood-Corey Industrial Institute.[26]

The following Sunday, at another local weekly meeting, Fred Toote, acting president general of the UNIA, appealed to UNIA members worldwide to support the Smallwood-Corey Industrial Institute project. He further assured the enthused crowd that the purchase of an institution founded and endowed by Negroes was right and proper, as it would enable the Negro race to have an institute of higher learning of its own.[27] What was more, the location of the school was ideal, in light of the back-to-Africa movement advocated by Marcus Garvey and other members of his organization: it was located on the very spot where the second cargo of Negro slaves to America had landed in 1622, and its wharf, once used to unload shipments of Negro slaves from Africa, could now return Negroes to Africa to build an independent Negro nation.

Equally appealing to the new owners of the property was the fact that the place where Negroes had once landed, illiterate and enslaved, was now a university that had been founded to eliminate illiteracy among Negroes and teach them self-pride, self-respect, self-reliance, and the principles of liberty and freedom.[28] With the UNIA's purchase of the institute, the possibility of establishing an international institution, as envisioned by President General Marcus Garvey, was becoming a reality. The UNIA believed that the newly acquired property had the potential to become one of the greatest, if not the greatest, educational institutions founded by a Negro, and now owned and operated by and for Negroes.[29] And in honor of the memory of Dr. Smallwood, the UNIA vowed to continue the work that he had begun—training young Negro men and women to be of service to their race for generations to come and nurturing and inculcating the highest ideals of racial development within the Negro race.[30]

As early as July 31, 1926, the parent body of the UNIA began to stress to its members the importance of making monetary contributions in support of the school, and a donation of $10,000 was immediately requested.[31] Regular advertisements in the *Negro World* reiterated the urgent need for donations. In bold print, the advertisements read, "$10,000.00 needed now. This is the time to show your loyalty to the U.N.I.A. and give substantial assistance to the educational program by immediately making a liberal contribution to help meet the first payment on property brought for the site of our university. No race-loving Negro can afford to miss this opportunity to help such a laudable cause. Make donations payable to Parent Body-U.N.I.A. 56 West 135th Street, New York."[32]

Two months after purchasing the institute, in August 1926, the executive council of the UNIA met to organize a new board of trustees, a new charter, and a new name for the school, which they decided to call Liberty University.[33] Additionally, the executive council desired to meet with the Educational Commission of the State of Virginia to establish standards and guidelines in an effort to adhere to the commission's expectations and demands in the operation of the institute.[34] It was the intent of the university's new management to recruit students from all over the world, but at the same time, the board recognized a need to give special consideration for admission to residents of Virginia, and particularly Surry County.[35]

It was the belief of the UNIA that providing a systematic education to the Negro people was essential. This education would enable Negroes to obtain valuable knowledge and would thoroughly inculcate in them, as a basic principle, consciousness of the social, civil, and economic values of their race. What better place for this to happen, the UNIA asked, than at a great university such as Liberty? Like Dr. Smallwood before them, the UNIA desired, in establishing Liberty, to develop a quality, international Negro university that would appeal to Negro youth not only in the United States, but also in the West Indies, Africa, and the islands of the sea.[36] With this philosophy as their driving force, the UNIA's parent body solicited requests for donations, posted announcements of the school's opening, and printed advertisements suggesting that "every division or chapter [of the UNIA] should grant a scholarship to a deserving boy or girl and enable them to secure a liberal education" in the *Negro World* and other newspapers throughout the country.[37] It was the UNIA's desire that each of its local divisions have at one least student enrolled at Liberty University.[38] Soon after, the UNIA's slogan became "Every division a student."[39]

The school term for the first year of operation of Liberty University began on September 15, 1926.[40] Tuition, which included board, room, light, heat, bath, and laundry, was $16 per month, while tuition for day students was $2. Students were also requested to pay an entrance fee of $5 at the beginning of each year.[41] To promote enrollment, the UNIA's weekly newspaper provided detailed information on various routes, exchanges, costs of fares, and modes of transportation to the school.[42] Advertisements in the *Negro World* also described courses covering a wide range of subject areas, including business, domestic science, vocal and instrumental music, Bible training, physical culture, dressmaking, plain sewing, typewriting, stenography, and bookkeeping. Students could receive instruction in the industrial, scientific, or agricultural fields. Interested students and parents were asked to contact the school's president, Caleb G. Robinson, for particulars regarding the curriculum.[43]

When the UNIA opened Liberty University, Marcus Garvey was imprisoned in Atlanta, Georgia; he was never able to see the school in operation. Fred Toote visited Garvey frequently during his confinement and, on May 15, 1927, after returning from a visit to the penitentiary, informed UNIA members at their weekly meeting of Garvey's grave health concerns. Toote warned that "unless they redouble[d] their efforts to secure the immediate release of their revered leader," Garvey would die in Atlanta.[44]

Two weeks after Toote returned from his visit with Garvey, Liberty University, now renamed Universal Liberty University, held its first commencement exercises on Sunday, May 29, 1927, in Claremont, Virginia. The Rev. J. B. Brown, DD, pastor of Zion Baptist Church of Petersburg, Virginia, delivered the Baccalaureate sermon at 2:30 p.m. Addresses were delivered by Fred Toote, Dr. J. St. Clair Drake, and Dr. C. S. Morris, former president of the school and pastor of the Fifth Baptist Church of Richmond Virginia. Much like commencement exercises conducted in years past at Temperance, Industrial and Collegiate Institute, Universal Liberty University's ceremonies continued over several days and featured an oratorical contest, a play, an alumni dinner, and an alumni meeting.[45]

On the day of Liberty's first commencement exercises, a large excursion party arrived from New York, New Jersey, Norfolk, Virginia, and Philadelphia. The UNIA offered such excursions to give its members the opportunity to tour the school buildings and grounds.[46] In this case, over a thousand people were in attendance, and the large size of the crowd forced school officials to hold the commencement services outdoors instead of in the school's auditorium, as planned.

As the UNIA celebrated the success of Universal Liberty University, Marcus Garvey continually pleaded for his release from prison. He wrote three separate pleas requesting pardon from President Calvin Coolidge, but his pleas went unanswered. Garvey's supporters, too, sent innumerable telegrams to President Coolidge, to express their feelings regarding the continued imprisonment of their leader. To show support for Garvey's release, Fred Toote suggested that members of the UNIA and other Garvey supporters designate the week of June 12–19, 1927, as Marcus Garvey Release Week. His purpose was to unify efforts in urging the president of the United States against the continued imprisonment of Marcus Garvey.[47] Two months later, on August 15, 1927, Toote resigned as acting president general of the UNIA. Garvey, still conducting UNIA business from his prison cell, appointed as his personal representative Mr. E. B. Knox, president of the Chicago Division.[48]

In November 1927, President Coolidge pardoned Garvey under condition of immediate deportation to Jamaica. Garvey would not be allowed to remain in the United States because the federal government had declared him a convicted criminal.[49] And so, without having a chance to visit his headquarters in New York to say good-bye to his loyal supporters and fellow UNIA members, Garvey was quickly put on a ship headed to Panama, then Jamaica, where he continued his message of uplifting the Negro race.[50] On November 29, in a letter to the UNIA, he stated, "I am forced to leave you, but I am going to prepare a greater and grander U.N.I.A. Keep up your courage and faith." After his deportation, however, the organization began to weaken.[51]

By January 1928, less than two months after the deportation of their leader, the UNIA was frequently publishing "Special Appeals" to its members in the *Negro World*. Mr. E. B. Knox, personal representative of President General Garvey, urged the members of the association to contribute one dollar or more in an effort to carry on the work of the university. He reminded members that Universal Liberty University was their university and that, therefore, they should not hesitate to support it. He requested that financial donations be sent to the secretary of the school, Mr. Balfour Williams.[52] In February 1928, the *Negro World* began listing the names of donors, with their divisions and the amount of money donated. Donations ranged from ten cents to ten dollars. Those who sent in twenty-five dollars or more were asked to send in a photograph for publication.[53] Monies to support the university were also generated from "plays" and "musicals" sponsored by Universal Liberty University.[54]

By May 1928, Universal Liberty University was continually plagued by debt and a general lack of funds. The board of trustees authorized President Robinson and Secretary Williams to solicit funds in an effort to pay off the school's debts and make necessary improvements for the upcoming fall term.[55] Despite continuous advertisements and appeals for help, however, Universal Liberty University continued to suffer financially.

Only two months later, after a grueling struggle with financial difficulties, President Robinson, the school's seventh and final administrator, departed the university, never to return. With him went the faculty and student body.[56] Four months afterward, in October 1928, when the fall session opened at most other schools, Universal Liberty University was closed.[57] The following year, on October 12, 1929, approximately seventeen days before the stock market crash that hurtled the United States into the Great Depression, a notice was published in the *Negro World* that read, "Owing to Contemplated Reorganization of Liberty University at Claremont, Va. The School Will Not Be Opened Until Further Notice, By Order of Board of Directors."[58]

Already grappling with a lack of sufficient funds to operate the school, the board's financial woes were compounded by the devastating effects of the failed economy, which made it virtually impossible for the university to survive. Even so, Amy Jacques Garvey, wife of Marcus Garvey, claimed that "[d]espite Garvey's imprisonment and the financial straits of the organization, they bravely carried on until 1930."[59] If they did, in fact, "bravely carry on," it was undoubtedly an arduous task. Shortly after its closing, the school was severely vandalized and rendered unsuitable for further use.[60] Because of a lack of any type of security or custodial staff on the property,[61] looters took truckloads of items, such as desks, laboratory equipment, heating apparatuses, and various other portable objects, and either sold the stolen goods or kept them for personal use.[62]

For several years, Universal Liberty University remained the property of the trustees.[63] But time and nature eventually took their toll on the buildings. Sawyer Hall, together with the other wooden buildings on campus, began to deteriorate and collapse. The once-imposing Lincoln Hall decayed as well, with its windows smashed out and its brickwork torn away.[64] What was once the heart and soul of Dr. Smallwood's vision for the young men and women of his race came to a halt once his body, hands, and mind were motionless. Soon after his death, the school's Northern patronage ceased. For twenty years (1892–1912), the ambitious Dr. Smallwood worked unselfishly for his school, giving all of himself for the benefit of others. As T. Thomas Fortune, editor of the *Negro World* and close friend of Dr. Smallwood's, once stated, "[Dr. Smallwood] let his imagination run riot, for he was young and saw visions and dreamed dreams. He hardly looked so far ahead as to envisage the realization of the visions and the dreams."[65] After his death, the school struggled to survive for another near twenty-year period (1912–1928).[66] Its closure marked a cruel end to a once-brilliant dream.

What was at one time a thriving and immaculate campus became a harvest for nature's prey. And what was once a promising educational institution, as one contemporary writer stated, was "buried under the fallen ruins, blended with the soil its founder had hoped would bear an everlasting monument of his labors."[67] Had it not been for Dr. Smallwood's untimely death, the Temperance, Industrial and Collegiate Institute might have become one of the world's premier institutes of higher education:[68] even though the institute was relatively short-lived, it is estimated to have educated over 2,500 students.[69]

Nearly ten years after Universal Liberty University ceased its operations, the mortgages held in trust had not been paid. In accordance with the terms in the deeds of trust, the property was advertised on May 14, 1937, and sold at public auction on the premises of the former school(s). Mr. H. C. Redd, of Hanover County, Virginia, purchased the 65¾ acres, including remaining structures on it, for a mere $100.[70] Soon after the purchase, Dr. Smallwood's monument overlooking the James River was moved to Gravel Hill Baptist Church between Claremont and Cabin Point, Virginia.[71]

Never again used for educational purposes, in June 1941, Universal Liberty University, formerly Liberty University, formerly Smallwood-Corey Industrial Institute, formerly Smallwood-Corey Memorial Industrial and Collegiate Institute, formerly Smallwood Memorial Institute, formerly the Temperance, Industrial and Collegiate Institute, was dynamited.[72]

Moonlight on the James

The shadows are black 'mid the moonbeams
On the crest of this lonely hill,
Below, not a ripple on its breast
The river lies, calm and still.

The trees respond with a murmur,
To the night wind's plaintive sigh,
And far above the stars keep watch
In the purple midnight sky.

All nature is hushed and sleeping,
Not a sound of the night is heard.
And the sad complaint of the waving trees
Or the cry of some waking bird.

The tumult of hearts that are throbbing,
With human pain or bliss,
Is hushed to a stiller happier pulse,
On a placid night like this.

And home on the sobbing night wind;
On each heart comes crowding fast,
Like ghosts of the dead as this solemn hour,
The memories of the past.

But hope descends from the far-off stars
Their promise eternal to bring
And banish the phantoms of the night,
With the touch of a seraph's wing.

And Peace, with the breath of its presence,
Like an angel in its flight,
Dispels the fear and the tumult
On this calm midsummer night.

A peaceful spell of the midnight,
  Sink, thou, deep into each heart;
Stilling its pain with thy balmy touch,
  Bidding each fear depart!

And 'mid the heat of the noontide
  And the cares that will come tomorrow,
May be recalled thy lesson and charm;
  To while away the sorrow.

O, the fragrance, the balm and the verdure,
  O, the stars, serenely bright;
O, the dew and calm and the silence,
  And the promise of the night!

O, stars, to whose silent music,
  To whose language mute is given,
That title grand by a gifted bard,
  "The poetry of heaven."

O, south wind, blowing gently,
  O, river, flowing free,
Bearing the message of ages
  From the mountains to the sea.

Teach me thy lesson of beauty,
  Let they spirit of duty fill
With a purpose true, a restless heart
  And whisper, "Peace be still."

—John J. Smallwood
Claremont, Virginia
November 1903
Courtesy of Hampton University Archives

DR. SMALLWOOD'S SPEECH

DELIVERED ON THE FIFTY-FIRST BIRTHDAY OF LINCOLN

D r. John Jefferson Smallwood delivered this speech commemorating the fifty-first birthday of Lincoln, and it was later printed in the June 13, 1896, issue of the *Monthly Advocate*, the semimonthly campus newspaper of the Temperance, Industrial and Collegiate Institute.

Our Progress Since His Edict Issue—
A few Words in His Honor, and his Memory

President Smallwood said the following:

Ladies and gentlemen—It is a time honored custom in this great country in which we live and in which we, as American citizens form so conspicuous a part, to take pleasure in setting apart this day as the day upon which the great event, or one of the great events, occurred in the civilization of the American Republic. We meet today to celebrate the 51st anniversary of one of the greatest if not the greatest of American statesmen that has ever lived. From the dark and gloomy fields of the slave-stricken Kentucky sprang the son of no mean attainment, of great foresight, of limited education and yet of unbounded expression and intelligence. He was a coarse man in his general makeup, certain in his plans, vigorous in the discharge of his duty and always determined to do right. This man whose anniversary we meet to celebrate was that wonderful statesman, that self-made American; that born-lover of human freedom, that self-made orator, that wonderful patriot, that noble emancipator of human souls, Abraham Lincoln, who, after careful and deliberate thought, with long and conscientious preparation, surrounded by the advice of many friends, in the face of a slave-stricken country, dared to say that upon paper which, when issued, was known all over the civilized world as the Emancipation Proclamation; and this Emancipation Proclamation was the instrument known as the great Edict that freed four-and-a-half million souls from the shackles of human slavery and made it possible for them to become participants in the government over which the great Emancipator was presiding.

There has [*sic*] been many conflicts since the occasion of that unpleasant strife is still fresh in the memory of all those men and women who heard the roaring of all the cannons, who saw the tired forms of the Northern and Southern heroes as they met upon the field of battle to fight and by that fight to decide whether that Emancipation Proclamation, issued by that wonderful statesman, was legitimate or not. Those days, ladies and gentlemen, have passed; they will never come again. The secession of South Carolina and the hasty expression of her sons have long been forgotten and no politician of this generation or before could make Massachusetts or Rhode Island look upon North Carolina and South Carolina with secessional hatred and fear. Thank God, the Civil War is over. We, the American Negroes, are free and free forever. The Union is united; the dead soldier, who fought upon the battle fields, representing the side of the Southern Confederacy and the brave hero from Massachusetts and New England, who fought in the interest of the Federal flag are today legislating at Washington for one common cause, in one common country, for one common people. But I am to speak today upon Mr. Lincoln because you represent a very conspicuous part of that purpose for which he lived. Grand in character, noble in purpose, lofty in ambition, wonderful in will-power, skilled in self-learning and trade and well-trained in man hood. He was a parliamentarian, who felt that the country, in which he lived, could not, under its constitution, hold men in one section free and hold them in another section in human bondage. Such could not have been the educational talents, the religious forbearance nor the patriotic desire; it was simply a mistaken idea, that was all. That feeling in this republic will never come again, but let me speak today frankly and practically. We, as negroes, are to play a part in this country that shall be so true in its motive, so earnest in its plan, so judicious in its purpose and so effectual in its influence upon the general public, that every white man in this country, be he Northerner or Southerner, whatever his prejudice may be shall see and see so plainly that we have proven ourselves worthy of the citizenship given us. We are not to look upon America as the home of someone else; we are not to look upon America as being the accidental home of the negro, we are not to look upon America as being the white man's country upon whose shores we have no right to come. Instead of clamoring over the past, instead of speaking of our 250 years of enslavement, instead of sitting for hours at a time talking of the old whipping post and the lash, instead of going over the country preaching that we should build monuments to Lincoln, let us become intelligent men and women; let us build colleges, blacksmith shops, carriage shops; let us establish banks and bank accounts; let us buy fine horses and carriages; let us teach our sisters and our wives and daughters to become shrewd business women, noble mothers, faithful advocates of the right and great moral powers in the great community in which they live. Let us teach our young men to buy land, to build up the waste places on this ancient and historic James, where once their fathers labored as slaves. Let us see to it that in every ditch and hamlet in the republic we shall have a school house on the hill side and the church in the valley and here we shall have built the greatest monument possible to the greatest statesman that America has ever produced. I am glad, ladies and gentlemen, to be a negro, a representative of the suffering and the final death of that wonderful patriot. And let us review these few years past and ask our American friends what we have done, what are we doing, what are we going to do with a fair chance in the race of life.

As a result of the Emancipation Proclamation in the United States, the negroes have 872 negro lawyers, 789 negro doctors, 444 negro merchants, 22,000 school teachers, 1894 regular classical college graduates, $63,000 invested in steamboat stock, $51,000 invested in city street railway, 996 ministers of the gospel, who come from the best colleges of this country and of Europe, four banks, with a capital stock of two and a half million dollars, 27 negro women in the United States practicing dentistry, 14 negro women of the United States as doctors, practicing medicine, and 12 of the most powerful and intellectual women in the ministry; we have 72 colleges and academies and high schools in which Latin, Greek, German, French and Hebrew are being taught by negro professors. In the United States in thirty years after the celebrated issuing of the Emancipation Proclamation from that wonderful friend of the negro race, Abraham Lincoln, the negroes of this country pay taxes upon $360,000,000 of taxable property. In Maryland he owns 1 1-7 acres of land in every 29; in Virginia he owns 1 1-8 of every 37; in North Carolina he owns 2 1-3 in every 54; in southern and democratic Georgia, he pays taxes upon $32,000,000 of taxable property; in South Carolina he pays taxes upon $29,000,000 of taxable property. This is the greatest argument in favor of Mr. Lincoln's philanthropy and his determination to emancipate the slaves by issuing of his Edict in the form of the Emancipation Proclamation.

Let us do our duty. We cannot honor Mr. Lincoln however, not even by the accumulation of the property just named; we are compelled to go back to the fields of industry and commencement anew. The busy hum of the factory wheels can be heard when it belongs to the negro; the train laden with its cargo of human souls drawn through this world at almost lightning speed, the whistle upon that train must belong to the negro; the electricity that is being discovered and so generally used, the great natural facilities of these idle fields of the south must be taken up by the black man and utilized. The negro must become President of his own college, the historian of his own race, and, by continual arguments upon the line of intelligence, by constant accumulation of property, by a strong and wonderful moral line drawn between the Judases and Isaiahs of the race, we must honor that man who has honored us. Again, ladies and gentlemen, Mr. Lincoln expected of us great things. It has been said in history that we cannot learn, that we possessed such incapabilities that we were unable to take care of ourselves. It has been said by the historian that there was no mental capacity in the race to fit it for the great duties and chances of life and when Mr. Lincoln made it possible by the issuing the Emancipation Proclamation for the Negro to become a freed man, he then expected the greatest thing possible of us.

Selected Bibliography

Books

Alexander, S. L. T. *Thomas Fortune, the Afro-American Agitator: A Collection of Writings, 1880–1928*. Gainesville: University Press of Florida, 2008.

Atkins, J. E. Adam Boykin: *Slave, Soldier, Citizen*. Surry County, VA: privately printed, 2008.

—. *Surry County, Virginia Historical Timeline with Addendums: Events, Places, and People that Shaped the History of Surry County, Virginia. In time Sequence: Prehistoric, 1400s, 1500s, 1600s, 1700s, 1800s, 1900s, 2000s*. Richmond, VA: privately printed, 2008.

Baird, M. S. Jr. *Claremont on the James: Its Beginning and Early Years, Circa 1880–1920*. Zuni, VA: Pearl Line, 2002.

Baugham, S. G. *The Town of Rich Square: A History, 1717–1983*. Jackson, NC, 1983.

Bennett, L. Jr. *Before the Mayflower: A History of the Negro in America, 1619–1964*. Rev. ed. Baltimore: Penguin, 1964.

Bisson, T. *Nat Turner, Slave Revolt Leader*. New York: Chelsea House, 1988.

Blackmon, D. A. *Slavery by Another Name: The Re-Enslavement of Black Americans from the Civil War to World War II.* New York: Doubleday, 2008.

Brown, W. W. *The Narrative of William W. Brown: A Fugitive Slave.* New York: Dover, 2003.

Buni, A. *Robert L. Vann of Pittsburgh Courier: Politics and Black Journalism.* Pittsburgh, PA: University of Pittsburgh Press, 1974.

Carter, W. A. *Shaw's Universe: A Monument to Educational Innovation.* Rockville, MD: D. C. National, 1973.

Cheek, W., and A. L. Cheek. *John Mercer Langston and the Fight for Black Freedom,* 1829–65. Urbana: University of Illinois Press, 1996.

Corbitt, D. L. *The Formation of the North Carolina Counties, 1663–1943.* 5th ed. Raleigh: North Carolina State Department of Archives and History, 1996.

Corey, C. H. *A History of Richmond Theological Seminary, with Reminiscences of Thirty Years' Work among the Colored People of the South.* Richmond, VA: J. W. Randolph, 1895.

Craft, W., and E. Craft. *Running a Thousand Miles for Freedom.* 1860; repr., London: William Tweedie, 2000.

Cronon, E. D. *Black Moses: The Story of Marcus Garvey and the Universal Negro Improvement Association.* 1969; repr., Madison: University of Wisconsin Press, 1995.

Crow, J. J., P. D. Escott, and F. J. Hatley. *A History of African Americans in North Carolina.* Raleigh, NC: Raleigh Division of Archives and History, North Carolina Department of Cultural Resources, 1992.

Daugherty, J. *Abraham Lincoln.* 4th ed. New York: Viking Press, 1963.

Douglass, F. *The Life and Times of Frederick Douglass*. 1892; repr., Mineola, NY: Dover, 2003.

Douglass, Frederick. *Narrative of the Life of Frederick Douglass, an American Slave*. Edited by J. W. Blassingame, J. R. McKivigan, and P. P. Hinks. New Haven: Yale University Press, 2001.

Edwards, J. *Nat Turner's Slave Rebellion in American History*. Berkeley Heights, NJ: Enslow, 2000.

Eicher, J. H., and Eicher, D. J. *Civil War High Commands*. Stanford University Press, 2001.

Farmer, W. M., and C. A. Keen. *The Surry County, Virginia, 1776 Bicentennial Committee Guide to the Buildings of Surry and the American Revolution*. Surry, VA: Bicentennial Committee, 2007. (Originally published in 1976 by author James D. Kornwolf.)

Franklin, J. H. *The Free Negro in North Carolina 1790-1860*. Chapel Hill, NC: The University of North Carolina Press, 1943.

Frazier, E. F. *The Negro Family in the United States*. Notre Dame, IN: University of Notre Dame Press, 2001.

Freedman, R. *Lincoln: A Photobiography*. Boston: Houghton Mifflin, 1987.

French, S. *The Rebellious Slave: Nat Turner in American Memory*. Boston: Houghton Mifflin, 2004.

Garvey, A. J. *Garvey and Garveyism*. New York: Collier-Macmillan, 1963.

Garvey, M. *Selected Writings and Speeches of Marcus Garvey*. Edited by B. Blaisdell. Mineola, NY: Dover, 2004.

Goerch, C. *Down Home.* Raleigh: Edwards & Broughton, 1943.

Gregory, E. S. *Claremont Manor: A History.* Petersburg, VA: Ann and Lewis Kirby & Plummer, 1990.

Greenburg, K. S. *Nat Turner: A Slave Rebellion in History and Memory.* New York: Oxford University Press, 2003.

Gray, T. R. *The Confessions of Nat Turner, the Leader of the Late Insurrections in Southampton, Virginia.* Baltimore: Lucas & Deaver, 1831.

Harlan, L. *Booker T. Washington: The Wizard of Tuskegee, 1901–1915.* New York: Oxford University Press, 1983.

Hendrickson, A. M. *Nat Turner.* New York: Chelsea House, 1995.

Head, T. *Voices from the Civil War: Slaves.* Farmington, MI: Black Birch, 2003.

Hopper, B. *Cabin Point: The Forgotten Village.* Zuni, VA: Pearl Line, 2004.

Hopper, B. *Musings about Claremont.* Claremont, VA: Privately printed. No date.

Howard, O. O. *Autobiography of Oliver Otis Howard: Major General United States Army.* Vol, Two. New York, NY: Trow Press, 1907.

Huggins, N. I. *Slave and Citizen: The Life of Frederick Douglass.* New York: HarperCollins, 1980.

Jacobs, H. *Incidents in the Life of a Slave Girl.* Written by Herself. Published for the Author, 1861. Edited by L. M. Child. 1862; repr., New York: Literary Classics of the United States, Inc. 2000.

Johnson, F. R. *The Nat Turner Slave Insurrection*. Murfreesboro, NC: Johnson Publishing, 1966.

———. *The Nat Turner Story: History of the South's Most Important Slave Revolt, with New Material Provided by Black Tradition and White Tradition*. Murfreesboro, NC: Johnson Publishing, 1970.

Johnson, M. P., ed. *Abraham Lincoln, Slavery, and the Civil War.* Selected Writings and Speeches. Boston: St. Martin's, 2001.

Jones, A. E. *Black America Series: Hertford County North Carolina*. Charleston, SC: Arcadia Publishing, an imprint of Tempus Publishing, 2002.

Kantrowitz, S. *Ben Tillman and the Reconstruction of White Supremacy*. Chapel Hill: University of North Carolina Press, 2000.

Kornwolf, J. D. *The Surry County, Virginia, 1776 Bicentennial Committee Guide to the Buildings of Surry and the American Revolution*. 1976; repr. Surry, VA: Carolyn A. Keen & W. Michael Farmer, 2007.

Lewter, M. *Marcus Garvey, Black Nationalist Leader.* New York: Chelsea House, 2005.

Logan, R. W. *The Betrayal of the Negro from Rutherford B. Hayes to Woodrow Wilson*. 1954; repr., New York. Da Capo, 1997.

Logan. E. G. *Army of Amateurs. General Benjamin F. Butler and the Army of the James, 1863–1865*. Mechanicsburg, PA: Stackpole Books, 1997.

McKissack, P. C. and F. L. McKissack. *Rebels against Slavery: American Slave Revolts*. New York: Scholastic, 1996.

Miers, E. S. *Abraham Lincoln. In Peace and War.* New York: American Heritage, 1964.

Mohamed, P. A *Man Called Marcus: The Life and Times of the Great Leader Marcus Garvey.* Dover, MA: Majority, 2003.

Moore, R. B. *Reconstruction the promise and betrayal of democracy.* New York, N.Y: CIBC, 1983.

Morgan, L. *Abraham Lincoln: What Made Him Great.* Englewood Cliffs, NJ: Silver Burdett, 1990.

Murray, E. R. *Wake Capital County of North Carolina: Prehistory through Centennial.* Raleigh: Capital County Publishing, 1983.

Oates, S. B. *The Fires of Jubilee: Nat Turner's Fierce Rebellion.* New York: HarperCollins, 1975.

Parramore, T. C. *Murfreesboro, North Carolina, and the Roots of Nat Turner's Revolt 1820–1831.* Zebulon, NC: Theo Davis & Sons, 2004.

Peabody, F. G. *Education for Life: The Story of Hampton Institute, Told in Connection with the Fiftieth Anniversary of the Foundation of the School.* New York. Doubleday, Page, & Co., 1918.

Perkins, D., ed. *The News and Observer's Raleigh: A Living History of North Carolina.* Winston Salem, NC: J. F. Blair, 1994.

Pleasant, M. Barbee Boone. *Our Home by the Sea: An Illustrated History.* Virginia, Beach, VA: Donning, 1992.

Puryear, B. N. *Hampton Institute: A Pictorial Review of Its First Century, 1868–1968.* Hampton, VA: Prestige, 1962.

Richings, G. F. *Evidences of Progress among Colored People.* Philadelphia: Ferguson, 1903.

Russell, L. F. *Black Baptist Secondary Schools in Virginia, 1887–1957: A Study in Black History.* Metuchen, NJ: Scarecrow, 1901. Virginia Union University Archives, Richmond, VA.

Sherman, D. *History of Wesleyan Academy at Wilbraham, Massachusetts, 1817–1890.* Boston: McDonald & Gill, 1893.

Slave Narratives. Volume compilation, Notes and Chronology. Literary Classics of The United States. New York. 2000

Slave Narratives from the Federal Writer's Project, 1936–1938: North Carolina. North Carolina Slave Narratives: A Folk History of Slavery in North Carolina from Interviews of Former Slaves. Bedford, MA: Applewood Books, 2003.

Slave Narratives from the Federal Writer's Project, 1936–1938: South Carolina. South Carolina Slave Narratives: A Folk History of Slavery in South Carolina from Interviews of Former Slaves. Bedford, MA: Applewood Books, 2003.

Slave Narratives from the Federal Writer's Project, 1936–1938: Alabama. Alabama Slave Narratives: A Folk History of Slavery in Alabama from Interviews of Former Slaves. Bedford, MA: Applewood Books, 2003.

Smallwood, J. *Smallwood and Carter Connections to Family Histories and Royalty Featuring the Ancestry of Elmer Eugene Smallwood (Husband) and Jean Marie Carter (Wife).* Bowie, MD: Heritage Books, 2002.

Smallwood, M. B. *Some Colonial and Revolutionary Families of North Carolina.* Vol. 1. Macon, GA: Southern Press, 1964.

Talbot, E. A. *Samuel Chapman Armstrong: A Biographical Study.* New York, NY: Doubleday, Page & Co., 1904.

Tragle, H. I. *Nat Turner's Slave Revolt, 1831.* Kit #44. Jackdaw no. A1. New York: Grossman, 1972.

U.S. Department of the Interior, Bureau of Education. Bulletin, 1916, No. 38. *Negro education: A Study of the Private and Higher Schools for Colored People in the United States. Prepared in Cooperation with the Phelps-Stokes Fund under the Direction of Thomas Jesse Jones, Specialist in the Education of Racial Groups, Bureau of Education.* Vol. 1. 1917; repr., New York: Arno, 1969.

Vickers, J. *Raleigh City of Oaks: An Illustrated History.* Woodland Hills, CA: Windsor, 1982.

Ward, A. *The Civil War in the Words of Former Slaves: The Slaves' War.* Boston: Houghton Mifflin, 2008.

Ward, G. C. and K. Burns. *Not for Ourselves Alone: The Story of Elizabeth Cady Stanton and Susan B. Anthony.* New York: Alfred A. Knopf, 1999.

Washington, B. T. *Up From Slavery: An Autobiography.* 1901; repr., New York: Barnes & Noble, 2003.

Weaver, J. D. *The Brownsville Raid.* New York: Norton, 1970.

Woodward, C. Vann. *The Strange Career of Jim Crow.* 1955; repr., New York: Oxford University Press, 2002.

Yetman, N. R. *When I was a Slave: Memoirs from the Slave Narrative Collection.* Mineola, NY: Dover, 2002.

Archival Collections

"Abraham Lincoln Memorial Hall." Unidentified clipping. Courtesy of Hampton University Archives. Hampton University, Hampton, VA.

Annual Circular of Information of the Temperance, Industrial and Collegiate Institute. Claremont, VA, 1905–06. Hampton University Archives. Hampton, VA.

Bradley, C. D. "Controversial Ben Butler." Hampton University Archives. Hampton, VA.

The Butler School: Its Establishment and Development as a School for Freedmen. Hampton University Archives. Hampton, VA.

Catalogue of Hampton Normal and Agricultural Institute, 1870–1871. Courtesy of Hampton University Archives. Hampton University. Hampton, VA.

Certificate for Amendment to the Charter of Smallwood Memorial Institute. May 24, 1917. State Corporation Commission. Charter Book 95. The Library of Virginia, Richmond, VA.

Charter to the Smallwood-Corey Memorial Industrial and Collegiate Institute. March 22, 1921. State Corporation Commission. Charter Book 111. The Library of Virginia. Richmond, VA.

Charter to the Smallwood-Corey Memorial Industrial and Collegiate Institute. October 18, 1924. State Corporation Commission. Charter Book 129. The Library of Virginia. Richmond, VA.

Charter to the Smallwood Memorial Institute. February 7, 1913. State Corporation Commission. Charter Book 80. The Library of Virginia. Richmond, VA.

Circular of Information of the Temperance, Industrial and Collegiate Institute, 1902. Claremont, VA. Hampton University Archives. Hampton, VA.

Commonwealth Ex Rel Moore, Auditor, et al. v. Smallwood Memorial Institute. Record 381. From the Circuit Court of Surry County. Report of the Supreme Court of Virginia, November 1918–January 16, 1919. Courtesy of Virginia State Library, Richmond, VA.

Commonwealth v. Smallwood Memorial Institute. Supreme Court of Virginia. 124 Va. 142; 97 S.E. 805: 1919 Va. 17. January 16, 1919. Courtesy of Virginia State Library, Richmond, VA.

D. J. Farrar (Plaintiff), et al. v. Rosa E. Smallwood (Defendants), Executrix, etc. et als. In the Chancery Court of the City of Richmond, Virginia, April 16, 1915. Surry County Virginia. Fiduciary Account Book 4, 1909–1922. Courtesy of Surry County Courthouse, Surry County, VA.

The Educational Leader. November 1903 issue. Hampton University Archives. Hampton, VA.

First Annual Catalogue of Virginia Union University, Richmond, Virginia, Combining Wayland Seminary, Formerly of Washington, D. C., and Richmond Theological Seminary, Richmond, Virginia, 1899–1900. Richmond, VA: Virginia Baptist Press, 1903. Virginia Union University Archives, Richmond, VA.

Fisher, M. M. *Virginia University and Some of Her Achievements: Twenty-Fifth Anniversary, 1899–1924.* Richmond, VA: Virginia Union University Press, 1924. Virginia Union University Archives. Richmond, VA.

Fourth Annual Catalogue of Virginia Union University, Richmond, Virginia, Combining Wayland Seminary, Formerly of Washington, D. C., and Richmond Theological Seminary, Richmond, Virginia, 1902–1903. Richmond, VA: Virginia Baptist Press, 1903. Virginia Union University Archives, Richmond, VA.

Frederick Douglass Papers. The Library of Congress. Manuscript Division. Washington, D. C.

Hampton: From the Sea to the Stars. Hampton, VA: Donning, 1985. Hampton University Archives. Hampton, VA.

Harlan, L., and R. W. Smock, eds. *Booker T. Washington Papers*. 14 Volumes. Urbana: University of Illinois Press, 1972. http://www. historycooperative.org/btw.

Hartshorn, W. N. *An Era of Progress and Promise, 1863–1910: The Religious, Moral and Educational Development of the American Negro Since his Emancipation*. Boston: Priscilla, 1910. Virginia State University Special Collections and Archives. Virginia State University Library. Petersburg, VA.

John J. Smallwood Papers. Hampton University Archives. Hampton, VA.

"Just a Word about Lincoln Memorial Hall." Unidentified newspaper clipping. Hampton University Archives. Hampton, VA.

Ludlow, H. W. "The Evolution of the Whittier School: The Butler's Predecessor." *Southern Workman* 36 (1906): 282–291. Hampton University Archives. Hampton, VA.

Map of Smallwood-Corey Industrial Institute. Surry County Courthouse, Surry County, VA.

North Carolina State Archives. Raleigh, NC.

"Politics Brought on Texas Race War." *The Scranton Republican*. Scranton, PA. William R. and Norma Harvey Library. Hampton University. Hampton, VA.

Records of the Richmond Theological Seminary. Virginia Union University Archives. Richmond, VA.

Reynolds, M. C. *Baptist Missionary Pioneers among Negroes Sketches*. Richmond, VA, n.d. Virginia Union University Archives. Richmond, VA.

Russell, L. F. *Black Baptist Secondary Schools in Virginia, 1887–1957: A Study in Black History*. Metuchen, NJ: Scarecrow, 1901. Virginia Union University Archives. Richmond, VA.

"Seventh Annual Commencement of the Temperance, Industrial and Collegiate Institute at Claremont, Surry Co., Va.: Commencing Sunday, June 11, 1899, at 10:30 a.m. and Continuing through Wednesday, June 14th." Southern Pamphlet Collection. Rare Book Collection. Wilson Library. University of North Carolina at Chapel Hill. Chapel Hill, NC.

Shaw University, 1874–1875: Catalogue of Shaw University. Raleigh, NC: Edwards, Broughton, & Co., 1875. Archives and Special Collections. Records Management Program Department. Shaw University Archives. Raleigh, NC.

Shaw University, 1875–1882: General Catalogue of the Officers and Students of Shaw University. Raleigh, NC. Edwards, Broughton, & Co., 1882. Archives and Special Collections. Records Management Program Department. Shaw University Archives. Raleigh, NC.

Sherman, D. *History of Wesleyan Academy at Wilbraham, Massachusetts, 1817–1890*. Boston: McDonald & Gill, 1893. Wesleyan Academy at Wilbraham Archives. Boston, MA.

Smallwood, John J. "Finding My Mother." Unidentified newspaper clipping. Hampton University Archives. Hampton, VA.

The Temperance, Industrial & Collegiate Institute Catalogue, 1906–07. Claremont, VA. Hampton University Archives. Hampton, VA.

"Tribute from Governor William Hodges Mann." Unidentified newspaper clipping. Hampton University Archives. Hampton, VA.

U.S. Census Records, 1850–1930. North Carolina State Archives. Raleigh, NC. (Also accessed online at http://www.ancestry.com.)

"What the Leading Virginians Say about Dr. Smallwood and the Building of Lincoln Hall." Unidentified newspaper clipping. Hampton University Archives. Hampton, VA.

Wood, J. P. *New England Academy, Wilbraham to Wilbraham and Monson.* Brattleboro, VT: R. L. Dothard Associates, 1971. Wesleyan Academy at Wilbraham Archives. Boston, MA.

1912 Wills Book. Surry County Courthouse, Surry County, VA.

Government Documents

Death Certificate for Dr. John J. Smallwood. September 29, 1912. Certificate #6521. Bureau of Vital Statistics. Richmond, VA.

United States Passport of John Jefferson Smallwood. December 10, 1891. North Carolina State Archives, Raleigh, North Carolina.

1850 Slave Census. Northampton County, North Carolina.

1850 Slave Census. Beaufort County, North Carolina, Town of Washington.

1850 United States Census. Beaufort County, North Carolina. July 25, 1850.

1850 United States Census. Northampton County, North Carolina. August 14, 1850.

1860 Slave Census. Beaufort County, North Carolina, Washington Township.

1860 Slave Census. Northampton County, North Carolina.

1860 United States Census. Beaufort County, North Carolina, Washington Township. September 8, 1860.

1860 United States Census. Northampton County, North Carolina. District No. 10. Green Plains P. O. June 18, 1860.

1870 United States Census. Northampton County, North Carolina, Rich Square Township, Rich Square. July 21, 1870.

1880 United States Census. Halifax County, North Carolina, Roseneath Township, E. D., 128. June 9, 1880.

1880 United States Census. Northampton County, North Carolina, Rich Square Township, E. D. 186. June 30, 1880.

1900 United States Census. Northampton County, North Carolina, Rich Square Township, Rich Square Town, E.D. 73. June 1, 1900.

1900 United States Census. Surry County, Virginia, Guilford Township, E. D. 69. Temperance, Industrial and Collegiate Institute. June 6, 1900.

1920 United States Census. Richmond City, Virginia, Lee Ward, E. D. 17. January 1920.

1920 United States Census. Richmond City, Virginia, Lee Ward, E. D. 86.

1930 United States Census. Richmond City, Virginia, Madison Ward, E. D. 126. April 5, 1930.

Journals, Pamphlets, Manuscripts, Speeches

Chickenbones: *A Journal for Literary and Artistic African-American Themes* (http://www.nathanielturner.com)

Nickens, Alice J. *Memories of C. S. Brown School, Part 1.* October 1, 1986. (http://www.roanoke-chowan.com/Stories/AliceNickens/MemoriesofCSBSchool)

Southern Workman

Southern Workman and Hampton School Record

Smallwood, John J. "The Fifty-First Birthday of Lincoln." *The Monthly Advocate: The Semi-Monthly Issue* 1, no. 2 (June 13, 1896): 4.

Turner, Lucy. The Family of Nat Turner, 1831 to 1954. *Negro History Bulletin* 18 (1954-1955): 127-132.

Turner, Lucy M., and Fannie V. Turner. The Story of Nat Turner's Descendants. *Negro History Bulletin* 10 (April 1947): 155-165.

Zogry, Kenneth J. *An American Success Story: The Pope House of Raleigh, NC* (http://www.nps.gov/nr/twhp/wwwlps/lessons/124popehouse/index.htm).

Newspapers

Afro-American Churchman
Crisis
Colored American
Daily Press
Detroit Journal
Educational Appeal
Journal and Guide
The *Monthly Advocate*
National Leader
The *Negro World*
The *New York Times*
Norfolk Landmark
Portsmouth Star

Richmond Afro-American
The *Richmond Planet*
Richmond Reformer
Richmond Times-Dispatch
Richmond Virginia Times
Roanoke Weekly Press
Southern News
Southern Workman
The *Star*
True Southerner
Virginia Star
The *(Daily) Times*

Libraries

Bluford Library, North Carolina Agricultural and Technical State University, Greensboro, NC
Library of Virginia, Richmond, VA
North Regional Library, Raleigh, NC
Shepard Library, North Carolina Central University, Durham, NC
Virginia Historical Society, Richmond, VA
Surry County Historical Society, Surry County, VA
Library of Congress, Washington DC
Cameron Village Library, Raleigh, NC
Virginia State University Library, Petersburg, VA
Bostock Library, Duke University, Durham, NC
Wilson Library, University of North Carolina at Chapel Hill, Chapel Hill, NC
Surry County Library, Branch of Blackwater Original Library, Surry, VA
Northampton County Library, Jackson, NC
William R. and Norma Harvey Library, Hampton University, Hampton, VA
Hampton University Archives, Hampton, VA
Virginia State Library, Richmond, VA
Virginia Union University Archives, L. Douglas Wilder Library, Richmond, VA
University of Virginia, Charlottesville, VA
W. E. B. Du Bois Library, University of Massachusetts Amherst, Amherst, MA
Olivia Raney Library, Raleigh, NC

Photography Credits

FRONTISPIECE (background)   F. Roy Johnson, *The Nat Turner Slave Insurrection* (Murfreesboro, NC: Johnson Publishing, 1966), Front cover.

(foreground)   Image used by permission of M. D. Harrison

COVER INSERT   Map drawn by Tom Ludwig

1 (full page)   Courtesy of Willie L. Lassiter

2 (top)   Courtesy of the Library of Congress LC-USZ62-48923

2 (bottom)   Courtesy of Hampton University Archives

3 (full page)   Courtesy of Hampton University Archives

4 (full page)   Courtesy of Hampton University Archives

5 (top left)   Courtesy of Hampton University Archives

5 (top right)   Courtesy of Shaw University Archives and Special Collections

5 (bottom)   Courtesy of Shaw University Archives and Special Collections

6 (left)   Courtesy of Flora Tann-Chambliss

6 (top right)   Courtesy of Shaw University Archives and Special Collections

6 (bottom right)   Courtesy of Shaw University Archives and Special Collections

7 (top)	Courtesy of Archives Department, Wilbraham & Monson Academy, Wilbraham, MA
7 (bottom left)	Courtesy of Archives Department, Wilbraham & Monson Academy, Wilbraham, MA
7 (bottom right)	Courtesy of Archives Department, Wilbraham & Monson Academy, Wilbraham, MA
8 (top)	Courtesy of Archives Department, Wilbraham & Monson Academy, Wilbraham, MA
8 (bottom)	Courtesy of Archives Department, Wilbraham & Monson Academy, Wilbraham, MA
9 (top)	Courtesy of Archives Department, Wilbraham & Monson Academy, Wilbraham, MA
9 (bottom left)	Courtesy of Archives Department, Wilbraham & Monson Academy, Wilbraham, MA
9 (bottom right)	Courtesy of Archives Department, Wilbraham & Monson Academy, Wilbraham, MA
10 (top)	Courtesy of Flora Tann-Chambliss
10 (bottom)	Courtesy of Willie L. Lassiter
11 (full page)	Image used by permission of M. D. Harrison
12 (top)	Courtesy of Hampton University Archives
12 (bottom)	Courtesy of the Surry County Historical Society

13 (top)   Courtesy of Flora Tann-Chambliss

13 (bottom)   Courtesy of Hampton University Archives

14 (top left)   Courtesy of Hampton University Archives

14 (top right)   Courtesy of Hampton University Archives

14 (bottom)   Courtesy of Hampton University Archives

15 (top)   Courtesy of Jackson Davis Collection, Special Collections, University of Virginia Library

15 (bottom)   Image used by permission of M.D. Harrison

16 (full page)   Courtesy of Jackson Davis Collection, Special Collections, University of Virginia Library

17 (top)   Courtesy of Jackson Davis Collection, Special Collections, University of Virginia Library

17 (bottom)   Courtesy of Hampton University Archives

18 (top left)   Courtesy of Flora Tann-Chambliss

18 (top right)   Courtesy of Willie L. Lassiter

18 (bottom left)   Courtesy of Flora Tann-Chambliss

18 (bottom right)   Courtesy of Dorothy Ruffin

19 (full page)   From a copy in the Rare Book Collection, The University of North Carolina at Chapel Hill

20 (left)	Courtesy of Hampton University Archives
20 (top right)	Courtesy of the Library of Congress LC-USZ62-48334
21 (full page)	Courtesy of Hampton University
22 (full page)	Author's collection
23 (top left)	Courtesy of the Library of Congress LC-DIG-cwpbh-05089
23 top right	http://www/cayugacounty.us/history/friends/pg9p.html
23 (bottom right)	Courtesy of the Library of Congress LC-USZ62-28195
24 (full page)	[No. 407]. [W.E.B. DuBois Papers] ([MS 312]), Special Collections and University Archives, W.E.B. DuBois Library, University of Massachusetts Amherst
25 (full page)	Courtesy of the Library of Virginia
26 (full page)	Courtesy of Willie L. Lassiter
27 (top)	Courtesy of Barbara Hopper
27 (bottom)	Image used by permission of M.D. Harrison
28 (full page)	Author's collection
29 (top left)	Courtesy of Marvin T. Jones

29 (bottom)   Courtesy of Virginia Union University
                           Archives

30 (full page)   Courtesy of the *Negro World,* Bostock
                           Library, Duke University. Map drawn by
                           Tom Ludwig

31 (full page)   Courtesy of the *Negro World,* Bostock
                           Library, Duke University

32 (top)   http://www.gutenberg.org/
                           files/15041/15041-h/images/ fortune.png

32 (center)   Courtesy of the Library of Congress
                           LC-USZ61-1854

32 (bottom)   Courtesy of Virginia Union University
                           Archives

33 (top)   Courtesy of Willie L. Lassiter

33 (bottom)   Courtesy of Dr. Genora Lassiter-Shaw

34 (top left)   Courtesy of Joyce Lawrence

34 (bottom left)   Courtesy of Flora Tann-Chambliss

34 (top right)   Courtesy of Joyce Lawrence

34 (bottom right)   Courtesy of Clarence Lassiter

35 (Back cover)   Courtesy of Jackson Davis Collection,
                           Special Collections, University of Virginia
                           Library

ENDNOTES

Notes to Introduction

1 On July 13, 2010, the Marker Editorial Committee of the Department of Historic Resources, Richmond, Virginia, approved to erect a historical highway marker on Route 10 in Surry County, Virginia, to commemorate Dr. Smallwood's life and works as founder and president of Temperance, Industrial and Collegiate Institute.

2. From a speech delivered by Dr. Smallwood to commemorate the fifty-first anniversary of Abraham Lincoln's birth, later published in the June 13, 1896 issue of the *Monthly Advocate.*

3. "Temperance and Morality, Industry and Economy, Intelligence and Race Pride: Love for the Home and Country makes a nation its own Controlling Power" was the motto of the *Monthly Advocate,* the semimonthly campus newspaper of the Temperance, Industrial and Collegiate Institute.

4. Dr. John J. Smallwood to Rev. Dr. H. B. Frissell, Principal of the Hampton Normal and Agricultural Institute, December 26, 1903, John J. Smallwood Papers, Hampton University Archives, Hampton, VA, p. 2 (hereafter cited as Letter: Dr. Smallwood to Dr. Frissell).

Notes to Chapter One

1. S. G. Baugham, *The Town of Rich Square: A History, 1717–1983* (Rich Square, NC: privately printed, 1983), 1. Before white settlers migrated to the area, Native Americans, predominantly the Meherrin tribe, had long inhabited the land that came to be known as Northampton County. Their settlements varied in size as well as custom, although each had its own leader

or head man. Like their English neighbors, the native inhabitants survived mainly on hunting, fishing, and farming. For more on the native inhabitants of Northampton County, see *Footprints in Northampton 1741–1776–1976: Northampton County Bicentennial Committee* (Jackson, NC: Northampton County Bicentennial Committee, 1976), 6.

2. D. L. Corbitt, *The Formation of the North Carolina Counties, 1663–1943*, 5th ed. (Raleigh: North Carolina State Department of Archives and History, 1996), xvii, xviii, xxvii, 26, 123, 163–166, 215.

3. Baugham, *Rich Square*, 1.

4. *Footprints in Northampton*, 5. According to David L Corbitt, Northampton County was named for James Compton, Earl of Northampton, not George, Earl of Northampton (*Formation of North Carolina Counties*, xxvii).

5. Baugham, *Rich Square*, 3; *Footprints in Northampton*, 4.

6. T. Bisson, *Nat Turner: Slave Revolt Leader* (New York: Chelsea House, 1988), 23.

7. Roy F. Johnson, *The Nat Turner Story: History of the South's Most Important Slave Revolt, with New Material Provided by Black Tradition and White Tradition* (Murfreesboro, NC: Johnson Publishing, 1970), 29; Bisson, *Nat Turner*, 21.

8. Rudolph Lewis, "The Uncertain Identity of Nathaniel Turner: The Scholars Debate," *ChickenBones: A Journal for Literary and Artistic African-American Themes*, http://www.nathanielturner.com/uncertainidentity.htm.

9. Bisson, *Nat Turner*, 23; see also Lewis, "Uncertain Identity."

10. M. B. Smallwood, *Some Colonial and Revolutionary Families of North Carolina*, vol. 1 (Macon, GA: Southern Press, 1964), 415–444. In 1632, the Smallwood patriarch, Matthew Smallwood, lived in Virginia, where, in 1639, his son James (later a colonel in the British army) was the first of the Smallwood line to be born in the New World. By 1664, James had relocated to Charles County, Maryland. In 1680, James's son Prior (or Pryor) was born. Prior Smallwood, who also resided in Maryland, had five children. One of his sons was named James Smallwood. This James Smallwood later had a son named Charles Smallwood, born around 1755/1765. By 1790, Charles had married Sally Smaw, and the couple moved to Beaufort County, North Carolina. During this time, the Smallwood family was prospering across three states: William Smallwood, a cousin of Charles Smallwood, who had served as a Revolutionary War officer and was a friend of George

Washington, was about to become the fourth governor of Maryland, a position he held from 1785 to 1788. By 1800, Charles and Sally, still residing in Beaufort County, North Carolina, lived on the west side of Bath Creek about halfway between the town of Bath and the Pamlico River. Their family consisted of four sons—Erusties, John Smaw, Marcus W., and Samuel Smaw—and one girl named Rebecca. They also owned seven slaves. By 1810, Charles Smallwood owned fifteen slaves, and Sally had borne two more sons, Thomas and T. T. Piladese.

11. Smallwood, *Some Colonial and Revolutionary Families*, 415–444.

12. Baugham, *Rich Square*, 1. In 1717, Timothy Cunningham of Albemarle County, Chowan Precinct, was the first English settler to purchase the 640-acre parcel of land. Soon after his purchase, in 1724, Cunningham sold the tract to one Edward Howcott, Chowan precinct. Only one year later, Howcott turned over the parcel again, to John Perry of Nansemond County, Virginia. In 1737, the land—now known as the Rich Square—was sold yet again, this time to Isaac Hunter of Chowan Precinct. In 1753, Hunter sold 100 acres of the original Rich Square tract to one David Rice; later, in 1759, Hunter sold a single additional acre to Quakers for a Meeting House. He willed the remaining 539 acres of the Rich Square land to his son Demcy in 1761, but it was soon thereafter deeded to another son, Thomas. In 1766, Thomas Hunter sold the entire 539 acres to Marmaduke Norfleet of Bertie County. Norfleet, in turn, willed the Rich Square plantation to his daughter, Sarah Jeffries, who inherited it upon his death in 1777. Rice later sold his 100-acre portion to a man named Stephen Josey.

13. Baugham, *Rich Square*, 1–5. In 1815, Sarah Jeffries sold the 539-acre plantation in one parcel to her son, Anson Jeffries, who later sold it intact to a man named Bryan Randolph in 1821. Upon Randolph's death in 1838, his wife and four children inherited the plantation, but Mrs. Randolph and two of her children died a short time later. Eventually, the last surviving Randolph son divided the 539 acres and began to sell off the pieces. Most of them were purchased and reconsolidated by Marcus W. Smallwood.

14. Baugham, *Rich Square*, 1–5. Northampton County maps of the 1820s identify the Rich Square plantation variously as "the Randolph's" and (by 1830) "the square." However, the 100-acre portion of Rich Square that had been purchased by Stephen Josey in the early 1750s is also labeled on these

maps as "the square." In 1817, the only house standing on Josey's portion of Rich Square was his own home.

15. Smallwood, *Some Colonial and Revolutionary Families*, 448. C. Goerch, *Down Home* (Raleigh, NC: Edwards & Broughton, 1943), 319, suggests that the name of the town derived from the fact that Marcus W. Smallwood owned most of the land in the area: since local townspeople often referred to Smallwood as the "rich squire," his land came to be known as the Rich Square.

16. Baugham, *Rich Square*, 5.

17. *Footprints in Northampton*, 133.

18. *Footprints in Northampton*, 115.

19. On Marcus Smallwood's various occupations, see, e.g.: 1860 United States Census, Northampton County, NC, District No. 10, 18 June 1860 (accessed online at http://www.ancestry.com); *Footprints in Northampton*, 32; Baugham, *Rich Square*, 5.

20. Goerch, *Down Home*, 319. See also Smallwood, *Some Colonial and Revolutionary Families*, 448.

21. Smallwood, *Some Colonial and Revolutionary Families*, 448.

22. Smallwood, *Some Colonial and Revolutionary Families*, 451.

23. 1850 United States Census, Beaufort County, NC, July 25, 1850, p. 340 (accessed online at http://www.ancestry.com).

24. Smallwood, *Some Colonial and Revolutionary Families*, 468.

25. 1850 United States Census, Beaufort County, NC, July 25, 1850, p. 340. (accessed online at http.www.ancestry.com).

26. 1860 United States Federal Census, Slave Schedule, Bertie County, NC, July 7, 1860, p. 59 (accessed online at http://www.ancestry.com).

27. Bisson, *Nat Turner*, 15.

28. J. Edwards, *Nat Turner's Slave Rebellion in American History* (Berkeley Heights, NJ: Enslow, 2000), 35. An article printed in the *Times* in Richmond, VA, in 1891 stated that Turner "was gifted with uncommon intelligence, was the favorite of his master" ("Turner's Insurrection: Sequel to that Bloody Event of Virginia History," The *Times* [Richmond, VA], February 18, 1891).

29. T. Gray, *The Confessions of Nat Turner, the Leader of the Late Insurrections in Southampton, VA* (Baltimore: Lucas & Deaver, 1831), 9.

30. Gray, *Confessions*, 7–11.

31. T. C. Parramore, *Murfreesboro, North Carolina, and the Roots of Nat Turner's Revolt, 1820–1831* (Zebulon, NC: Theo Davis & Sons, 2004), 59.

32. Gray, *Confessions*, 9.

33. Gray, *Confessions*, 11.

34. Edwards, *Nat Turner's Slave Rebellion*, 48.

35. Parramore, *Murfreesboro*, 59.

36. Bisson, *Nat Turner*, 56–57.

37. Edwards, *Nat Turner's Slave Rebellion*, 37.

38. Bisson, *Nat Turner*, 55.

39. Edwards, *Nat Turner's Slave Rebellion*, 34.

40. Bisson, *Nat Turner*, 55; Edwards, *Nat Turner's Slave Rebellion*, 48.

41. Parramore, *Murfreesboro*, 60.

42. Bisson, *Nat Turner*, 13.

43. Edwards, *Nat Turner's Slave Rebellion*, 49.

44. Bisson, *Nat Turner*, 62.

45. Edwards, *Nat Turner's Slave Rebellion*, 52.

46. Bisson, *Nat Turner*, 63.

47. Bisson, *Nat Turner*, 62.

48. Bisson, *Nat Turner*, 11.

49. Bisson, *Nat Turner*, 11, 39.

50. Edwards, *Nat Turner's Slave Rebellion*, 53, 59.

51. H. I. Tragle, Nat Turner's Slave Revolt, 1831, Kit #44, Jackdaw no. A1 (New York: Grossman, 1972); Bisson, 75.

52. Edwards, *Nat Turner's Slave Rebellion*, 67.

53. Tragle, *Nat Turner's Slave Revolt*.

54. Johnson, *The Nat Turner Story*, 111n.50; Parramore, *Murfreesboro*, 60, 51.

55. Parramore, *Murfreesboro*, 60.

56. Parramore, *Murfreesboro*, 60–63.

57. Parramore, *Murfreesboro*, 61.

58. Parramore, *Murfreesboro*, 64.

59. Parramore, *Murfreesboro*, 61.

60. Edwards, *Nat Turner's Slave Rebellion*, 61; Tragle, *Nat Turner's Slave Revolt*.

61. Edwards, *Nat Turner's Slave Rebellion*, 62, 66.

62. A. M. Hendrickson, *Nat Turner* (New York: Chelsea House, 1995), 54.

63. Hendrickson, *Nat Turner*, 56, 57.

64. "Turner's Insurrection: Sequel to that Bloody Event of Virginia History," the *Times* (Richmond, VA), February 18, 1891.

65. Parramore, *Murfreesboro*, 63.

66. Bisson, *Nat Turner*, 105.

67. Johnson, *Nat Turner Story*, 188.

68. Johnson, *Nat Turner Story*, 188.

69. Bisson, *Nat Turner*, 104.

70. "Turner's Insurrection: Sequel to that Bloody Event of Virginia History," the *Times* (Richmond, VA), February 18, 1891.

71. L. Bennett, Jr. *Before the Mayflower: A History of Black America, 6th Edition* (New York: Johnson Publishing Co., 1987), 139.

72. S. B. Oates, *The Fires of Jubilee: Nat Turner's Fierce Rebellion* (New York: HarperCollins, 1975), 126; Bisson, *Nat Turner*, 105; Lucy M. Turner, "The Family of Nat Turner, 1831 to 1954," *Negro History Bulletin* 18, (1954-1955): 127-132; Lucy M. Turner and Fannie V. Turner, "The Story of Nat Turner's Descendants," *Negro History Bulletin* 10, (1946-47): 155-165.

Notes to Chapter Two

1. Bruce Lawrence Turner, interview by Mary E. C. Drew, October 2008, Southampton County, VA. In my search for any documented information that could support Dr. Smallwood's claim to be the grandson of Nat Turner, I interviewed Bruce Lawrence Turner, who claims to be the great-great-great-grandson of Nat Turner. In Mr. Turner's records of his family tree, he had a sheet of paper on which he had written this description of Nat Turner's daughter.

2. 1850 United States Federal Slave Census Report, Northampton County, North Carolina (accessed online at http://www.ancestry.com).

3. 1850 United States Federal Slave Census Report, Northampton County, North Carolina (accessed online at http://www.ancestry.com). William was later killed in the Civil War, along with the husband of his sister, Martha Indiana Josey (Baugham, *Rich Square*, 7–8).

4. Baugham, *Rich Square*, 3–4.

5. 1850 United States Federal Slave Census Report, Northampton County, North Carolina (accessed online at http://www.ancestry.com).

6. J. Carver-Hardie, *Bishop-Josey Family Reunion. 25–27 July 2008*. Courtesy of Joanne Carver-Hardie. Oral family records indicate that Oscar Josey was the slave son of Stephen Josey, who bequeathed to his wife, Martha, three slaves, one of whom was Oscar Josey's mother, Venus (Stephen Josey Will, in *Will Book 3*, Northampton County, NC, October 17, 1823, p. 291). Oscar Josey married Emma Smallwood, daughter of Mary Eliza Smallwood and sister to John Jefferson Smallwood.

7. Baugham, *Rich Square*, 31; *Footprints in Northampton*, 123.

8. Baugham, *Rich Square*, 31.

9. Baugham, *Rich Square*, 16.

10. Norwood was elected mayor "along with four town commissioners: Everette Baugham, J. W. Baxton, L. J. Davis, and Watkins Roberts, a black man" (*Footprints in Northampton*, 114).

11. 1860 United States Federal Slave Census Report, Northampton County, North Carolina, district no. 10, Green Plains, PO June 18, 1869, dwelling #563, family #563, line 10, p. 35A (accessed online at http://www.ancestry.com).

12. Willie L. Lassiter (niece to Dr. Smallwood), interview by Mary E. C. Drew, June 9, 2007, Philadelphia, PA.

13. 1900 United States Census, Rich Square Town, Rich Square, Northampton County, NC (accessed online at http://www.ancestry.com).

14. W. W. Brown, *The Narrative of William Wells Brown: A Fugitive Slave* (Reading, MA: Addison-Wesley, 2002).

15. Willie L. Lassiter (niece to Dr. Smallwood), interview by Mary E. C. Drew, June 9, 2007, Philadelphia, PA.

16. 1900 United States Census, Rich Square Town, Rich Square, Northampton County, NC (accessed online at http://www.ancsetry.com).

17. On January 9, 1932, The *Afro-American* newspaper published an article entitled "Nat Turner, Va. Slave Hero, Has 7 Living Grandchildren." The article listed the names of Nat Turner's grandchildren as follows: one grandson, John R. Jones (Deweyville, VA); six grand-daughters, Charity Lockley and Mittie Whitfield (Washington, D.C.), Mason Dean (Franklin, VA), Mary E. Jones and Margaret Jones (Capron, VA), and Ella Coleman (Newport News, VA). Another article obtained in 2007 from a descendant of Nat Turner in Baltimore, Maryland, referred to the Rev. John W. Jones as a great grandson of Nat Turner. Jones was pastor of Ebenezer Baptist Church

in Baltimore and a leading figure in the organization of Clayton Williams University (now extinct) in 1902. He later organized the Williams-Jones Institute in 1923 and served as its president until his death in December 1931. Rev. Jones's father was named Thomas Jones. Interestingly, the names of three of Nat Turner's grandchildren who were listed as residing in Virginia (Thomas, John R, and Mary E.) are very similar to the names of three of the children who were either sold with their mother, Mary Eliza (Bryant or Smallwood), into Northampton County, North Carolina, or were born after she arrived: Thomas, John J., and Mary Eliza. In the 1800s, it was common practice for a mother who had lost a child—or, in Mary Eliza's case, several children—to name another child after the one she had lost. It is also possible that, prior to Mary Eliza's purchase by the Bryant family of North Carolina, she could have belonged to a Jones family in Virginia.

18. 1900 United States Census, Rich Square Town, Rich Square, Northampton County, NC; Russell Lassiter (nephew to Dr. Smallwood), interview by Maudie Chambers (great-great-niece to Dr. Smallwood), 1984, Woodland, NC; "Smallwood-Lassiter Family Tree," interview with Flora Tann-Chambliss (great-niece to Dr. Smallwood), interview by Mary E. C. Drew, October 2007, Cairo, IL. The 1900 census lists Elizabeth "Betty" Smallwood's birth date as 1859, but family records indicate her birth year as 1858.

19. 1900 United States Census, Rich Square Town, Rich Square, Northampton County, NC.

20. C. Vann Woodard, *The Strange Career of Jim Crow* (1955; repr., New York: Oxford University Press, 2002), 16.; see also http://www.spartacus. schoolnet.co.uk/USA.mulatoo.htm.

21. Elaine Tann, "Smallwood Family Tree (1991)," courtesy of Flora Tann-Chambliss; Dr. Gloria Williams, interview by Mary E. C. Drew, descendant of Dr. Smallwood, March 2008, Austin, TX.

22. 1850 United States Federal Slave Census Report, Northampton County, North Carolina (accessed online at http://www.ancestry.com).

23. *Footprints in Northampton*, 133. "Bryant" is often spelled as "Bryan." Around the mid-1800s, several land transactions occurred between Marcus W. Smallwood and some of the Bryans/Bryants who resided on Bryantown Road. In 1848, Marcus W. Smallwood sold land to a Miles Bryan (Northampton County, NC, Deed Book 32, p 355), and in 1849 he sold land to a Harrison Bryant (Northampton County, NC, Deed Book

33, p 176). In 1850, Harrison Bryant (b. 1824) lived fourteen houses to the west of Marcus W. Smallwood and Martha Josey (1850 United States Census). Ten houses to the east of Marcus W. Smallwood lived another Bryant, Willie Bryant (b. 1825) (1850 United States Census). A little farther down Bryantown Road lived several families of Bryants (1850 United States Census).

24. United States Passport of Dr. John Jefferson Smallwood, December 10, 1891, Virginia Bureau of Vital Statistics and Marriages. Prior to becoming the property of Marcus W. Smallwood, it is possible that, because of the surname of Lawrence, David (slave husband of John Jefferson's mother, Mary Eliza) was perhaps the property of a Lawrence family. He is listed as "David Lawrence" in some records and as "David Smallwood" in others.

25. *North Carolina Slave Narratives: A Folk History of Slavery in North Carolina from Interviews with Former Slaves—Typewritten Records Prepared by the Federal Writers' Project, 1936–1938* (Bedford, MA: Applewood Books, 2003), 133–134.

26. Brown, *Narrative of William Wells Brown*, 15, 52.

27. Letter: Dr. Smallwood to Dr. Frissell.

28. William and Ellen Craft, *Running a Thousand Miles for Freedom: Slave Narratives* (1860; repr., London: William Tweedie, 2000), 337.

29. H. Jacobs, *Slave Narratives: Incidents In the Life of a Slave Girl*, ed. L. Maria Child (1861; repr., New York: Literary Classics of the United States, 2000), 760.

30. Brown, *The Narrative of William Wells Brown*, 50.

31. Brown, *The Narrative of William Wells Brown*, 50.

32. Willie L. Lassiter (niece to Dr. Smallwood), interview by Mary E. C. Drew, June 9, 2007, Philadelphia, PA.

33. Letter: Dr. Smallwood to Dr. Frissell.

34. Russell Lassiter (nephew to Dr. Smallwood), interview by Mary E. C. Drew, 1984, Northampton County, NC; Willie L. Lassiter (niece to Dr. Smallwood), interview by Mary E. C. Drew, June 9, 2007, Philadelphia, PA.

35. United States Passport of Dr. John Jefferson Smallwood, December 10, 1891, Virginia Bureau of Vital Statistics and Marriages; and letter: Dr. Smallwood to Dr. Frissell.

36. Frederick Douglass, *Narrative of the Life of Frederick Douglass, An American Slave*, ed. J. W. Blassingame, J. R. McKivigan, and P. P. Hinks (New Haven: Yale University Press, 2001), 48.
37. "Finding My Mother," article written by Dr. John Jefferson Smallwood to an unidentified newspaper. Courtesy of Hampton University Archives, Hampton, VA.

Notes to Chapter Three

1. Interview with Andrew Boone, ex-slave, Northampton County, NC, in *A Folk History of Slavery in North Carolina*, 136–137.
2. E. S. Miers, *Abraham Lincoln. In Peace and War* (New York: American Heritage, 1964), 120.
3. Miers, *Abraham Lincoln*, 122.
4. *Population of the United States in 1860, Compiled from the Original Returns of the Eighth Census, Under the Direction of the Secretary of the Interior by Joseph C. G. Kennedy, Superintendent of Census* (1864; repr., New York: Norman, 1990).
5. 1860 United States Census, Northampton County, North Carolina; *The History of Rich Square Baptist Church*, Rich Square, North Carolina, obtained from Northampton County Museum, Jackson, NC.
6. *Footprints in Northampton*, 4.
7. J. J. Crow, P. D. Escott, and F. J. Hatley, *A History of African Americans in North Carolina* (Raleigh, NC: Raleigh Division of Archives and History, North Carolina Department of Cultural Resources, 1992), 53.
8. *Footprints in Northampton*, 4.
9. Interview with Andrew Boone, ex-slave, Northampton County, NC, in *A Folk History of Slavery in North Carolina*, 136–137.
10. Crow, Escott, and Hatley, *A History of African Americans in North Carolina*, 63.
11. Interview with Andrew Boone, ex-slave, Northampton County, NC, in *A Folk History of Slavery in North Carolina*, 133.
12. Interview with Andrew Boone, ex-slave, Northampton County, NC, in *A Folk History of Slavery in North Carolina*, 134.
13. T. C. Parramore, "The Burning of Winton," *Hertford County, NC, Summer 2008 Visitor's Guide* 1, no. 1 (July 2008): 42–43; excerpted from T. C.

Parramore, "The Burning of Winton in 1862," *The North Carolina Historical Review* (Winter 1962): 18–31.

14. *Footprints in Northampton*, 38.

15. Boone's Mill is located between Jackson, NC, and Verona, NC; Ransom's troops were on the road to Weldon, North Carolina, when they stopped at Boone's Mill. For more on the locations of the battle, see, e.g., http://www.historicjacksonnc.com/jackson_nc_history.php.

16. *Footprints in Northampton*, 38.

17. On Lincoln's appointment of Grant, see, e.g., L. Morgan. *Abraham Lincoln: What Made Him Great* (Englewood Cliffs, NJ: Silver Burdett, 1990), 67; R. Freedman, *Lincoln: A Photobiography* (Boston: Houghton Mifflin, 1987), 107.

18. Freedman. *Lincoln: A Photobiography*, 107.

19. Freedman, *Lincoln: A Photobiography*, 111.

20. Morgan, *Abraham Lincoln*, 70.

21. Freedman, *Lincoln: A Photobiography*, 112.

22. Freedman, *Lincoln: A Photobiography*, 115.

23. *Footprints in Northampton*, 36.

24. *Footprints in Northampton*, 39.

25. *Footprints in Northampton*, 38.

26. Willie L. Lassiter (niece to Dr. Smallwood), interview by Mary E.C. Drew, June 9, 2007, Philadelphia, PA

27. Interview with Andrew Boone, ex-slave, Northampton County, NC, in *A Folk History of Slavery in North Carolina*, 136.

28. Willie L. Lassiter (niece to Dr. Smallwood), interview by Mary E.C. Drew, June 9, 2007, Philadelphia, PA

29. Willie L. Lassiter (niece to Dr. Smallwood), interview by Mary E.C. Drew, June 9, 2007, Philadelphia, PA.

30. Willie L. Lassiter (niece to Dr. Smallwood), interview by Mary E C Drew, June 9, 2007, Philadelphia, PA

31. Willie L Lassiter (niece to Dr. Smallwood), interview by Mary E.C. Drew, June 9, 207, Philadelphia, PA

Notes to Chapter Four

1. Letter: Dr. Smallwood to Dr. Frissell. In June 1870, as soon as Hampton Normal and Agricultural Institute received its charter, the American

Missionary Association turned full ownership of the Butler School over to
General Armstrong and the board of trustees. In 1930, the name Hampton
Normal and Agriculture Institute was changed to Hampton Institute, and
in 1984, the name was changed to Hampton University. M. Barbee Boone
Pleasant, *Our Home by the Sea: An Illustrated History* (Virginia Beach,
VA: Donning, 1992), 9.

2. B. T. Washington, *Up From Slavery: An Autobiography* (1901; repr., New
York: Barnes & Noble, 2003), 26.
3. Washington. *Up from Slavery*, 24.
4. On Butler and his role in forming the Butler school, see L. Bennett Jr., *Before
the Mayflower: A History of the Negro in America, 1619–1964* (Baltimore,
MD: Penguin, 1966), 167–168; and "The Butler School: Its Establishment
and Development as a School for Freedmen," research paper in the Hampton
University Archives, Hampton, VA, pp. 11, 20–22.
5. "Butler School," 20–22.
6. C. D. Bradley, "Controversial Ben Butler," the Casement Papers, Fortress
Monroe, VA, p. 1. Courtesy of Hampton University Archives, Hampton, VA.
7. "Butler School," 20–22.
8. Bradley, "Controversial Ben Butler," 1.
9. "Butler School," 20–22.
10. Bradley, "Controversial Ben Butler," 1.
11. "Butler School," 20–22.
12. Bennett, Jr., *Before the Mayflower*, 167–168.
13. Bradley, "Controversial Ben Butler," 1.
14. Bennett, *Before the Mayflower*, 167–168.
15. Bradley, "Controversial Ben Butler," 4.
16. "Butler School," 18.
17. "Butler School," 20–22.
18. "Butler School," 23–26.
19. "Butler School," 23–24.
20. Bradley, "Controversial Ben Butler," 1-2
21. "Benjamin Franklin Butler (politician)" http://en.wikipedia.org/wiki/
Benjamin_Franklin_Butler_(politician). Retrieved March 15, 2010.
22. "Butler School," 26.
23. "Butler School," 11.
24. Pleasant, *Our Home by the Sea*, 24.

25. "Butler School," 12.

26. *Hampton: From the Seas to the Stars* (Hampton, VA: Donning, 1985), 98.

27. Pleasant, *Our Home by the Sea*, 24.

28. "Butler School," 11.

29. *Hampton: From the Seas to the Stars*, 98–101.

30. "Butler School," 11.

31. "Butler School," 18.

32. Bradley, "Controversial Ben Butler," 4.

33. Bradley, "Controversial Ben Butler," 5.

34. *Hampton: From the Seas to the Stars*, 98. Oliver Otis Howard was born on November 8, 1830, in Leeds, Maine. He was a career United States Army officer and a Union general in the American Civil War. He is credited for his role in founding Howard University where he served as president from 1869 to 1874. He died in Burlington, Vermont, on October 26, 1909.

35. *Hampton: From the Seas to the Stars*, 101.

36. H. W. Ludlow, "The Evolution of the Whittier School: The Butler's Predecessor," *Southern Workman* 36 (1906): 288.

37. J. H. Eicher and D. J. Eicher, *Civil War High Commands*, (2001; Stanford: CA: Stanford University Press), 306.

38. "Early Years," (http://en.wikipedia.org/wiki/Oliver O. Howard). Retrieved March 11, 2010.

39. "Law Creating the Freedmen's Bureau" (http://www.history.umd.edu/Freedmen/fbact.htm). Retrieved March 12, 2010.

40. "Freedman" (http://en.wikipedia.org/wiki/Freedman). Retrieved March 11, 2010.

41. R. B. Moore, *Reconstruction: the promise and betrayal of democracy*. (1983; New York, N.Y.: The Council on Interracial Books for Children), 11-30.

42. O. O. Howard. *Autobiography of Oliver Otis Howard: Major General United States Army*, Volume Two. (1907; New York, N.Y.: The Baker & Taylor Co., 1908; Trow Press), 375.

43. W. E. B. DuBois, *"The Freedmen's Bureau"*, (1901: *Atlantic Monthly 87*.) http://history.eserver.org/freedmens-bureau.txt. 354-365. Retrieved 2010-03-12.

44. Moore, *Reconstruction: The Promise and Betrayal of Democracy*, 17.

45. W. E. B. DuBois, *"The Freedmen's Bureau."* (1901: *Atlantic Monthly 87*). 354–365. http://history.eserver.org/freedmens-bureau.txt. Retrieved March 12, 2010.

46. Howard, *The Autobiography of Oliver Otis Howard: Major General United States Army*, 394–397.

47. *Hampton: From the Seas to the Stars*, 101.

48. Pleasant, *Our Home by the Sea*, 24.

49. Pleasant, *Our Home by the Sea*, 16–17.

50. Pleasant, *Our Home by the Sea*, 17.

51. Pleasant, *Our Home by the Sea*, 23.

52. *Hampton: From the Seas to the Stars*, 101.

53. Pleasant, *Our Home by the Sea*, 23.

54. *Hampton: From the Seas to the Stars*, 101; Ludlow, "Evolution of the Whittier School," 288.

55. Pleasant, *Our Home by the Sea*, 9.

56. Ludlow, "Evolution of the Whittier School," 288.

57. Washington, *Up from Slavery*, 24.

58. Ludlow, "Evolution of the Whittier School," 288. For the opening date of the fall 1870 term, see the *Catalogue of the Hampton Normal and Agricultural Institute, Hampton, Virginia 1870–1871*, Hampton University Archives, Hampton, VA, p. 12.

59. *Catalogue of the Hampton Normal and Agricultural Institute*, 3.

60. "Butler School," 26.

61. *Hampton: From the Seas to the Stars*, 98.

62. *Catalogue of the Hampton Normal and Agricultural Institute*, 4.

63. *Catalogue of the Hampton Normal and Agricultural Institute*, 14.

64. *Catalogue of the Hampton Normal and Agricultural Institute*, 4.

65. Pleasant, *Our Home by the Sea*, 24.

66. Baugham, *Rich Square*, 7.

67. Sale of Marcus W. Smallwood's lands by Sheriff Kadar Biggs on July 14, 1868, recorded May 14, 1875, Northampton County, Jackson, NC, Northampton County Deeds, Book 96, p. 518.

68. Willie L. Lassiter (niece to Dr. Smallwood), interview by Mary E. C. Drew, June 9, 2007, Philadelphia, PA. Mrs. Lassiter is the daughter of Mary Eliza Smallwood-Lassiter and the granddaughter of Marcus W. Smallwood.

69. Baugham, *Rich Square*, 6. Marcus W. Smallwood died in 1870 and was buried in a field belonging to Martha Josey on Bryantown Road in Rich Square, North Carolina.

70. Letter: Dr. Smallwood to Dr. Frissell. After providing an education for some five thousand freedmen, the Butler School served the community for twenty-five years (*Butler School*, 27). The Butler School closed in 1887 and was succeeded by the Whittier School, which was erected in 1887 and opened its doors on November 23, 1889 (Pleasant, *Our Home by the Sea*, 24). General Armstrong died on May 11, 1893, after having served as principal of Hampton Normal and Agricultural Institute for twenty-five years (Pleasant, *Our Home by the Sea*, 18). Dr. Hollis Burke Frissell succeeded him as principal in 1893 (*Hampton: From the Sea to the Stars*, 102).

71. Ludlow, "Evolution of the Whittier School. 288.

Notes to Chapter Five

1. Letter: Dr. Smallwood to Dr. Frissell, 2. In the letter, John J. Smallwood states that, in the fall of 1876, he went to Shaw University under the Rev. Dr. H. M. Tupper; however, in the Shaw University catalogue of 1874–1875, he is listed as a student in the preparatory department (p. 11); therefore, he must have entered Shaw in the fall of 1875.

2. Letter: Dr. Smallwood to Dr. Frissell, 2.

3. Bradshaw Vinson (great-great-nephew to Dr. Smallwood), interview by Mary E. C. Drew, April 2008, Northampton County, NC.

4. Letter: Dr. Smallwood to Dr. Frissell, 2. In the early nineteenth century, Noah Webster (1758-1843) compiled a dictionary that became the standard for American English. Revised several times, in 1786 the book was called *The American Spelling Book*, and in 1829 it was changed to *The Elementary Spelling Book*. Dr. Smallwood referred to this book as the *Old Webster Spelling Book*. http://en.wikipedia.org/wiki/Noah_Webster. Retrieved May 15, 2010.

5. Willie L. Lassiter (niece to Dr. Smallwood), interview by Mary E. C. Drew, August 2007, Philadelphia, PA.

6. Letter: Dr. Smallwood to Dr. Frissell, 2. Southampton County, Virginia, is located in the southeastern part of Virginia along the North Carolina border. The town of Franklin, Virginia, located in Southampton County, was developed in the early 1840s as a result of the railroad's bringing

commerce and people to the area. The railroad arrived in 1835 and bridged the Blackwater and Nottoway rivers with the Portsmouth and Roanoke Railroad, extending its line across the county. Franklin was chartered as an independent city in 1960. http://www.southamptoncounty.org/history.asp.

7. Letter: Dr. Smallwood to Dr. Frissell, 2.

8. O.O. Howard, *Autobiography of Oliver Otis Howard: Major General United States Army,* Volume Two. (New York, NY: the Trow Press, 1907), 262.

9. D. Perkins (ed.), *The News and Observer's Raleigh: A Living History of North Carolina's Capital* (Winston Salem, NC: J. F. Blair, 1994), 83.

10. W. A. Carter, *Shaw's Universe: A Monument to Educational Innovation* (Rockville, MD: D. C. National, 1973), 2. Dr. Tupper was born April 11, 1831, in Monson, Massachusetts. His academic career included attendance at Monson Academy (1855), Amherst College (1859) and Newton Theological Seminary (1862). After having enlisted to serve in the Union Army in July 1862, he received an honorable discharge on July 14, 1865 (Carter, *Shaw's Universe,* 1–2). Even as a boy, Dr. Tupper had definite convictions on slavery. He was converted while a student at Monson Academy and was ordained a few days after he had enlisted as a soldier in the army. His association with colored youths stemmed from his college days where he was employed as a Sunday school missionary by the Dudley Street Baptist Church of Boston. Whatever the reasons for his commitment to educating the colored people of the South, Dr. Tupper incessantly solicited philanthropic efforts from friends and in-laws to build an institution for ex-slaves after the Civil War (Carter, *Shaw's Universe,* 26).

11. Perkins, *News and Observer's Raleigh,* 84.

12. Carter, *Shaw's Universe,* 2.

13. Carter, *Shaw's Universe,* 2.

14. E. Reid Murray, *Wake, Capital County of North Carolina: Prehistory through Centennial,* vol. 1 (Raleigh, NC: Capital County, 1983), 611.

15. Carter, *Shaw's Universe,* 2.

16. Carter, *Shaw's Universe,* 23.

17. Carter, *Shaw's Universe,* 3.

18. Carter, *Shaw's Universe,* 26. The South Street estate of Daniel Barringer, former United States Minister to Spain, was purchased on May 3, 1870, and used as Shaw's campus. (E. R. Murray, *Wake Capital County of North Carolina: Prehistory through Centennial* [Raleigh, NC: Capital County

Publishing, 1983], 611.) As a result of fundraisers implemented by Dr. Tupper, philanthropic contributions were made by the Freedmen's Bureau, Tupper's friends, and other New Englanders, including Elijah Shaw of Wales, Massachusetts, whose name the university bears.

19. Carter, *Shaw's Universe*, 23. Shaw's students made bricks out of clay dug from the property, and the building was constructed out of these homemade bricks. Shaw Hall was erected on the same site where Dr. Tupper and his wife once hid from a lynch mob after he purchased the Barringer estate (Perkins, *News and Observer's Raleigh*, 84). It was also the same site where, during the closing months of the Civil War, Generals Grant and Sherman discussed terms of surrender with General Johnston's Confederate forces (Carter, *Shaw's Universe*, 4.)

20. Carter, *Shaw's Universe*, 4.

21. Carter, *Shaw's Universe*, 23.

22. *Shaw University, 1874–1875: Catalogue of Shaw University* (Raleigh, NC: Edwards, Broughton, & Co., 1875). Courtesy of Archives and Special Collections, Records Management Program Department, Shaw University Archives, Raleigh, NC. On March 8, 1875, Shaw Collegiate Institute, now incorporated as Shaw University (Carter, *Shaw's Universe*, 5), consisted of two major structures—Shaw Hall and Estey Seminary (Carter, *Shaw's Universe*, 23). Shaw University had been formerly called Raleigh Institute, but the name was changed to Shaw Collegiate Institute in honor of the prominent donor Elijah Shaw (Carter, *Shaw's Universe*, 4).

23. Letter: Dr. Smallwood to Dr. Frissell, 2.

24. J. Vickers, *Raleigh, City of Oaks: An Illustrated History* (Woodland Hills, CA: Windsor, 1982), 55. According to the 1870 Census, Raleigh, NC, had a total of 4,094 Negroes and 3,689 whites residing in the city. The influx of Negroes into the city after the Civil War contributed significantly to the city's population growth, with Negroes concentrated in the south section of the city.

25. Vickers, *Raleigh, City of Oaks*, 58.

26. Carter, *Shaw's Universe*, 27. A Street in the town of Rich Square, North Carolina, bears the name "Roberts" in honor of the Roberts family.

27. Carter, *Shaw's Universe*, 28. Dr. Manassa T. Pope attended Shaw University from 1874 to 1879. He then studied at Shaw University's Leonard School of Medicine and was a graduate of its first medical class in 1886. Dr. Pope

became the first African-American man to receive a medical license in the state of North Carolina. On July 4, 1898, during the Spanish-American War, he enlisted as first assistant surgeon in the Third Regiment, serving until his discharge in February 1899. In 1919, he ran unsuccessfully for mayor in Raleigh, North Carolina. He died in 1934. (Kenneth J. Zogry, *An American Success Story: The Pope House of Raleigh, NC,* accessed online at http://www.nps.gov/nr//twhp/wwwlps/lessons/124popehouse/index. htm). Retrieved March 9, 2009. A street in the town of Rich Square, North Carolina, bears the name "Pope" in honor of the Pope family. The Pope House Museum was incorporated in 2000 and is located in Raleigh, North Carolina. The museum contains family books, artifacts, and other papers of historical value.

28. http://thepopehousemuseum.org.

29. Dr. Smallwood, in his December 26, 1903, letter to Dr. Frissell, Principal of Hampton Normal and Agricultural Institute, stated that he enrolled in Shaw University in the fall of 1876 (letter: Dr. Smallwood to Dr. Frissell); however, the Shaw University catalog, located in Shaw's Archival and Special Collections department, lists him as a student of the 1875 class.

30. *Shaw University, 1875–1882: General Catalogue of the Officers and Students of Shaw University* (Raleigh, NC: Edwards, Broughton, and Co., 1882), 30. Courtesy of Archives and Special Collections, Records Management Program Department, Shaw University Archives.

31. *Shaw University, 1874–1875*, 11.

32. *Shaw University, 1874–1875*, 11–12.

33. *Shaw University, 1874–1875*, 15.

34. *Shaw University, 1874–1875*, 15–16.

35. *Shaw University, 1874–1875*, 16–17.

36. *Shaw University, 1875–1882*, 26.

37. *Shaw University, 1875–1882*, 7. A Degree of AB was conferred on students in the college department who met the requirements for a Religious and Missionary Education (Carter, *Shaw's Universe*, 156).

38. *Shaw University, 1874–1875*, 16.

39. Letter: Dr. Smallwood to Dr. Frissell, 2.

40. *Shaw University, 1875–1882*, 30.

41. *Shaw University, 1875–1882*, 31. As John Jefferson was completing his studies, Shaw University continued to grow (Carter, *Shaw's Universe*, 23). In 1879, a

third building was erected, the Greenleaf Building (Carter, *Shaw's Universe*, 26). In 1881, the Leonard Medical School was in operation at Shaw, and the School of Law opened its doors in 1888 (Carter, *Shaw's Universe*, 27, 29). Two years later, in 1890, a building was erected for a school of pharmacy. By 1919, all three schools had closed (Perkins, *News and Observer's Raleigh*, 85.)

42. 1880 United States Census, Halifax County, NC, Roseneath Township, E. D. 128, June 9, 1880, p. 367 (accessed online at http://www.ancestry.com).

43. Letter: Dr. Smallwood to Dr. Frissell, 2. See also http://en.wikipedia.org/wiki/ Temperance Movement. During the 1800s, the high rate of alcohol consumption affected both men and women and was indiscriminate among age and social groups. By 1840, alcohol consumption contributed to many social ills, such as poverty, joblessness, immorality, crime, and unemployment. The temperance movement was initiated to educate Americans about the effects of alcohol consumption and to prevent drunkenness; thus it emphasized complete abstinence from intoxicating liquors.

44. 1870 United States Census, Halifax County, NC, October 31, 1870, p. 22 (accessed online at http://www.ancestry.com). In 1870, Palmyra was located in Halifax County, with a post office in Scotland Neck, North Carolina.

45. 1870 United States Census, October 31, 1870, p. 22. Living in the household with David Lawrence (Smallwood) was a woman, presumably his wife, and five children ranging in age from seven to eighteen. In 1870, David Lawrence (Smallwood) was fifty years old. Prior to residing in Palmyra, in the county of Halifax, he lived in the township of Deep Creek, Edgecombe County, North Carolina, in what is now Tarboro. He lived in the household of an Augustus Bryant, a Negro, who was employed as a farm laborer (1870 United States Federal Census, July 9, 1870, p. 37). It is reasonable to assume that Augustus Bryant, since he had the surname of Bryant, could have been owned by one or some of the white Bryants from Bryantown Road in Rich Square, North Carolina. Perhaps, after slavery ended, he left the area of Rich Square and migrated to Edgecombe County, North Carolina. In 1920, one-hundred-year-old David Lawrence (Smallwood), a widower and head of household, was residing in the township of Roseneath in Halifax County, North Carolina (1920 United States Federal Census), where he had lived for over twenty years (1900 United States Federal Census). Online data accessed at http://www.ancestry.com.

46. Letter: Dr. Smallwood to Dr. Frissell, 3.

Notes to Chapter Six

1. D. Sherman, *History of Wesleyan Academy at Wilbraham, Massachusetts, 1817–1890* (Boston: McDonald & Gill, 1893), 459.
2. *Richmond Planet*, May 12, 1912. Courtesy of William R. and Norma Harvey Library, Hampton University, Hampton, VA.
3. Sherman, *History of Wesleyan Academy*, 452. Dr. Loranus Crowell was born in 1815 and died in 1889. He was a financial agent for the academy.
4. Sherman, *History of Wesleyan Academy*, 439. Dr. G. M. Steele was a prominent clergyman and educator in the Methodist Episcopal Church for more than fifty years. He was president of Lawrence University in Appleton, Wisconsin, until 1879, when he became principal of the Wesleyan Academy at Wilbraham, Massachusetts. He died in 1901 at the age of seventy-eight in Kenilworth, IL (The *New York Times*, January 18, 1902).
5. Sherman, *History of Wesleyan Academy*, 441.
6. Sherman, *History of Wesleyan Academy*, 446.
7. Letter: Dr. Smallwood to Dr. Frissell.
8. "Imposing Exercises at Claremont: Governor Mann speaks. Lincoln Memorial Hall Dedicated. Northern Philanthropy and Southern Generosity," *Richmond Planet*, May 25, 1912. Courtesy of William R. and Norma Harvey Library, Hampton University, Hampton, VA.
9. "A Young Negro Orator in Luck," unidentified newspaper clipping dated March 14, Boston. Courtesy of Wilbraham and Monson Academy Archives.
10. Letter: Dr. Smallwood to Dr. Frissell, 3.
11. John J. Smallwood, "Finding My Mother," unidentified newspaper clipping. Courtesy of Hampton University Archives, Hampton, VA.
12. Smallwood, "Finding My Mother."

Notes to Chapter Seven

1. Benjamin Harrison, twenty-third President of the United States (1889–1893), was born August 20, 1833, in North Bend, Ohio. He later moved to Indianapolis, Indiana, where he practiced law and campaigned for the Republican Party. He died March 13, 1901, in Indianapolis. See http://en.wikipedia.org/wiki/Benjamin_Harrison (accessed August 10, 2008).

2. James G. Blaine (January 31, 1830–January 27, 1893) served as secretary of state under Presidents James A. Garfield and Chester A. Arthur. He also served in the House of Representatives, as Speaker of the House, and as U.S. senator from Maine. He was a dominant Republican leader of the post–Civil War period and obtained the Republican nomination in the 1884 presidential election, but lost to Democrat Grover Cleveland. See http:// en.wikipedia.org/wiki.James_G_Blaine (accessed August 10, 2008).

3. Nothing else is known about the man identified as "Huston."

4. Governor Alvin Peterson Hovey was a Union general during the American Civil War and Governor of Indiana from January 14, 1889, to November 23, 1891. He died in office in 1891 in Indianapolis. See http://en.wikipedia. org/wiki/Alvin_P_Hovey (accessed August 15, 2007).

5. Rev. W. T. Perrin was a friend of John Jefferson's.

6. "Sister Perrin," the wife of Rev. W. T. Perrin, assisted John Jefferson in finding his mother.

7. Mr. Johnson resided in Alabama and was the slave trader who had last sold John Jefferson's mother. He contacted John Jefferson in May 1889, after having received a letter from him asking for assistance in locating his mother. Mr. Johnson told him that he had sold his mother in 1864 to a slave speculator in Texas and offered to assist him in finding her for the sum of $100.

8. Mrs. Vaughan, an unidentified friend of John Jefferson Smallwood, had very little confidence in Mr. Johnson. Johnson had sold Dr. Smallwood's mother to a slave speculator in Texas in 1864 and offered to assist him in finding her for the sum of $100. Dr. Smallwood could not share this information with Mrs. Vaughan because of her lack of confidence in Mr. Johnson.

9. Willie L. Lassiter (niece to Dr. Smallwood), interview by Mary E. C. Drew, August 10, 2007, Philadelphia, PA. Dr. Smallwood's mother, Mary Eliza Smallwood, remained in Rich Square, North Carolina, until her death in 1904.

10. Willie L. Lassiter (niece to Dr. Smallwood), interview by Mary E. C. Drew, August 10, 2007, Philadelphia, PA. Dr. Smallwood's three sisters, Emma Smallwood-Josey, Elizabeth "Betty" Smallwood, and Mary Eliza Smallwood-Lassiter, remained in Rich Square, North Carolina, until their deaths. Smallwood Street, named in honor of the Smallwood family, marks the general vicinity where they resided.

11. In July 1870, David Lawrence (Smallwood), Mary Eliza Smallwood's slave husband, lived in the township of Deep Creek, Edgecombe County, North

Carolina, located in what is now Tarboro, North Carolina. He was employed as a farm laborer. In October 1870, David moved to Halifax County, North Carolina, to the township of Palmyra. In 1920, David was one hundred years old, a widower and head of household, and lived in the township of Roseneath in Halifax County (1920 United States Census), where he lived for over twenty years (1900 United States Census). (Census data accessed online at http://www.ancestry.com.)

12. Tobias, one of John Jefferson's brothers, was sold to a slave owner in Scotland Neck, North Carolina, at the time of the slave auction. According to oral family histories, Tobias was never seen again by his family. In 1920, Tobias lived in Northampton County, North Carolina, in the township of Occoneechee Neck, approximately twenty-six miles from Scotland Neck and twenty miles from Rich Square. He was sixty-eight years old, a widower, and worked as a farmer (1920 Census Record, January 8, 1920; accessed online at http://www.ancestry.com). He married an Anna Smallwood on January 9, 1873, in Northampton County, North Carolina (North Carolina State Archives, Raleigh, North Carolina). He died on July 23, 1928, of nephritis and was buried in Chapel Hill Cemetery in Rich Square, North Carolina (Standard Death Certificate, North Carolina State Archives, Raleigh, NC). Thomas, another of John Jefferson's brothers, was sold to a slave owner in Scotland Neck, North Carolina, at the time of the auction, according to oral family histories, and was never seen again by his family. As John Jefferson Smallwood stated in this letter, Thomas had already died before John Jefferson was reunited with his mother and sisters. There are no records for Thomas Smallwood that indicate his life and death dates, or the cause of his death.

13. John Jefferson was perhaps lecturing in Hamburg, Germany, in July 1889 during his tour with the United Literary and Lecturing Society of England. While on the tour, he studied at England's Trinity College for a year before returning to America. He traveled again to Continental Europe in 1890 and remained in France, Germany, and Britain until the spring of 1891 (Letter: Dr. Smallwood to Dr. Frissell).

Notes to Chapter Eight

1. Letter: Dr. Smallwood to Dr. Frissell, 3; "A Young Negro Orator in Luck," unidentified newspaper clipping, courtesy of Wilbraham and Monson Academy Archives, Wilbraham, MA. Rev. John J. Smallwood was paid the sum of $6,980 by the United Literary and Lecturing Society of England to go to Europe in October 1889 and deliver lectures on "The Race problem in America" and "The Negro in American Politics."

2. Letter: Dr. Smallwood to Dr. Frissell.

3. Letter: Dr. Smallwood to Dr. Frissell.

4. Mr. Arrington, in addition to owning large tracts of farmland, owned and operated the Southern Cooperage Company and Virginia Heading Company. His company was interested not only in merchandise and manufacturing slack cooperage and heading, but also shipped pulp wood and lumber (M. S. Baird, Jr., *Claremont on the James: Its Beginning and Early Years, Circa 1880–1920* (Zuni, VA: Pearl Line, 2002), 112).

5. J. J. Smallwood to H. J. Arrington (Trust Deed), August 11, 1891, *Surry County Deeds*, Surry County, VA, Deed Book 25, pp. 95–97.

6. Baird, Jr., *Claremont on the James*, 5.

7. Baird Jr., *Claremont on the James*, 2. The Quiyoughcohannock Indians (Powhatan tribe) initially inhabited the site that later became known as Claremont Colony.

8. Baird, Jr., *Claremont on the James*, 13. Claremont was known for its crops of corn, clover, potatoes, vegetables, grain, and other agricultural products.

9. Baird, Jr., *Claremont on the James*, 45.

10. Baird, Jr., *Claremont on the James*, 2.

11. Baird, Jr., *Claremont on the James*, 27.

12. Baird, Jr., *Claremont on the James*, 29.

13. Baird, Jr., *Claremont on the James*, 41.

14. United States Passport of John Jefferson Smallwood, December 10, 1891, North Carolina State Archives, Raleigh, NC.

15. "Vindicated: Mr. Smallwood Holds His Work," *Monthly Advocate* 1, no. 2 (June 13, 1896): 2. The *Monthly Advocate* was the semi-monthly campus newspaper of the Temperance, Collegiate and Industrial Institute. All copies of the *Monthly Advocate* were obtained courtesy of the Surry County Historical Society, Surry County, VA.

16. E. S. Gregory, *Claremont Manor: A History* (Petersburg, VA: Ann and Lewis Kirby & Plummer, 1990), 100; "Vindicated: Mr. Smallwood Holds His Work," 3.

17. "Vindicated: Mr. Smallwood Holds His Work," 3.

18. Willie L. Lassiter (niece to Dr. Smallwood), interview by Mary E. C. Drew, June 2007, Philadelphia, PA.

19. Dr. John Jefferson Smallwood to Mr. E. W. Fox, printed in B. Hopper, *Musings about Claremont* (Claremont, VA: privately printed, n.d.), 18.

20. Dr. Smallwood to Elizabeth Cady Stanton, November 11,1893, Frederick Douglass Papers, Library of Congress, Washington, DC, http://memory.loc.gov/ammem/doughtml/doughome.html (accessed September 20, 2008).

21. G. C. Ward and K. Burns, *Not for Ourselves Alone: The Story of Elizabeth Cady Stanton and Susan B. Anthony* (New York. Alfred A. Knopf, 1999), 38–39. In 1848, Mrs. Stanton and Jane Hunt, Mary Ann McClintock, Martha Wright, and Lucretia Mott organized the first women's rights convention in the United States. Later, Mrs. Stanton worked closely with Susan B. Anthony to advocate for women's suffrage, founding the National Woman Suffrage Association in 1869. Mrs. Stanton died in 1902.

22. Ward and Burns, *Not for Ourselves Alone*, 39.

23. Dr. John Jefferson Smallwood to Mr. E. W. Fox, printed in Hopper, *Musings about Claremont*, 18.

24. Dr. Smallwood to Frederick Douglass, March 24, 1894, Frederick Douglass Papers, Library of Congress, Washington DC, http://memory/loc.gov/ammem/doughtml/doughome.html (accessed September 20, 2008).

25. Douglass, *Narrative of the Life of Frederick Douglass: An American Slave, Written by Himself* (1845; repr., New York: Literary Classics of the United States, 2000), 269–368. Mr. Douglass was born a slave in February of 1818 in Talbot County, Maryland. He successfully escaped from Maryland on September 3, 1838, and was in New York within twenty-four hours. He continued traveling until he reached Massachusetts. During his lifetime, he published three versions of his autobiography, each expanding on the previous one. He also published a series of newspapers, including the *North Star, Frederick Douglass Weekly, Frederick Douglass' Paper, Douglass' Weekly*, and the *New National Era*. Mr. Douglass died February 20, 1895, at the age of seventy-seven in Washington DC.

26. Susie Bransford, "A Pupil of Three-Score (Editorial)," *Southern Workman* (February 2, 1891): 174. (Susie Bransford, a graduate of Hampton Normal and Agricultural Institute, class of 1889, was a teacher in Northampton County, North Carolina, in the township of Woodland. In her article in the *Southern Workman*, she described the deplorable conditions to which Negroes in her hometown were subjected, conditions that made it almost impossible for them to seek out an education and for her to teach them. In keeping with the motto of her alma mater, however, Ms. Bransford was committed to the mission of Hampton, to "gather and scatter" her knowledge among her people.)

Notes to Chapter Nine

1. H. S. Chesbro and Husband, (Deed Bargain and Sale) to J. J. Smallwood, April 24, 1895, Surry County, VA, *Surry County Deeds*, Deed Book 26, pp. 538–540.

2. H. S. Chesbro and Husband, (Deed Bargain and Sale) to J. J. Smallwood, April 24, 1895, Surry County, VA, *Surry County Deeds*, Deed Book 21, pp. 287–289.

3. *Circular of Information of the Temperance, Industrial and Collegiate Institute, Claremont, VA, 1902*, Hampton University Archives, Hampton, VA. Hereafter cited as *Circular (1902)*.

4. *Annual Circular of Information of the Temperance, Industrial and Collegiate Institute, Claremont, VA, 1905–06*, Hampton University Archives, Hampton, VA. Hereafter cited as *Annual Circular (1905–06)*.

5. *Circular (1902)*.

6. *Annual Circular (1905–06)*.

7. Dr. Smallwood to Mr. E. W. Fox, printed in Hopper, *Musings about Claremont*, 18.

8. Dr. Smallwood to Mr. E. W. Fox, printed in Hopper, *Musings about Claremont*, 18.

9. W. N. Hartshorn, *An Era of Progress and Promise, 1863–1910: The Religious, Moral and Educational Development of the American Negro Since his Emancipation* (Boston: Priscilla, 1910), 363. Courtesy of Virginia State University Special Collections and Archives, Virginia State University Library, Petersburg, VA.

10. "Money Received. By Mr. Smallwood from His Friends during the School Year of 1895 to 1896. Commencing with the Months of August 1895 and Ending June 1896," *Monthly Advocate* 1, no. 2 (June 13, 1896): 1.

11. Dr. Smallwood to Mr. E. W. Fox, printed in Hopper, *Musings about Claremont*, 18.

12. "Vindicated: Our Growth and Work," *Monthly Advocate* 1, no. 2 (June 13, 1896): 3.

13. "Vindicated: Our Growth and Work," 1–4.

14. L. Harlan, *Booker T. Washington: The Wizard of Tuskegee, 1901–1915* (New York: Oxford University Press, 1983), 163.

15. Unidentified newspaper clipping, courtesy of Hampton University Archives, Hampton, VA.

16. Unidentified newspaper clipping, courtesy of Hampton University Archives, Hampton, VA.

17. C. T. McDaniels, "Declares Dr. Smallwood is one the men to whom the Negro must turn as an example of Race Pride and Practical Industry," *Journal and Guide* (July 29, 1911): 137. Courtesy of Hampton University Archives, Hampton, VA. Mr. Sawyer was born September 22, 1816, and died in 1900 at the age of eighty-three. Sawyer County, Wisconsin, is named in his honor. http://www.wisconsinhistory.org.

18. Letter: Dr. Smallwood to Dr. Frissell.

19. Surry County, VA, *Surry County Deeds*, Deed Book 27, p. 256.

20. Harlan, *Booker T. Washington*, 308.

21. L. R. Harlan and R. W. Smock, *The Booker T. Washington Papers, Vol. 3: 1889–95* (Urbana: University of Illinois Press, 1972), 23.

22. See http://www.aaheritageva.org/search/sites and Harlan and Smock, *Booker T. Washington Papers, Vol. 3*, 23. Throughout her 102 years of life, Ms. Howland continued to be a strong activist for Negroes, in addition to women's rights, temperance, and civil liberties. She died in 1929.

23. Surry County, VA, *Surry County Deeds*, Deed Book 27, pp. 53–54. Owing to Dr. Smallwood's inability to pay the notes for the thirty-six-acre wharf property on time, the trustees for Ms. Howland sold the land at public auction on December 20, 1902, to D. Wilson Moore of Clayton, New Jersey, for $3,500. (*Surry County Deeds*, Deed Book 29, p. 618). As a result, the title to the school property was temporarily lost, and the name "Howland" was removed from the building (Gregory, *Claremont Manor*, 100). D. Wilson

Moore, in turn, leased the land to Dr. Smallwood under the stipulations that he would conduct a school upon the property and pay semiannual rents of $93 over a period of six years, with no more than six months to elapse without payment (*Surry County Deeds*, Deed Book 29, p. 639). Six years later, the deed of trust was satisfied on February 23, 1909 (*Surry County Deeds*, Deed Book 33, p. 534).

24. Flora Tann-Chambliss (great niece to Dr. Smallwood), interview by Mary E. C. Drew, June 2007, Cairo, IL; Clarence Lassiter (great nephew of Dr. Smallwood), interview by Mary E. C. Drew, June 2007, Woodland, NC.

25. United States Federal Census, Surry County, VA, Temperance, Industrial and Collegiate Institute, June 6, 1900 (accessed online at http://www.ancestry.com). Marcus W. Smallwood was a graduate of the class of 1899.

26. J. J. Smallwood to (Deed Trust) Mrs. H. H. Cook, Trustee, July 1, 1897, *Surry County Deeds*, Deed Book 27, pp. 628–630. John W. Patterson, in 1903, served as business manager for the Institute.

27. "Vindicated: Mr. Smallwood Holds His Work," 3.

28. "Vindicated: Mr. Smallwood Holds His Work," 3.

29. "Vindicated: Mr. Smallwood Holds His Work," 3.

30. "Vindicated: Mr. Smallwood Holds His Work," 3.

31. "Vindicated: Mr. Smallwood Holds His Work," 3.

32. Washington, *Up From Slavery*, 68.

33. On this accusation, see Harlan and Smock, *Booker T. Washington Papers, Vol. 12: 1912–14* (Urbana: University of Illinois Press, 1972), 160n.3. Available online at http://www.historycooperative.org/btw/Vol.12/html/160.html.

34. Booker T. Washington to Emily Howland, October 13, 1901, printed in L. R. Harlan and R. W. Smock, *The Booker T. Washington Papers, Vol. 6: 1901–02* (Urbana: University of Illinois Press, 1972), 240–241.

35. Harlan and Smock, *Booker T. Washington Papers, Vol. 4: 1895–1898* (Urbana, IL: University of Illinois Press, 1972), 235–236. (Available online at http://www.historycooperative.org/btw/ Vol.4/html/235.html.) Daniel Augustus Straker was born in Bridgetown, Barbados, in 1842 and later moved to the United States shortly after the Civil War, around 1867 or 1868. Before entering Howard University Law School, from which he graduated in 1871, he taught for two years in a freedmen's school in Louisville, Kentucky. He held several positions throughout his career, serving as stenographer to General O. O. Howard and a clerk in the United States Treasury Department,

in addition to practicing law in Orangeburg, South Carolina, after having resigned from an appointed position in 1875 as inspector of customs in Charleston, South Carolina. In 1876, he was elected to three successive terms with the South Carolina legislature but was later denied his seat because of accusations that he was not an American citizen. He later served as dean of the law school at Allen University in Columbia, South Carolina from 1882–1887. His aspirations for public office were hindered during a period of disenfranchisement in the South.

36. *Monthly Advocate* 1, no. 2 (June 13, 1896): 3.
37. *Monthly Advocate* 1, no. 2 (June 13, 1896): 3.
38. *Monthly Advocate* 1, no. 2 (June 13, 1896): 3.
39. *Monthly Advocate* 1, no. 2 (June 13, 1896): 3.
40. *Monthly Advocate* 1, no. 2 (June 13, 1896): 3.
41. Letter: Dr. Smallwood to Dr. Frissell.
42. Hartshorn, *Era of Progress and Promise*, 363.
43. Bennett, Jr., *Before the Mayflower*, 229.
44. C. Vann Woodward, *The Strange Career of Jim Crow* (1955; repr., New York: Oxford University Press, 2002), back cover.
45. Bennett, Jr., *Before the Mayflower*, 236.
46. http://en.wikipedia.org/wiki/Lynchings_in_the_United_States (accessed June 4, 2008).
47. Bennett, Jr., *Before the Mayflower*, 236.
48. *Richmond Planet* 15, no. 7 (January 29, 1898): 3.
49. "The Reign of Lawlessness," *Richmond Planet* 16, no. 3 (December 31, 1898): 4.

Notes to Chapter Ten

1. Letter: Dr. Smallwood to Dr. Frissell.
2. *Annual Circular (1905–06)*.
3. Dr. John J. Smallwood to Mr. E. W. Fox, printed in Hopper, *Musings About Claremont*, 18.
4. "Smallwood's Speech: Delivered on the Fifty-First Birthday of Lincoln," *Monthly Advocate* 1, no. 2 (June 13, 1896): 4.
5. "Smallwood's Speech," 4.

6. "Seventh Annual Commencement of the Temperance, Industrial and Collegiate Institute at Claremont, Surry Co., Va.: Commencing Sunday, June 11, 1899, at 10:30 a.m. and Continuing through Wednesday, June 14th," Southern Pamphlet Collection, Rare Book Collection, Wilson Library, University of North Carolina at Chapel Hill, Chapel Hill, NC. (Hereafter cited as "Seventh Annual Commencement.")

7. Fannie E. Smallwood was one of four of Dr. Smallwood's nieces who attended his school. She had attended a school in New England at a very early age and was now on the faculty at the Institute (Flora Tann-Chambliss [great-niece to Dr. John Jefferson Smallwood], interview by Mary E. C. Drew, October 2007, Cairo, IL; "Seventh Annual Commencement"). Among Dr. Smallwood's other nieces, Lizzie Josey, Reddie Josey, Hattie Lassiter, and Lucille A. Smallwood also attended and graduated from the institute; they were all natives of Rich Square, North Carolina. Two of Dr. Smallwood's nephews also graduated from the institute—Marcus W. Smallwood and Johnnie Lassiter, also natives of Rich Square (Willie L. Lassiter [niece to Dr. Smallwood], interview by Mary E. C. Drew, June 9, 2007, Philadelphia, PA; 1900 United States Census, Surry County, VA, Guilford Township, E. D. 69, Temperance, Industrial & Collegiate Institute, June 6, 1900, p. 5A).

8. "Seventh Annual Commencement."

9. "Seventh Annual Commencement."

10. "Seventh Annual Commencement."

11. "Seventh Annual Commencement."

12. "Seventh Annual Commencement."

13. "Seventh Annual Commencement." Dumbbell drills were a popular form of exercise during the early 1900s and were often set to music or performed as an exhibition.

14. "Seventh Annual Commencement."

15. "Seventh Annual Commencement."

16. "Seventh Annual Commencement."

17. "Seventh Annual Commencement."

18. Unidentified newspaper clipping, dated January 8, 1899, Hampton University Archives, Hampton, VA.

19. "Money Received By Mr. Smallwood from His Friends," 1.

20. "Hewitt's Millions for Charity and Arts," the *New York Times*, September 4, 1908.

21. *Commonwealth Ex Rel. Moore, Auditor, et al. v. Smallwood Memorial Institute*, Record 381, Circuit Court of Surry County, VA, in *Report of the Supreme Court of Virginia, November 1918 through January 16, 1919*, Virginia State Library, Richmond, VA, p. 52. (Hereafter cited as *Moore v. Smallwood Memorial Institute*.)

22. *Moore v. Smallwood Memorial Institute*, 49.

23. *Moore v. Smallwood Memorial Institute*, 49.

24. "Letters of Commendation," *Monthly Advocate* 1, no. 2 (June 13, 1896): 2.

25. 1900 United States Census, Surry County, VA, Guilford Township, E. D. 69, Temperance, Industrial & Collegiate Institute, June 6, 1900, p. 5A.

26. Bennett, Jr., *Before the Mayflower*, 240.

27. Marriage license for John J. Smallwood and Rosa E. Banks, Virginia Bureau of Vital Statistics and Marriages, Richmond City, VA, 1895–1908, microform reel 69: 1900 #523.

28. *Annual Circular (1905–06)*.

29. Gregory, *Claremont Manor*, 100.

Notes to Chapter Eleven

1. *Catalogue of the Temperance, Industrial and Collegiate Institute, 1906–07, Claremont, VA*, Hampton University Archives, Hampton, VA. Hereafter cited as *Catalogue (1906–07)*.

2. *Circular (1902)*.

3. *Circular (1902)*. Members of the board of trustees included Professor J. J. Smallwood, president; Professor J. H. Blackwell, secretary; Mr. P. Emmett Ellis, treasurer; Dr. W. F Graham, DD; Professor R. Kelser; Honorable J. W. Peterson; Honorable W. W. Lawrence; Mr. Willis R. Wright; and Ms. Joseph S. Gray. Faculty members included Rev. W. H. Willis, AB BA, principal; Mrs. Rosa E. Smallwood, lady president; Mrs. W. H. Willis; Ms. D. S. Chadwick; and Ms. Nannie C. Morris.

4. *Circular (1902)*.

5. *Circular (1902)*.

6. *Circular (1902)*.

7. *Circular (1902)*.

8. *Circular (1902)*.

9. "The Temperance, Industrial and Collegiate Institute, Claremont, VA," *The Educational Leader* (November 1903): 1. Courtesy of Hampton University Archives, Hampton, VA.

10. Letter: Dr. Smallwood to Dr. Frissell.

11. "The Temperance, Industrial and Collegiate Institute," 1.

12. Letter: Dr. Smallwood to Dr. Frissell.

13. "The Temperance, Industrial and Collegiate Institute," 1.

14. "The Temperance, Industrial and Collegiate Institute," 2.

15. "The Temperance, Industrial and Collegiate Institute," 2.

16. Letter: Dr. Smallwood to Dr. Frissell.

17. "The Temperance, Industrial and Collegiate Institute," 1.

18. "The Temperance, Industrial and Collegiate Institute," 1.

19. "The Temperance, Industrial and Collegiate Institute," 1.

20. Rev. A. C. Skinner, "T. I. and C. Institute: Founded by Prof. John J. Smallwood, Began Its Closing Exercises," The *Star*, Newport News, VA, June 20, 1903. (Hereafter cited as Skinner, "Closing Exercises."). Courtesy of Hampton University Archives, Hampton, VA.

21. Skinner, "Closing Exercises."

22. Skinner, "Closing Exercises."

23. Skinner, "Closing Exercises."

24. Skinner, "Closing Exercises."

25. Skinner, "Closing Exercises."

26. Skinner, "Closing Exercises." Lafayette Hershaw was born in North Carolina in 1863. He was the son of a slave mother and his father was of French descent. He was a civil rights activist and devoted his life to making a difference in the lives of fellow Negroes. He received a bachelor of arts from Atlanta University and a law degree from Howard University. In 1890, he was appointed to a position in the U.S. Department of the Interior and was one of twenty-nine founding members of the Niagara movement.

27. Orations by the four female graduates were as follows: "The Need of an Industrial Education," Ms. Emma Watkins of Toano, Virginia; "The Injustice of Caste Legislation," Ms. Gladys M. Baker of Phoebus, Virginia; "Woman's Influence in the Social and Political World," Ms. Lena A. Williams of Providence Forge, Virginia; and "Competition Must be the Victor of the

20th Century," Ms. Eudora M. Baker of Phoebus, Virginia. Cited in *The Star*, Newport News, VA, June 20, 1903.

28. "Colored Men Acquiring Property," *Southern Workman and Hampton School Record* 20, no. 2 (October 1891): 239. Courtesy of North Carolina Central University Library, Durham, NC.

29. Bennett, Jr., *Before the Mayflower*, 240.

30. W. Cheek and A. L. Cheek, *John Mercer Langston and the Fight for Black Freedom, 1829–65* (Urbana: University of Illinois Press, 1996). The names "Douglas[s] and Langston" refer to Frederick Douglass, editor of the abolitionist newspaper the *North Star*, and Charles Henry Langston, editor of the Lawrence, KS, *Historic Times*. Charles Henry Langston was the grandfather of the renowned African American poet Langston Hughes and older brother to John Mercer Langston, an accomplished attorney and activist, who had numerous appointed posts. Both Charles and John Langston worked for the abolitionist cause and helped lead the Ohio Anti-Slavery Society in 1858. In 1888, John was the first black elected to the United States Congress from Virginia (and the last for nearly a century).

31. "Colored Men Acquiring Property," 239.

32. Bennett, Jr., *Before the Mayflower*, 186–187.

33. "Smallwood's Speech," 4.

34. "Vindicated: Mr. Smallwood Holds His Work," 1–3.

Notes to Chapter Twelve

1. "Vindicated: Mr. Smallwood Holds His Work," 1–4.

2. Willie L. Lassiter (niece to Dr. Smallwood), interview by Mary E. C. Drew, June 9, 2007, Philadelphia, PA.

3. Surry County, VA, *Surry County Deeds*, Deed Book 33, p. 186.

4. *Annual Circular (1905–06)*.

5. *Annual Circular (1905–06)*.

6. *Annual Circular (1905–06)*.

7. *Catalogue (1906–07)*.

8. *Catalogue (1906–07)*.

9. *Catalogue (1906–07)*.

10. *Catalogue (1906–07)*.

11. Unidentified newspaper clipping, Hampton University Archives, Hampton, VA.

12. J. D. Kornwolf, *The Surry County, Virginia, 1776 Bicentennial Committee Guide to the Buildings of Surry and the American Revolution* (Surry County, VA: Surry County 1776 Bicentennial Committee, 1976), 144. (Book reprinted in 2007 by authors M. W. Farmer and C. A. Keen.)

13. Unidentified newspaper clipping, Hampton University Archives, Hampton, VA.

14. Dr. John J. Smallwood to Mr. E. W. Fox, February 27, 1893, printed in Hopper, *Musings about Claremont*, 18; *Catalogue (1906–07)*.

Notes to Chapter Thirteen

1. "Politics Brought on Texas Race War," The *Scranton Republican*, Scranton, PA, 1906. Courtesy of William R. and Norma Harvey Library, Hampton University, Hampton, VA.

2. "Race War Begun in Texas: Killing of Five White Men Results in Organized Fight on Negroes," the *New York Times*, March 30, 1904.

3. "Race War Begun in Texas."

4. "Race War Begun in Texas."

5. "The Rise and Fall of Jim Crow: Jim Crow Stories: The Brownsville Affair (1906)," http://www.pbs.org/wnet/jimcrow/stories_events_browns.html.

6. "The Rise and Fall of Jim Crow"; J. D. Weaver, *The Brownsville Raid* (New York: Norton, 1970). The 167 black soldiers of the Twenty-fifth Regiment were discharged without honor, even though some had over twenty years of service with the army and were only a couple of years away from retirement with pensions. Because of President Roosevelt's decision, he fell out of favor with many blacks who had previously supported him for his occasional condemnation of lynchings and his association with Booker T. Washington. Mr. Washington, who was a friend of the president, spoke in defense of the soldiers at a White House dinner and tried to convince Roosevelt to reconsider his decision, but the president would not budge. For two years, from 1907–1908, the Brownsville Affair was heard before the United States Senate Committee, whose members reached the same decision as President Roosevelt. It was not until 1970 when the Brownsville Affair was investigated in depth by J. D. Weaver that the U.S. Army conducted a new investigation of

the affair. In 1972, the army found the accused members of the Twenty-fifth Regiment innocent and reversed President Roosevelt's 1906 order. Under the Nixon administration, the accused soldiers' dishonorable discharges were overturned, but the administration refused to grant their families the back pay owed them on their pensions. The last surviving veteran of the Twenty-fifth Regiment, Dorsie Willis, received a meager pension of $25,000.

7. "Politics Brought on Texas Race War."

8. "Politics Brought on the Texas Race War."

9. "Politics Brought on the Texas Race War."

10. S. Kantrowitz, *Ben Tillman and the Reconstruction of White Supremacy* (Chapel Hill: University of North Carolina Press, 2000), 41. Tillman was a member of the U.S. Senate in 1906. Prior to serving in the Senate, he was governor of South Carolina from 1890 to 1894. In 1894, he was elected to the U.S. Senate and was reelected in 1901, 1907, and 1913, and he served as senator until his death on July 3, 1918.

11. R. W. Logan, *The Betrayal of the Negro from Rutherford B. Hayes to Woodrow Wilson* (1954; repr., New York: Da Capo, 1997), 91. (This is an expanded edition of Logan's 1954 book, *The Negro in American Life and Thought: The Nadir, 1877–1901.*)

12. "Politics Brought on Texas Race War."

13. Bennett Jr., *Before the Mayflower*, 240.

14. "Politics Brought on Texas Race War."

15. Logan, Betrayal of the Negro, 13–15.

16. Logan, *Betrayal of the Negro*, 12. Presidents between 1877 and 1901 included Hayes, Garfield, Arthur, Cleveland, Harrison, and McKinley.

17. Logan, *Betrayal of the Negro*, 12–15.

18. B. Lapucia, "Migration North on the Promised Land," http://www.yale. edu/ynhti/curriculum/ units/1978/2/78.02.05.x.html (accessed October 21, 2008). In the deep South, from 1868 to 1876 and 1889 to 1923, there were 50 to 100 lynchings annually across the South. According to the NAACP, between 1889 and 1922, lynchings were at their worst level in U.S. history, with almost 3,500 people lynched, mostly Negro men.

19. Lapucia, "Migration North on the Promised Land."

20. "Politics Brought on Texas Race War."

Notes to Chapter Fourteen

1. McDaniels, "Declares Dr. Smallwood," 137.
2. "Hon. Marcus Garvey in Able Article Explains the Aims and Objects of the U.N.I.A.," the *Negro World*, April 4, 1926. All copies of the *Negro World* courtesy of Bostock Library, Duke University, Durham, NC.
3. "Discouragements," *Monthly Advocate* 1, no. 2 (June 13, 1896): 2. The presidential cottage was built some time after 1896, though the exact date of its construction is unknown.
4. McDaniels, "Declares Dr. Smallwood," 137.
5. McDaniels, "Declares Dr. Smallwood," 137.
6. McDaniels, "Declares Dr. Smallwood," 137.
7. "Dr. Smallwood, Here-Noted Negro Educator. Says People of His Race Do Best in South—Must Work Out Own Salvation," *Richmond Reformer*, December 5, 1908. Courtesy of William R. and Norma Harvey Library, Hampton University, Hampton, VA.
8. "Dr. Smallwood Here-Noted Negro Educator."
9. "Dr. Smallwood Here-Noted Negro Educator."
10. "Dr. Smallwood Here-Noted Negro Educator."
11. "Dr. Smallwood Here-Noted Negro Educator."
12. "Dr. Smallwood Here-Noted Negro Educator."
13. Willie L. Lassiter (niece to Dr. Smallwood), interview by Mary E. C. Drew, June 9, 2007, Philadelphia, PA.
14. 1910 United States Census, Surry County, VA, Guilford District, Claremont Town, E. D. 116, April 15, 1910, p. 1B, Cabin Point Road, Dwelling #20, Family #12, lines 84–88. In 1910, Dr. Smallwood and his family were living in Claremont, Surry County, Virginia, on Cabin Point Road. By 1910, Mrs. Smallwood had given birth to two other children, both of whom died in infancy. Thelma, age eight, had begun attending school. Dr. and Mrs. Smallwood owned a farm, free of debt. A farm laborer and his wife, Erastus and Lula Lucas, were living with Dr. Smallwood and his family.

Notes to Chapter Fifteen

1. McDaniels, "Declares Dr. Smallwood," 138.

2. Willie L. Lassiter (niece to John Jefferson Smallwood), interview by Mary E. C. Drew, July 2007, Philadelphia, PA.

3. "Vindicated: Mr. Smallwood Holds His Work," 2.

4. *Moore v. Smallwood Memorial Institute*, 48.

5. McDaniels, "Declares Dr. Smallwood," 137.

6. *Moore v. Smallwood Memorial Institute*, 48.

7. McDaniels, "Declares Dr. Smallwood," 137.

8. McDaniels, "Declares Dr. Smallwood," 137.

9. Surry County, VA, *Surry County Deeds*, Deed Book 25, pp. 94–95.

10. James Boyce and Susan Boyce (Deed Bargain Sale) to Rosa E. Smallwood, Surry County, VA, *Surry County Deeds*, Deed Book 33, September 9, 1905, p. 186.

11. McDaniels, "Declares Dr. Smallwood," 137.

12. McDaniels, "Declares Dr. Smallwood," 137–138.

13. Hartshorn, *Era of Progress and Promise*, 363.

14. McDaniels, "Declares Dr. Smallwood," 138.

15. "Vindicated: Mr. Smallwood Holds His Work," 3.

16. McDaniels, "Declares Dr. Smallwood," 138.

17. "River Front and Wharf," unidentified newspaper clipping, courtesy of Hampton University Archives, Hampton, VA.

18. McDaniels, "Declares Dr. Smallwood," 137.

19. McDaniels, "Declares Dr. Smallwood," 137.

20. Frederick Maglott and Eva S. Maglott (Deed Bargain and Sale) to J. J. Smallwood, Surry County, VA, *Surry County Deeds*, Deed Book 33, January 23, 1911, p. 185.

21. Maria Stone and Daniel Stone (Deed Book) to J. J. Smallwood, Surry County, VA, *Surry County Deeds*, Deed Book 33, November 24, 1911, pp. 400–401. Dr. Smallwood purchased this 13 -acre tract of land from Daniel and Maria Stone on November 11, 1911.

22. Maria Stone and Daniel Stone (Deed Book) to J. J. Smallwood, Surry County, VA, *Surry County Deeds*, Deed Book 33, p. 399. Dr. Smallwood purchased the 7,500 square feet of land from Daniel and Maria Stone on November 24, 1911.

Notes to Chapter Sixteen

1. "Just a Word about Lincoln Memorial Hall," unidentified newspaper clipping, Hampton University Archives, Hampton, VA.
2. "Just a Word about Lincoln Memorial Hall."
3. "Just a Word about Lincoln Memorial Hall."
4. McDaniels, "Declares Dr. Smallwood," 138.
5. *The Columbia Electronic Encyclopedia*, 6th edition (New York: Columbia University Press, 2007). Mr. Hay was born in 1838 and died July 1, 1905.
6. McDaniels, "Declares Dr. Smallwood," 138.
7. McDaniels, "Declares Dr. Smallwood," 137–138.
8. "Imposing Exercises at Claremont."
9. "Abraham Lincoln Memorial Hall," unidentified newspaper clipping, Hampton University Archives, Hampton, VA.
10. McDaniels, "Declares Dr. Smallwood," 137–138.
11. McDaniels, "Declares Dr. Smallwood," 137–138.
12. McDaniels, "Declares Dr. Smallwood," 137–138.
13. "Just a Word about Lincoln Memorial Hall."
14. "Smallwood's Speech," 4.
15. "Tribute from Governor William Hodges Mann," unidentified newspaper clipping, Hampton University Archives, Hampton, VA.
16. "What the Leading Virginians Say about Dr. Smallwood and the Building of Lincoln Hall," unidentified newspaper clipping, Hampton University Archives, Hampton, VA.
17. "What the Leading Virginians Say." James S. Sherman was the twenty-seventh Vice President of the United States. He served under President William Howard Taft and was in office from March 4, 1909, to October 30, 1912. He was the last vice president to die in office. His death was caused by health-related problems. http://en.wikipedia.org/wiki/James_S._Sherman.
18. McDaniels, "Declares Dr. Smallwood" 137–138.
19. *Moore v. Smallwood Memorial Institute*, 48.
20. Unidentified newspaper clipping, Hampton University Archives, Hampton, VA.

Notes to Chapter Seventeen

1. "Imposing Exercises at Claremont." The party from Richmond was one of several groups to come to the institute from various cities across the nation to observe the dedication ceremonies.
2. "Imposing Exercises at Claremont."
3. "Imposing Exercises at Claremont."
4. "Imposing Exercises at Claremont."
5. Kornwolf, *Surry County Bicentennial Committee Guide*, 144. After Mr. Hay's death in 1905, his wife, Mrs. Clara Hay, continued to make generous donations to the Temperance, Industrial and Collegiate Institute.
6. "Negro Education Faded Out When founder Died," unidentified newspaper clipping, courtesy of James Atkins, Richmond, VA.
7. "Imposing Exercises at Claremont."
8. "Imposing Exercises at Claremont."
9. Kornwolf, *Surry County Bicentennial Committee Guide*, 144.
10. Gregory, *Claremont Manor*, 101.
11. Gregory, *Claremont Manor*, 101.
12. Baird, Jr., *Claremont on the James*, 60. All monetary profits were deposited into the institute's revenue account (Kornwolf, *Surry County Bicentennial Committee Guide*, 144).
13. Kornwolf, *Surry County Bicentennial Committee Guide*, 144.
14. Kornwolf, *Surry County Bicentennial Committee Guide*, 144.
15. Gregory, *Claremont Manor*, 101. By 1917, a sum of $90–$100 per month was generated by the sale of electricity to the Town of Claremont.
16. "Imposing Exercises at Claremont."
17. "Imposing Exercises at Claremont."
18. "Imposing Exercises at Claremont."
19. "Imposing Exercises at Claremont."
20. "Imposing Exercises at Claremont."
21. "Imposing Exercises at Claremont."
22. "Imposing Exercises at Claremont."
23. "Imposing Exercises at Claremont."
24. Certificate of Incorporation, Temperance, Industrial & Collegiate Institute, State Corporation Commission, Charter Book 78, Virginia State Library, Richmond, VA, p. 502. See also *Moore v. Smallwood Memorial Institute*, 48.

25. Certificate of Incorporation, Temperance, Industrial & Collegiate Institute, 502–503. Work study could be carried out under the supervision of officers and instructors of the institution on any property under the control of the Board.

26. *Moore v. Smallwood Memorial Institute*, 48.

27. Certificate of Incorporation, Temperance, Industrial and Collegiate Institute, 503.

28. Certificate of Incorporation, Temperance, Industrial and Collegiate Institute, 502.

29. "Negro Educator Stricken Here," *Richmond Times-Dispatch*, September 30, 1912.

30. "Imposing Exercises at Claremont."

Notes to Chapter Eighteen

1. "Negro Educator Stricken Here."

2. *Moore v. Smallwood Memorial Institute*, 50–51.

3. *Moore v. Smallwood Memorial Institute*, 52.

4. *Moore v. Smallwood Memorial Institute*, 49.

5. Gregory, *Claremont Manor*, 101.

6. *Moore v. Smallwood Memorial Institute*, 51.

7. *Moore v. Smallwood Memorial Institute*, 105–106.

8. *Moore v. Smallwood Memorial Institute*, 52.

9. "Negro College Faded Out When Founder Died. Crumbling Ruins are Mute Evidence of School of Culture that Faded Out," unidentified newspaper clipping, courtesy of James Atkins, Richmond, VA.

10. "John J. Smallwood Dies after Brief Illness: Tragic Ending of a Brilliant Career: Orations Delivered Here and at Claremont," *Richmond Planet*, October 5, 1912; "Negro Educator Stricken Here."

11. Death Certificate for Dr. John J. Smallwood, 29 September 1912, Certificate #6521, Bureau of Vital Statistics, Richmond, VA.

12. "Negro College Faded Out When Founder Died."

13. "John J. Smallwood Dies after Brief Illness."

14. "John J. Smallwood Dies after Brief Illness."

15. Kornwolf, Surry County Bicentennial Committee Guide, 144; "Negro Educator Stricken Here."

16. "Negro Educator Stricken Here."

17. "John J. Smallwood Dies after Brief Illness."
18. Kornwolf, Surry County Bicentennial Committee Guide, 144; "Negro Educator Stricken Here."
19. Dr. George R. Hovey was born in Newton Center, Massachusetts, and graduated with honors from Brown University in 1885. He served as president of Virginia Union University from 1905 to 1919. Dr. Hovey was a conscientious and devoted teacher, and "nothing less than a high course of study for Negro students was in harmony with his wish" (M. C. Reynolds, *Baptist Missionary Pioneers among Negroes: Sketches Written by Mary C. Reynolds and Others* [Richmond, VA, n.d.], 45–47; courtesy of Virginia Union University Archives and Special Collections, Richmond, VA). John Mitchell Jr., born a slave in Richmond, Virginia, on July 11, 1863, was appointed editor of the weekly paper the *Richmond Planet* in 1884 at the age of twenty-one. Under his tenure, the *Planet* gained a reputation as a proponent of racial equality and of rights for the African American community. Mitchell himself quickly gained a reputation as a man determined to expose racial injustice whenever and wherever it lurked. For forty-five years, the *Planet* addressed, attacked, and exposed the harsh realities of race relations on the local, national, and worldwide levels. Much of the paper's focus was on segregation, lynchings, and the rise of the Ku Klux Klan. The February 22, 1887, issue of the *New York World* described Mitchell as "a man who would walk into the jaws of death to serve his race" ("Born in the Wake of Freedom," the *Richmond Planet*, August 13, 1898).
20. Dr. Calvin Scott Brown, a native of Salisbury, North Carolina, was born on March 23, 1859, and entered Shaw University in 1880 (G. F. Richings, *Evidences of Progress Among Colored People* [Philadelphia, PA: George S. Ferguson Co., 1903], 67). His first job while attending Shaw was as secretary to Dr. Henry Martin Tupper, who was at that time president of the university. Tupper recognized Brown's great potential and foresaw a bright future for him, but recognized that his poor financial situation would probably not allow him to remain in school. To help cover the cost of Brown's education at Shaw, Dr. Tupper sought help from some of his white friends, and they began providing scholarships to Brown, who also received financial assistance from a Northern white church. Six years later, in 1886, Brown graduated valedictorian of his class (Alice Jones Nickens, "Memories of C. S. Brown School, Part I," http://www.roanoke-chowan.

com/stories/AliceNickens/MemoriesofCSBSchool1.htm retrieved January 19, 2010). Dr. Brown was also instrumental in founding a school in the area of Winton, North Carolina. In 1885, Dr. Brown preached at Winton's Pleasant Plains Baptist Church, which was founded and led by the family of Milly Weaver of the Winton Triangle area. Milly herself was married to Rich Square native James Walden, who had served in the Second Calvary, U.S. Colored Troops. The eldest of the Waldens' seven daughters, Lydia, married Dr. Manassa T. Pope around the time they were both attending Shaw, although their families probably knew each other before that time, as Dr. Pope's father hailed from Rich Square. It was Pope who introduced Brown to the community around Winton, where he was persuaded to establish a school. Levi Brown, Sr., of Winton donated land for the school and he and his sons cleared it before Dr. Brown had even left Winton (Alice Eley Jones, *Black America Series: Hertford County, North Carolina* [Charleston, SC: Arcadia Publishing, 2002], 77). When Dr. Brown left Winton, he returned to Raleigh, where he met with Dr. Tupper. Tupper immediately produced $10 from his pocket and said, "I want you to go to Winton and start a school with this money" (Reynolds, *Baptist Missionary Pioneers*, 69). Dr. Brown then returned to Winton and established a normal school called the Chowan Academy (1886–1893), which graduated its first class in 1890 (Jones, *Black America Series*, 75). Manassa T. Pope taught at Chowan Academy in its first year and became a board member. James and Milly Walden were supporters of the school's founding organization, the Chowan Educational Association (Marvin T. Jones, interview by Mary E. C. Drew, January 19, 2010, Washington DC.). In 1893, the school's name was changed to Waters Normal Institute in appreciation of the $8,000 donated to the building fund of Reynolds Hall, which was completed in 1893 and named in honor of Ms. M. C. Reynolds, author of the book *Baptist Missionary Pioneers among Negroes: Sketches Written by Mary C. Reynolds and Others* (Jones, *Black America Series*, 77). In 1937, a year after Dr. Brown's death, the Waters school was renamed Calvin Scott Brown High School in his honor. Today, Brown Hall houses the Calvin Scott Brown Regional Cultural Arts Center and Museum, founded in 1986 (Jones, *Black America Series*, 80).

21. "John J. Smallwood Dies after Brief Illness." Dr. Smallwood was also a member of the Venus Lodge No. 46 (Knights of Pythias, NASAEAA and A).

22. "John J. Smallwood Dies after Brief Illness." Dr. P. B. Ramsey and Mr. J. R. Pollard attested to Dr. Smallwood's last will and testament on September 17, 1912: Will of Dr. John J. Smallwood, 1912 Wills Book, Surry County Courthouse, Surry County, VA.
23. Willie L. Lassiter (niece to Dr. Smallwood), interview by Mary E. C. Drew, June 10, 2007, Philadelphia, PA.
24. Kornwolf, Surry County Bicentennial Committee Guide, 144.
25. Kornwolf, Surry County Bicentennial Committee Guide, 144.
26. Dr. John J. Smallwood, "Moonlight on the James," *Educational Appeal*, Claremont, VA, November 1903. Courtesy of Hampton University Archives, Hampton, VA.
27. "John J. Smallwood Dies after Brief Illness."

Notes to Chapter Nineteen

1. "John J. Smallwood Dies after Brief Illness."
2. "Change Name of School at Claremont," *Journal and Guide*, December 21, 1912.
3. "Change Name of School at Claremont." Board members added by Mrs. Smallwood included Dr. C. S. Morris of Norfolk, Virginia; Mr. P. B. Young, also of Norfolk; Dr. E. R. Jefferson; Mr. George W. Bragg; Mr. D. J. Farrar; and Mrs. Rosa D. Bowser of Richmond, Virginia.
4. "Change Name of School at Claremont."
5. "Change Name of School at Claremont."
6. Charter to the Smallwood Memorial Institute, February 7, 1913, State Corporation Commission, Charter Book 80, pp. 219–221. Courtesy of the Library of Virginia, Richmond, VA.
7. Gregory, Claremont Manor, 102; *Rosa Smallwood Walton v. William Henry Walton, et al.*, file 360, Surry County Circuit Court, Surry County Courthouse, Surry County, VA.
8. *D. J. Farrar* (Plaintiff), *et al. v. Rosa E. Smallwood* (Defendants), *Executrix, etc. et al.* In the Chancery Court of the City of Richmond, Virginia, April 16, 1915, Surry County Courthouse, Surry County, VA, Fiduciary Account Book 4 (1909–1922), pp. 240–241. Hereafter cited as *Farrar v. Smallwood*.
9. U.S. Department of the Interior, Bureau of Education, Bulletin 1916, no. 38, vol. 1: *Negro Education: A Study of the Private and Higher Schools*

for Colored People in the United States. Prepared in Cooperation with the Phelps-Stokes Fund under the Direction of Thomas Jesse Jones, Specialist in the Education of Racial Groups, Bureau of Education, vol. 1 (1917; repr., New York: Arno, 1969), 665. Hereafter cited as Jones, *Negro Education*.

10. Jones, *Negro Education*, 665.
11. Jones, *Negro Education*, 665.
12. Jones, *Negro Education*, 665.
13. *Farrar v. Smallwood*, 238–239.
14. Will of Dr. John J. Smallwood, 1912 Wills Book, Surry County Courthouse, Surry County, VA. Dr. Smallwood's creditors included various business associates who had done work on the school: W. H. Jenks for work done on the electric power house; Henry Holmes for installing chairs in the dining hall; Robert Bass, electrician, for work in the power house; Irvin Sutherland for feed for the institute's livestock; and Carl Ruehrmund, architect of Lincoln Hall. Dr. Smallwood also owed money for groceries used to feed the school's students, stationery, typewriters, teachers' salaries, hospital expenses, pay of the school's matron and laundress, pictures, chairs, plumbing and steam fitting, cement work on sidewalks, travel stipends for board members to attend various meetings (locally and in New York), freight for coal, and payment of the nurses who cared for him during his illness.
15. *Farrar v. Smallwood*, 238–239.
16. *Farrar v. Smallwood*, 238–239.
17. *Farrar v. Smallwood*, 238–239.

Notes to Chapter Twenty

1. *Moore v. Smallwood Memorial Institute*, 1–2.
2. *Moore v. Smallwood Memorial Institute*, 1.
3. The school had already paid the taxes for 1913, so the money was ultimately refunded to Smallwood Memorial Institute, pursuant to the court's ruling.
4. *Moore v. Smallwood Memorial Institute*, 4–5.
5. *Moore v. Smallwood Memorial Institute*, 3.
6. *Moore v. Smallwood Memorial Institute*, 3.
7. *Moore v. Smallwood Memorial Institute*, 1, 4.
8. *Moore v. Smallwood Memorial Institute*, 5–6.

9. *Moore v. Smallwood Memorial Institute*, 6. (Emphasis added). The Constitution further stated that all property belonging to "incorporated colleges and academies and to free schools, theological seminaries and library companies, or used for college or school purposes" was exempt from taxation. Pages 8 and 9 of the opinion outlining Moore's arguments include examples of real estate considered exempt from taxation.

10. *Moore v. Smallwood Memorial Institute*, 6–7. (Emphasis added).

11. *Moore v. Smallwood Memorial Institute*, 7.

12. Representatives of the Smallwood Memorial Institute argued that the school had acquired the farmland by donations of money and property and had used it for school purposes, cultivating it, in part, to defray the costs of operation. Moore countered that the mere use of land for school purposes did not exempt the institute from taxation. Furthermore, he said, Smallwood Memorial Institute's claim that it was not conducted for profit did not entitle it to exemption status. (*Moore v. Smallwood Memorial Institute*, 11–13.)

13. Smallwood Memorial Institute argued, however, that it had received all rights to the property from Temperance in February 1913.

14. *Moore v. Smallwood Memorial Institute*, 13.

15. The taxes and levies on this tract of land were paid for 1913, but the circuit court directed that the money be refunded.

16. *Moore v. Smallwood Memorial Institute*, 14–16.

17. There are no indications that the institute actually sold any of the Boyce tract; Moore's argument was based entirely on allegations.

18. *Moore v. Smallwood Memorial Institute*, 16. In the letter, John J. Smallwood states, "and, of course, I have to pay taxes on the A. J. Holloway place and the James Boyce farm on the Cabin Point Road."

19. Surry County, VA, *Surry County Deeds*, Deed Book 26, pp. 538–540. Dr. Smallwood originally purchased the Old Wharf property from Hale H. and Hattie S. Chesbro of Nansemond, Virginia, on April 24, 1895. Mr. and Mrs. Chesbro had purchased the property on the Claremont estate known as Claremont and Wharf Property around 1885 from J. Frank and Lillie Mancha. The tract (also known as the Chesbro Farm) contained a farm and the wharf that Dr. Smallwood later renovated and named for his friend John Hay; it was also the site on which Howland Hall was constructed.

20. *Moore v. Smallwood Memorial Institute*, 17.

21. Surry County, VA, *Surry County Deeds*, Deed Book 27, p. 256. During the summer of 1895, Dr. Smallwood borrowed an unspecified sum of money

from Emily Howland of Sherwood, New York, and granted her trustee, J. C. Asbury, a deed of trust on property to secure the debt. In appreciation for Ms. Howland's moral support and financial contribution to his school, Dr. Smallwood named a building on his campus "Howland Hall" in her honor (Surry County, VA, *Surry County Deeds*, Deed Book 27, pp. 53–54). After the construction of Howland Hall, Dr. Smallwood had trouble paying the note on the property, and on December 20, 1902, the land was sold at public auction to D. Wilson Moore of Clayton, New Jersey, for $3,500 (Surry County, VA, *Surry County Deeds*, Deed Book 29, p. 618). As a result, the title to the school property was temporarily lost, and the name "Howland" was removed from the building (Gregory, *Claremont Manor*, 100). D. Wilson Moore, in turn, leased the land to Dr. Smallwood under the stipulations that he would conduct a school upon the property and pay semiannual rents of $93 over a period of six years, with no more than six months to elapse without payment (Surry County, VA, *Surry County Deeds*, Deed Book 29, p. 639). Dr. Smallwood finally satisfied the deed of trust on February 23, 1909 (Surry County, VA, *Surry County Deeds*, Deed Book 33, p. 534).

22. *Moore v. Smallwood Memorial Institute*, 18.
23. *Moore v. Smallwood Memorial Institute*, 21.
24. *Moore v. Smallwood Memorial Institute*, 21–22.
25. *Moore v. Smallwood Memorial Institute*, 26–27.
26. *Moore v. Smallwood Memorial Institute*, 27.
27. *Moore v. Smallwood Memorial Institute*, 29.
28. *Moore v. Smallwood Memorial Institute*, 48–53. If ownership of the plant reverted to anyone after Burt's forfeiture, it would have been the town of Claremont, not the Smallwood family or the Temperance, Industrial and Collegiate Institute.
29. *Moore v. Smallwood Memorial Institute*, 20.
30. *Moore v. Smallwood Memorial Institute*, 54–62.
31. *Moore v. Smallwood Memorial Institute*, 64–68.
32. *Moore v. Smallwood Memorial Institute*, 68–76.
33. *Moore v. Smallwood Memorial Institute*, 82–84.
34. *Moore v. Smallwood Memorial Institute*, 76–82.
35. *Moore v. Smallwood Memorial Institute*, 84–87.
36. *Moore v. Smallwood Memorial Institute*, 105–106.

37. *Moore v. Smallwood Memorial Institute*, 108–110. The appraisal represents the value of Dr. Smallwood's property as of October 28, 1912; Dr. Smallwood had died almost exactly a month before, on September 29.

38. *Moore v. Smallwood Memorial Institute*, 108–110.

39. Certificate for Amendment to the Charter of Smallwood Memorial Institute, May 24, 1917, State Corporation Commission, Charter Book 95, p. 533.

40. Certificate for Amendment to the Charter of Smallwood Memorial Institute (1917), 533.

41. Certificate for Amendment to the Charter of Smallwood Memorial Institute (1917), 533.

42. Baird Jr., *Claremont on the James*, 61.

43. *Commonwealth v. Smallwood Institute, Supreme Court of Virginia 124 Va. 142, 97 S. E. 805; 1919 Va.*, January 16, 1919, pp. 147–148.

44. *Commonwealth v. Smallwood Institute, Supreme Court of Virginia*, 148.

Notes to Chapter Twenty-One

1. M. M. Fisher, *Virginia University and Some of Her Achievements: Twenty-Fifth Anniversary, 1899–1924* (Richmond, VA: Virginia Union University Press, 1924), 31. Courtesy of Virginia Union University Archives, Richmond, VA.

2. C. H. Corey, *A History of the Richmond Theological Seminary, with Reminiscences of Thirty Years' Work Among the Colored People of the South* (Richmond, VA: J. W. Randolph, 1895), 74.

3. Corey, *History of the Richmond Theological Seminary*, 47.

4. Fisher, *Virginia University and Some of Her Achievements*, 31.

5. Fisher, *Virginia University and Some of Her Achievements*, 32.

6. Fisher, *Virginia University and Some of Her Achievements*, 58.

7. "Death List of A Day: The Rev. Charles Henry Corey, D. D.," the *New York Times*, September 6, 1899.

8. M. C. Reynolds, *Baptist Missionary Pioneers Among Negroes Sketches* (n.p., n.d.), 36. Courtesy of Virginia Union University Archives, Richmond, VA.

9. Reynolds, *Baptist Missionary Pioneers*, 36.

10. Records of the Richmond Theological Seminary, Virginia Union University Archives, Richmond, VA.

11. Reynolds, *Baptist Missionary Pioneers*, 36. The Augusta Institute is now Morehouse College.

12. Reynolds, *Baptist Missionary Pioneers*, 35–38.
13. Records of the Richmond Theological Seminary, Virginia Union University Archives, Richmond, VA.
14. Fisher, *Virginia University and Some of Her Achievements*, 34.
15. Fisher, Virginia University and Some of Her Achievements, 34.
16. Fisher, *Virginia University and Some of Her Achievements*, 34.
17. Fisher, *Virginia University and Some of Her Achievements*, 36.
18. Reynolds, *Baptist Missionary Pioneers*, 38
19. Reynolds, *Baptist Missionary Pioneers*, 38.
20. Records of the Richmond Theological Seminary, Virginia Union University Archives, Richmond, VA.
21. Reynolds, *Baptist Missionary Pioneers*, 38; "Death List of a Day: The Rev. Charles Henry Corey, D. D."
22. Russell, *Black Baptist Secondary Schools in Virginia, 1887–1957: A Study in Black History* (Metuchen, NJ: Scarecrow, 1901), 101.
23. Russell, *Black Baptist Secondary Schools*, 102.
24. *First Annual Catalogue of Virginia Union University, Richmond, Virginia, Combining Wayland Seminary, Formerly of Washington, D. C., and Richmond Theological Seminary, Richmond, Virginia, 1899–1900* (Richmond, VA: Virginia Baptist Press, 1903), 54.
25. Russell, *Black Baptist Secondary Schools*, 102.
26. Russell, *Black Baptist Secondary Schools*, 102.
27. Russell, *Black Baptist Secondary Schools*, 102–103; Charter to the Smallwood-Corey Memorial Industrial and Collegiate Institute, March 22, 1921, State Corporation Commission, Charter Book 111, pp. 441–444. Courtesy of the Library of Virginia, Richmond, VA.
28. Charter to the Smallwood-Corey Memorial Industrial and Collegiate Institute, 441–444.
29. Charter to the Smallwood-Corey Memorial Industrial and Collegiate Institute, 441–444. All other bylaws under the new charter remained similar to those under previous charters.
30. Charter to the Smallwood-Corey Memorial Industrial and Collegiate Institute, 441–444.
31. Russell, *Black Baptist Secondary Schools*, 103. Born in Nansemond County, Virginia, on July 17, 1879, Rev. Langston lived on a farm until he was twenty-one years of age. At sixteen, he was converted and felt called

to become a minister. In 1900, he was licensed as a minister at Mineral Springs Baptist Church, where he was ordained to the ministry in 1907. He was a graduate of Virginia Union University and was pastor of the Bank Street Baptist Church in Norfolk in 1916. (On Langston, see also Hopper, *Musings about Claremont*, 21.)

32. Because Temperance, Industrial and Collegiate Institute experienced several mergers and name changes in the decades following Dr. Smallwood's death, it is difficult to keep track of the changes in administration. What follows is a breakdown of the succession of principals (or presidents, since the titles were interchangeable) at Temperance and its affiliated schools. Dr. John Jefferson Smallwood was, of course, the first president of Temperance (1892–1912); upon his death in 1912, his wife, Rosa E. Smallwood, served as acting president for several months. In January 1913, Temperance, Industrial and Collegiate Institute was renamed Smallwood Memorial Institute; its first principal (under the new name) was Dr. Charles Morris, who was replaced later that same year by J. R. Pollard. Pollard served as principal until May 1914, when Caleb G. Robinson became the last president of Smallwood Memorial Institute. The Corey Memorial Institute, founded in Norfolk County, Virginia, in 1906, was first headed by Rev. Benjamin McWilliams, who resigned his post as principal in 1912. After Williams's resignation, Corey Memorial was governed by a series of principals: Rev. J. Early Wright (1912–1915), Rev. Charles H. Morton (1915–1918), and Rev. H. M. Henderson (1918–1921). During the merger with the Smallwood Memorial Institute in 1921, F. W. Williams served as acting principal of the Corey Memorial Institute. After the merger, Rev. Robert J. Langston became the first principal of the newly created Smallwood-Corey Memorial Industrial and Collegiate Institute. (First principal under the school's *new* name, he was actually the fifth administrator that both the Temperance/ Smallwood Memorial and Corey Memorial institutes had seen.) In 1923, while Langston was still principal, the name of the school changed again, to Smallwood-Corey Industrial Institute. In September of 1924, F. W. Williams became acting principal, but within a short period of time, Rev. H. M. Henderson (formerly principal of Corey Memorial Institute from 1918–1921) became principal and served from 1924–1926. In June 1926, the UNIA purchased the Smallwood-Corey Industrial Institute and renamed it Liberty University. After another change of name in 1927, the school

became known as Universal Liberty University. Its principal/president was Caleb G. Robinson, who filled the position until 1928, when the university closed its doors for good.

33. Russell, *Black Baptist Secondary Schools*, 103.

34. The board of trustees consisted of thirty-five members, with a quorum of fifteen needed to conduct business.

35. Charter to the Smallwood-Corey Memorial Industrial and Collegiate Institute, October 18, 1924, State Corporation Commission, Charter Book 129, p. 496. Courtesy of the Library of Virginia, Richmond, VA.

36. Russell, *Black Baptist Secondary Schools*, 103.

Notes to Chapter Twenty-Two

1. M. Lewter, *Marcus Garvey, Black Nationalist Leader* (New York: Chelsea House, 2005), 4–9.

2. Lewter, *Marcus Garvey*, 11.

3. Lewter, *Marcus Garvey*, 13.

4. Lewter, *Marcus Garvey*, 18.

5. Lewter, *Marcus Garvey*, 21.

6. Lewter, *Marcus Garvey*, 21.

7. Lewter, *Marcus Garvey*, 25–26.

8. *Speeches and Writings*, vi.

9. Lewter, *Marcus Garvey*, 41.

10. Lewter, *Marcus Garvey*, 42.

11. Lewter, *Marcus Garvey*, 41.

12. Lewter, *Marcus Garvey*, 35.

13. B. Blaisdell, introduction to *Selected Writings and Speeches of Marcus Garvey*, by Marcus Garvey, ed. B. Blaisdell (Mineola, NY: Dover, 2004), vi; P. Mohamed, *A Man Called Marcus: The Life and Times of the Great Leader Marcus Garvey* (Dover, MA: Majority, 2003), 23.

14. Lewter, *Marcus Garvey*, 47.

15. "U.N.I.A. Buys Quarter Million Dollar Property for Great Negro University: Garvey's Dream of Belting the World with Universities for the Training of Negro Youth Begins to Materialize," the *Negro World*, July 24, 1926.

16. Lewter, *Marcus Garvey*, 59–60.

278 MARY E. C. DREW

17. Blaisdell, introduction to *Selected Writings and Speeches of Marcus Garvey*, viii.

18. Lewter, *Marcus Garvey*, 70.

19. Cobb was a prominent attorney in Washington, D. C. Vann, a native of Ahoskie, Hertford County, North Carolina, was born on August 27, 1879. The story of his education is quite remarkable: as a child, he walked twenty-four miles to school and graduated valedictorian of his grammar school class; later, he attended Virginia Union University, from which he received a Pitt scholarship (1903) because of his diligent work and study ethics. In 1903, he entered the University of Pittsburgh and earned a bachelor of arts degree after only three years of study. Then, in 1909, Vann received his law degree; he began practicing as an attorney in 1910. In the same year, he went into the newspaper business and became one of the founders of the *Pittsburgh Courier,* which gained national prominence after its incorporation on March 10, 1910. In 1913, Vann became the editor of the *Courier* and remained such until his death in October 1940. The *Pittsburgh Courier* was once the country's most widely circulated black newspaper, with a national circulation of almost two hundred thousand. The *Courier's* mission was to empower African Americans economically and politically and to protest against misrepresentations of African Americans in the mainstream media. Vann was also involved in politics and influenced black voters to shift their political allegiance away from the Republican Party, still thought of as the party of President Lincoln, and to support the Democratic candidate Franklin D. Roosevelt. In late 1929, approximately two years after Marcus Garvey was released from Atlanta Penitentiary by President Coolidge's executive pardon, Vann contacted Garvey, now exiled in Jamaica, and invited him to write a weekly serialized account in the *Courier,* which would include a history of the UNIA and a discussion of the philosophy of Garveyism. Garvey agreed to begin installments of his story in late 1930 under the title *"Negro World,"* without compensation and exclusively for the Courier. The weekly articles began on February 15, 1930, but Garveyism was no longer of much interest to *Courier* readers in the depths of the Depression, and there was no objection when the series came to an end later that year. In addition to a number of other posthumous honors, in his childhood hometown of Ahoskie, North Carolina, a school was named in his honor. (For information on Vann, see esp. Andrew Buni, *Robert L. Vann*

of the Pittsburgh Courier: Politics and Black Journalism [Pittsburgh, PA: University of Pittsburgh Press, 1974].)

20. Buni, *Robert L. Vann*, 232–234.

21. Surry, County, VA, *Surry County Deeds*, Deed Book 39, pp. 399–404.

22. Surry, County, VA, *Surry County Deeds*, Book 39, pp. 399–404; Russell, *Black Baptist Secondary Schools*, 103.

23. Smallwood-Corey Industrial Institute Map (June 28, 1926), Claremont, Surry County, Virginia; "Map of Virginia Property acquired By U.N.I.A. Showing Landing Place of Slaves on James River," the *Negro World*, July 31, 1926.

24. "New York Members Cheer Wildly As Officer Announces Purchase of Valuable Virginia Property," the *Negro World*, July 24, 1926.

25. Surry County, VA, *Surry County Deeds*, Deed Book 6, pp 295–296.

26. "Educational Institute, Claremont, Virginia, Recently Acquired by U.N.I.A. To Open for Fall Term, September 15," *The Negro World*, August 28, 1926; and "Liberty University: Opened for Fall Term, September 15," the *Negro World*, October 20, 1926.

27. "Dr. J. G. St. C. Drake Gives Details of Property Purchase," the *Negro World*, July 31, 1926.

28. "New York Members Cheer Wildly As Officer Announces Purchase of Valuable Virginia Property."

29. "Dr. J. G. St. C. Drake Gives Details of Property Purchase."

30. "A University on the James River," the *Negro World,* July 31, 1926. Interestingly, T. Thomas Fortune, editor of the *Negro World,* had known Dr. Smallwood personally and had had the honor of speaking at one of the institute's commencement exercises. Fortune recalled that, under Dr. Smallwood's leadership, the Temperance, Industrial and Collegiate Institute prospered and was known throughout the United States and in many parts of Europe, but that, upon Dr. Smallwood's death, the institute suffered from poor management by various groups and individuals, ultimately resulting in extreme indebtedness.

31. "A University on the James River."

32. "The New University—Some Additional Pictures; Negroes Should Unite and Make University Project a Striking Success; Improving the Mind," the *Negro World*, August 7, 1926.

33. In 1927, the school was renamed Universal Liberty University, although Amy Jacques Garvey, wife of Marcus Garvey, described it as more of a "practical high school" than a college (A. J. Garvey, *Garvey and Garveyism* [New York: Collier Books, 1963], 173). The school was nonetheless given the designation "university" because the Parent Body of the UNIA intended to develop it into a university. According to Mrs. Garvey, the UNIA was already supporting other local schools at the time of the purchase of the Smallwood-Corey Institute.

34. "U.N.I.A. Buys Quarter Million Dollar Property."

35. "U.N.I.A. Buys Quarter Million Dollar Property."

36. "A University on the James River."

37. "Educational Institute, Claremont, Virginia, Recently Acquired by U.N.I.A."; and "Liberty University Open For Fall Term September 15."

38. "Parent Body Special," the *Negro World*, April 30, 1927.

39. "September 26, 1928! Opening Date, September 26, 1926. Universal Liberty University," the *Negro World*, September 29, 1928.

40. "Educational Institute, Claremont, Virginia Recently Acquired by U.N.I.A."

41. "Educational Institute, Claremont, Virginia Recently Acquired by U.N.I.A."

42. "Educational Institute, Claremont, Virginia Recently Acquired by U.N.I.A."

43. "Educational Institute, Claremont, Virginia Recently Acquired by U.N.I.A."

44. "Hon. Marcus Garvey Shall Not Die in Atlanta Penitentiary," the *Negro World*, May 21, 1927.

45. "Commencement Exercises at Universal University," the *Negro World*, May 29, 1927.

46. "Liberty University to Help Furnish the New Education for the Negro," the *Negro World*, September 4, 1926.

47. "Marcus Garvey Release Week, June 12–19," the *Negro World*, June 4, 1927.

48. "Hon. Fred A. Toote Resigns as Acting Head of U.N.I.A. To Lay Down Reins August 15; Hon. E. B. Knox Appointed Personal Representative of the President-General," the *Negro World*, August 6, 1927.

49. Blaisdell, introduction to *Selected Writings and Speeches of Marcus Garvey*, ix.

50. Lewter, Marcus Garvey, 73. Garvey died in England on June 10, 1940, at the age of fifty-three. More than twenty years later, his remains were moved to a gravesite in Kingston, Jamaica (Lewter, Marcus Garvey, 80).

51. "Marcus Garvey Sends Special Message to Members and Friends," the *Negro World*, December 10, 1927.

52. "Honorable Marcus Garvey Calls for Greater Effort in 1928," the *Negro World*, January 14, 1928.

53. "Special Appeal: List of Donors to the Universal Liberty University Appeal," the *Negro World*, February 11, 1928.

54. "Commencement Exercises at Universal University," the *Negro World*, May 28, 1927; "Specially Arranged Mass Meeting: Fine Musical Program to Be Held at Liberty Hall," the *Negro World*, September 1, 1928.

55. "The Why and Wherefore of Back to Africa," the *Negro World*, May 26, 1928.

56. Russell, *Black Baptist Secondary Schools*, 103.

57. Russell, *Black Baptist Secondary Schools*, 103.

58. "Notice: Owing to Contemplated Reorganization of Liberty University at Claremont, VA," the *Negro World*, October 12, 1929.

59. A. J. Garvey, Garvey and Garveyism (New York: Collier-Macmillan, 1963, 173).

60. Baird Jr., *Claremont on the James*, 62.

61. Baird Jr., *Claremont on the James*, 62.

62. "Negro College Faded Out When Owner Died."

63. Kornwolf, *Surry County Bicentennial Committee Guide*, 144.

64. "Negro College Faded Out When Owner Died."

65. "A University on the James River." Fortune had once had the honor of being the commencement orator at Temperance, Industrial and Collegiate Institute.

66. Kornwolf, *Surry County Bicentennial Committee Guide*, 144; Baird Jr., *Claremont on the James*, 61.

67. "Negro College Faded Out When Founder Died."

68. Kornwolf, *Surry County Bicentennial Committee Guide*, 144.

69. J. E. Atkins, *Surry County, Virginia, Historical Timelines with Addendums: Events, Places, and People that Shaped the History of Surry County, Virginia, In time sequence Pre-historic, 1400s, 1500s, 1600s, 1700s, 1800s, 1900s, 2000s* (Richmond, VA: privately printed, 2008).

70. Surry County, VA, *Surry County Deeds*, Deed Book 43, p. 17.

71. Baird Jr., *Claremont on the James*, 62.

72. Baird Jr., *Claremont on the James*, 62.

INDEX

A

A. J. Holloway tract, 158
Albemarle Precinct, 17
Albemarle Sound, 17
American Missionary Association
  (AMA), 39, 43
Annual Convention of the Negro
  Peoples of the World, 191
Annual Farmers and Landowners
  Congress, 107
Anthony, Susan B., 64, 214
Armstrong, 37, 41-43, 46, 70
Armstrong, Samuel Chapman, 41-
  43, 46, 93, 213
Arrington, H. J., 63, 88, 127, 151

B

Bagley Hall, 67, 69, 122, 159, 163
Baily (doctor and mentor of John
  Jefferson), 63, 70
Baker, William H., 127
Banks, Mat, 88

Banks, Phyllis, 88
Banks, Rosa E. *See* Smallwood, Rosa
Baptist General Association, 185-87
Beaufort County, North Carolina, 18-
  19, 219-20
Belding, O. D., 158
Bertie County, 17, 19
Binney, J. C., 183
Black Codes, 121
Black Star Line, 191
Blackwell, J. H., 105, 160, 187
board members, powers of, 105, 142,
  187
Bohannan, A. W., 157
Booker T. Washington University,
  191
Boone, Andrew, 27-28, 32-33, 35
Boyce, Susan, 113, 127
Boyce tract, 154, 157
Brooks, Phillip, 123
Brown, C. S., 146, 221
Brown, J. B., 195
Brown, William Wells, 28
Brownsville, 117-18

Bryan, W. H., 57
Bryant (surname given to Mary
    Eliza), 27
Bryantown Road, 19, 25, 27
Bureau of Refugees, Freedmen
    and Abandoned Lands. *See*
    Freedmen's Bureau
Burt, W. Stanley, 126, 136, 142, 144,
    156-57
Butler, 37-41, 44, 217
Butler, Benjamin Franklin, 37-41, 44
Butler School, 37, 39-41, 43-44, 46,
    90-92, 215

C

Carolina. *See* North Carolina
Charles, I, 17
Charles, II, 17
Cherry (Nat Turner's wife), 20, 25
Chesbro, Hale Hiram, 72
Chesbro, Hattie S., 72
Chowan County, 17
Civil War, 32, 34-35, 37, 41, 118,
    183
Clanton, H., 57
Claremont, Virginia, 63-64
Claremont and Wharf Property, 72,
    128, 165
Claremont Herald, 160
Cleveland, Grover, 116
Cobb, James, 191
Cockran, W. Burke, 132, 138
Colver, Nathaniel, 183-84
Colver Institute. *See* Richmond

Institute
*Commonwealth ex rel. Moore,
    Auditor, et al. v. Smallwood
    Memorial Institute*, 152
Compromise of 1877, *120*
Congressman Holland, 134
contraband of war, slaves referred to
    as, 38
Cook, Henry H., 75
Coolidge, Calvin, 180, 192, 196
Corey, Charles Henry, 184-85, 208
Corey Memorial Institute, 177, 185-
    87, 193
Craft, Ellen, 29
    *Running a Thousand Miles for
        Freedom*, 29, 208
Craft, William, 29
    *Running a Thousand Miles for
        Freedom*, 29, 208
Crowell, Loranus, 56, 58, 60, 95, 123
Crowell, W. R., 60

D

David (John Jefferson's slave-born
    father), 26-27, 30, 54-55
Davis, D. Webster, 84
Declaration of Rights of the Negro
    Peoples of the World, 191
Dolittle, P. B., 86
Dorchester, Daniel, 123
Douglass, Frederick, 14, 30, 68, 70,
    109, 171, 209-10, 216
Drake, J. G. St. Clair, 192, 195

E

Edgecombe County, 55
1899 Open Door policy, 131
Elizabeth (daughter of Mary Eliza), 27
Ellis, P. Emmett, 85, 104-5, 128
emancipation oak, 39, 91
Emancipation Proclamation, 38, 44, 133, 202, 204-5
Emma (daughter of Mary Eliza), 27
Estes, Fred M., 57, 138, 141-42
Estey Seminary, 50

F

Farmers' Congress, 85
Farrar, D. J., 132, 151, 160, 216
Federal Bureau of Investigation (FBI). *See* United States Bureau of Investigation
Fort Monroe, 37-40, 42, 44, 90
Fortune, T. Thomas, 198, 207
Fox, E. W., 64-65
Franklin, A. Q., 85
Freedmen's Bureau, 41-43, 184
Freedmen's Bureau Bill, 41
Freedom's Fortress. *See* Fort Monroe
Frissell, Hollis, 14, 169
Fugitive Slave Act, 38

G

Garvey, Amy Jacques, 192, 197
Garvey, Marcus, 180, 188-91, 195-
96, 208-9, 211-12
in Costa Rica, 180, 189-93, 195-97, 208-9, 211
deportation of, 196
in England, 190
founded the Universal Negro Improvement Association, 190
legal troubles of, 191, 196
Garvey's Watchman, 189
Gatling, George W., 132, 138
George (Earl of Northampton), 17
George, W. Hubert, 147
Gordon, M. W., 84
Graham, W. F., 105
Grant, Ulysses S., 34, 40, 44
Graves, Rhoda E., 85-86
Gray, Joseph N., 105
Great Emancipator. *See* Lincoln, Abraham
Gwaltney, W. L., 157

H

Halifax County, North Carolina, 54-55, 220
Hampton, Virginia, 37-39, 41, 43-44, 90-93, 100-101, 162, 165, 168-69, 212, 214-19, 221-26, 229
Hampton Hospital, 39
Hampton Normal and Agricultural Institute, 37, 43-44, 46, 70, 168-69, 215, 229
Hancock (judge), 126
Harlan, James E., 123
Harrison, 59, 99, 147-48, 163, 175,

223-26
Harrison (reverend in Surry County),
    147-48
Harrison, Benjamin, 99, 123, 163,
    223-26
Hay, Clara S., 131, 139, 165, 168
Hay, John Milton, 131, 157, 165, 168
Hayes, Rutherford B., 120, 211
Henderson, 187
Henderson, H. M., 185, 187
Henry, B., 132, 142
Hepler, T. H., 113
Hershaw, Lafayette, 107
Hewitt, Frederick Cooper, 87
Holloway, William, 154, 158
Holmes, R. R., 113
Home Mission Society, 183-84
Hoover, J. Edgar, 191
Hovey, George R., 146
Howard, 41-42, 75, 210
Howard, Oliver Otis, 41-42, 75, 210
Howard Theological Seminary.
    See Normal and Theological
    Institute for the Education of
    Preachers and Teachers
Howard University, 42, 182
Howland, Emily, 74-75, 77, 171
Howland Hall, 75, 155, 171

J

Jacobs, Harriet, 29
James Boyce Farm, 127, 158
James River, 40, 63, 138, 148, 175,
    198
Jamestown, Virginia, 17-18, 63, 72

Jim Crowism, 81-82, 108, 116, 118,
    120
John Hay Wharf, 131, 138-39, 141,
    146, 155, 165, 192
Johnson (former master of John
    Jefferson's parents), 60
Johnson, S. B., 127
Johnson, W. T., 105
Jones, David, 132, 142
Jones, R. Emmett, 86
Jones, S. L., 84
Josey, Lizzie, 85, 166
Josey, Martha, 25
Josey, Oscar, 25
Josey, Reddie E., 114
Josey, Stephen, 25
Josey, William, 25
Journal and Guide, 122, 127, 221

K

Kelley, J. K., 60
Kelser, R., 105, 107
Kitchin, Claude, 132, 138
Knox, E. B., 196
Ku Klux Klan, 121

L

land grants, 17
Langston, Robert J., 187
Lassiter, Hattie M., 85
Lassiter, Willie L., 10, 12, 72
Lawrence, David. See David (John
    Jefferson's slave-born father)
Lawrence, W. W., 105

Lee (general), 34, 40
Liberty University, 194-98. *See also*
  Universal Liberty University
Lincoln, 32, 34-35, 38, 41, 130-33,
  168, 201-5, 209, 221
Lincoln, Abraham, 32, 34-35, 38, 41,
  130, 133, 164, 168, 202, 208-9,
  211-12, 214, 221
Lincoln Memorial Hall, 129-33, 138-
  40, 144, 164, 175, 214, 217
Lincoln's Emancipation
  Proclamation. *See*
  Emancipation Proclamation
Lockwood, Lewis C., 39
Lumpkin, Mary Jane, 183
lynchings, 82, 120-21

M

Maglott, Eva, 129
Maglott, Frederick, 129
Mancha, Lillie, 72
Mann, 141-42
Mann, William Hodges, 133, 141-42,
  162, 218
Marcus Garvey Release Week, 196
Martin, Thomas, 132, 134-35, 138
Mary Eliza (daughter of Mary Eliza
  and Marcus W. Smallwood), 45
Mary Eliza (mother of John
  Jefferson), 26-30, 45-46, 98,
  112
  death of, 111
McDaniels, Charles Thomas, 122,

127
McKinley, William, 131
McMahon, George C., 132
McWilliams, Benjamin E., 185
Mitchell, John, Jr., 141, 146
Monthly Advocate, 73, 78, 81, 88,
  100, 130, 201, 221, 229
Moore, C. Lee, 152-56, 158, 212,
  215
Moore, D. Wilson, 126, 155
Moore, Putnam, 20
Moore, Sally Francis, 21
Moore, Thomas, 20-21
Morris, Charles S., 138, 140, 146,
  149-50, 195
Morton, Charles H., 185
Murfreesboro, North Carolina, 22,
  211-12, 223

N

Nancy of the Nile (mother of Nat
  Turner), 18-19
National Negro Educational
  Association, 142
National Theological Institute and
  University, 183
Negro Factories Corporation, 190
Negro World, 178-80, 190, 193-98,
  221, 227
Newsome, J. Thomas, 114
Nicolay, John G., 131
Norfolk, Virginia, 35, 63, 186
Norfolk Union Baptist Association,

185-86
Normal and Theological Institute
    for the Education of Preachers
    and Teachers. See Howard
    University
Northampton County, North
    Carolina, 17-18, 27, 32, 94,
    219-20
  agriculture in, 32
  main reason why it has a large
    slave population, 32
  typical scene of a slave auction in,
    27-28
North Carolina, 17, 32, 34
Norwood, William, 25

O

Old Bagley Hall. See Bagley Hall
Old Claremont Wharf. See
    Claremont and Wharf Property
Old Webster Spelling Book, 47-48, 52
Owen, Mary B., 113
Owens, Eleanor D., 84, 86

P

Patterson, John W., 75
Peake, Mary, 39, 44
Perrinr, W. T., 57, 60
Peterson, Catherine, 75
Peterson, John W., 105
Piladese, T. T., 19
Pittsburgh Courier, 180, 192, 208
Plessy v. Ferguson, 81
Pocahontas, 102, 138, 141, 146

Pollard, J. R., 145, 149-50, 155, 157-
    58, 160
Pope, Manassa T., 52, 94
precincts, 17
Proctor, Fannie E., 85
Prophet, the. See Turner, Nat

R

race wars, 116-18, 217
Ramsey, P. B., 134, 142, 145, 147
Ransom, Matt, 34
Reconstruction, 120, 211-12
Redd, H. C., 198
Reese, Giles, 25
Richmond Institute, 184-85. See
    also Richmond Theological
    Seminary
Richmond Planet, 138, 146, 222
Richmond Theological Seminary,
    185, 208, 216-17
Rich Square, 18-19, 25, 27
Rich Squire. See Smallwood, Marcus
    W.
Roberts, Nicholas Franklin, 52, 94
Robinson, Caleb G., 159, 193, 195
Roosevelt, Theodore, 117, 131, 168
Roseneath Township, 54, 220
Ruehrmund, Carl, 132
Running a Thousand Miles for
    Freedom (Craft), 29, 208

S

Santmyer, C. A., 157
Sawyer, Philetus, 74, 100

Sawyer Hall, 74, 100, 122, 126, 130, 159, 197
Shaw, Elijah, 50, 93
Shaw Hall, 50-51, 93
Shaw University, 47, 49-52, 54, 93-94, 177, 218, 223
Sherman, James S., 134-35
Sherman, William Tecumseh, 34-35
Silsbee, Texas, 116-18
Skinner, A. C., 106
slave revolt, 13, 18-25, 30, 48, 112, 169-70, 207, 209-13, 223
    aftermath of the, 21-23
slave system, 20, 29
Smallwood, Fannie E., 84
Smallwood, John Jefferson
    at the beating of Marcus Smallwood by Union soldiers, 35-36
    birth of, 28, 30, 32
    criticized by his opponents, 75-81
    death of, 145
    devotion to temperance work, 146
    founded the Temperance, Industrial and Collegiate Institute, 64
    marriage of, 88
    offered to give lectures in England about race relations, 57
    searching for his mother, 48-49, 58-61
    setback in his school, 83
    speech delivered on the fifty-first birthday of Lincoln, 201
    studying at Butler School, 37, 43-46
    studying at Shaw University, 49-54
    studying at Wesleyan Academy, 55-57
    vision of, 73, 75, 109, 198
Smallwood, John Smaw, 19
Smallwood, Lucy A., 85
Smallwood, Marcus W., 18-19, 25-27, 30, 43, 45
    being beaten by Union soldiers, 36
    death of, 46-47
Smallwood, Rosa, 88, 113-14, 124, 127, 145, 149-51, 158, 161
Smallwood, Sally Smaw, 18
Smallwood, Samuel Smaw, 19
Smallwood, Thelma, 88, 124, 152, 155, 158
Smallwood, Thomas, 19
Smallwood-Corey Industrial Institute, 178-80, 187, 192-93, 198, 217
Smallwood-Corey Memorial Industrial and Collegiate Institute, 183, 186-87, 198, 215
Smallwood Memorial Institute, 149-50, 152, 155-57, 159-60, 177, 186, 198, 215-16
Southampton County, Virginia, 13, 19, 63, 170
Southern Workman, 108, 217, 221-22
Spear, S. P., 34
Stanton, Elizabeth Cady, 14, 64, 67, 171, 214
Steele, George M., 55-60, 70, 95-96
Stewart, Sidney, 116
Stone, Daniel, 129
Stone, Maria, 129
Straker, Daniel Augustus, 78

Stryker, M. W., 132, 138
Surry County, Virginia, 11, 63, 124,
    178, 186, 194, 207, 209, 211,
    215-17, 220
Swanson, Claude W., 132, 134, 138

T

Tallman, L. B., 114
Taylor, W. L., 85
Temperance, Industrial and
    Collegiate Institute
  annual commencement exercises
    second, 68, 70, 72, 109
    seventh, 84, 86
  board members of, 142
  college course of study in, 103, 114
  fire at, 83
  founding of, 64
  normal preparatory programs in,
    102-3
Tennis, W. F., 128
Terrible Nineties, 82
Thirteenth Amendment, 35
Thomas (son of Mary Eliza and
    David), 27, 54
Threatt, Margaret E., 85-86
Tilden, Samuel J., 120
Tillman, Benjamin "Pitchfork," 118-
    19, 123, 211
Tobias (son of Mary Eliza and
    David), 27, 54
Toote, Fred, 192-93, 195-96
Travis, Joseph, 21
Trinity College, 57, 63
Tumber (judge), 134

Tupper, Henry Martin, 47, 49-50, 53,
    70
Turner, Benjamin, 18, 20
Turner, Nat, 13, 18-20, 23, 169-70,
    207, 209-13, 223
  capture and trial of, 23
  execution of, 23
  infamous revolt of. *See* slave revolt
Turner, Samuel, 20
Tuskegee Normal and Industrial
    Institute, 74, 77-78, 190
Tuskegee's model, 74

U

Union Troops, 33-34
United Literary and Lecturing
    Society of England, 57, 63
United States Bureau of
    Investigation, 191
United States Hotel, 184
Universal Liberty University, 189,
    195-98
Universal Negro Improvement and
    Conservation, 190
Universal Negro Improvement
    Association (UNIA), 179-80,
    190-96, 208
  founding of, 180, 188-93, 195-97,
    208-9, 211-12
Up from Slavery (Washington), 190,
    214

V

Vann, Robert L., 180, 191, 208

Vaughan, Mrs. (unidentified friend of John Jefferson), 60
Vincent, W. G., 127

W

Walton, William H., 150
Washington, Booker T., 37, 43, 74, 77, 190
Up from Slavery, 190, 214
Wesleyan Academy, 55-56, 60-61, 95-97, 141, 213, 218-19
West, A. S., 105

Westinghouse Company, 139
Westinghouse Electric Company, 72, 139
Williams, Archer, 85
Williams, Balfour, 196
Williams, F. W., 187
Willis, W. H., 187
Willow Oak (AME Church) Cemetery, 112, 146
Woodward, C. Vann, 82
Wright, J. Early, 185
Wright, Willis R., 105

Edwards Brothers,Inc!
Thorofare, NJ 08086
16 November, 2010
BA2010321